MINSTRELS, POET'S & VAGABONDS

Robert Fields

macdonald media publishing

First published in October 2009 by **macdonald** media publishing, 22 Roxburgh Road, Paisley, PA2 0UG. info@macdonald-media.co.uk

ISBN: 978-0-9553126-9-4

ISBN: 0-9553126-9-8

A CIP catalogue record for this book is available from the British Library.

Printed and bound by Thomson Litho, East Kilbride

Every effort has been made to contact the copyright owners of photographs and if we have missed anyone, please contact us. Thanks to all who let us use their photographs.

Cover design: Karla Heap

Production & Typesetting: Cameron Heggie.

FOREWORD

I AM very proud to have been asked by Robbie to write the foreword to his new book, Minstrels, Poets and Vagabonds. I've known Robbie for many a year. We first met when Uriah Heep were playing at the Maryland Club in Glasgow, way back in 1970. He is a great guy and has made himself a huge part of the music scene in Scotland, as a manager of bands, as a club owner, promoter, DJ and the like . . .

His enthusiasm for anything to do with music is immense and, when you read these pages, I know you will agree with me that this love shines through in this book.

We became such close friends that when he and his wife Carole had a baby boy, they named him after Lee Kerslake, Heep's drummer for many years and myself, calling him Lee Michael. This friendship extended through the entire Heep crew, including our lighting engineer, Del Roll, after whose wife Robbie and Carole named their little girl Cheryl.

Robbie has written this story from the viewpoint of how his own life has been entwined with the Glasgow music scene as he knows it and has lived it. He is, in this regard, a true historian of the Glasgow music scene and has many an interesting tale to tell.

And as for Uriah Heep, well Glasgow was always and remains, a very special place for us to play – Glaswegians are as passionate about their rock music as we are about playing it. Our shows in Glasgow took in the Maryland, Picasso, Electric Gardens, Strathclyde University, the QM, the Barrowlands and, lately, the Garage, but it was our nine shows at the

Apollo, when it was still called Greens, that were truly magical. Seeing the balcony bouncing up and down when we were on stage was unbelievable, but such was the excitement of each show.

I hope you enjoy this book as much as I will and many thanks to Robbie, who has lived through it all and now put it all into words and pictures for everyone to enjoy!

'Appy days!

Mick Box, guitarist Uriah Heep

INTRODUCTION

MINSTRELS, Poets and Vagabonds makes no claim to be the definitive book on the history of the rock scene in Glasgow over the last half century, but it does claim to sit nicely on the shelves along side such fine tomes as those by Russell Leadbetter, Martin C. Strong, Brian Hogg and Martin Kielty and to fill in any gaps left by them.

I've tried to remain loyal to my genre as I'm a rocker and I feel that this scene has been (I can exclusively reveal) almost totally ignored in most parts by the mainstream media over the past 50 years. So in this book you will not find any pop-rock meanderings because in allowing that the floodgates would surely open and rushing through would come the likes of Texas, Del Amitri, the Silencers, K.M.O., Simple Minds and Travis etc – all fine bands in their own right and, as fellow Glaswegians earning a crust in the very fraught arena of the music business, they have my 100 per cent respect. But their end product is not what this book is about.

Nor did I want to go down the indie rock route. I couldn't open the door for the likes of Glasvegas and Mogwai, or I would have had to include bands like Primal Scream, the Jesus and Mary Chain, the Fratellis, ac acoustics, Murmur, Kit Cumming's fantastic Said Florence, the Vaselines, Captain America, Teenage Fan Club, BMX Bandits, Michael Rooney's mega Primevals and the Gyres etc.

Nor did I try and 'adopt' any band, artist or trend which started in the early Seventies and has carried on to this day with the likes of Snow Patrol and Franz Ferdinand, all at some point featuring in various Scottish/Glasgow charts and polls although their Scottish/Glasgow links are tentative, to say the least.

When setting out the plan for this book I thought it would be cool to have a collection of free music for the readers, to enhance their journey through the five decades covered here and on putting pen to paper I ended up with a 115-track historical artefact listening post which in my humble opinion is quite unique and superb. So get the kettle on and download your listening post.

Are you sitting comfortably? Then let the journey begin . . .

Robert Fields, October 2009

THE SIXTIES

It's All In My Head

YOU could say that rock 'n' roll really went to my head when I was just 11 years old. For weeks I'd saved my pocket money until I had amassed 2/6. This princely sum was going to transform a wide-eyed 11-year-old into a bona fide music star . . . for it bought me a plastic Beatles wig. Unfortunately, that summer was one of the few in those good old days to be blessed with a heat wave, long before such events were associated with the tragedy of drowning polar bears, rather than the innocence of ice cream nougats and skinny dips in the Clyde.

Well, that false barnet grew so hot it promptly stuck fast to my own curls, surprising my young brain by entombing it entirely in a Darth Vader-style helmet. Never again, it seemed, would my young head see the light of day.

After much pulling by Dad and muffled squealing by his melted Beatle, we finally trundled off to the barber where, to the merriment of all waiting their turn, both helmet and hair were cut off.

Thankfully, this first dalliance with the dark side could not me put off rock 'n' roll for long.

It was, after all, the best of times for growing into music.

I'd come into this world, already screaming and shouting, on 10 December 1952, at Stobhill Hospital in Glasgow, ominously the year of the UK's first official music chart.

To this day I have a fond and vivid memory of listening to Elvis Presley's

'Jailhouse Rock' for the very first time at the age of five. I remember, too, that the atmosphere in our own house in Springburn was often electric: every week my mum and older sisters would bring new offerings of 45rpm discs into the house and from early on music was an integral part of our everyday entertainment.

This era, moving into the Sixties, was without doubt the happiest, musically and socially, of my life. Both Mum and Dad had jobs, there was always food on the table and somehow the summers were the longest, hottest wig-melters for years.

In 1958 my dad got a great job offer with the National Engineering Laboratory in Scotland's first new town, East Kilbride, so we packed our bags and moved from smoky Springburn to this new and wonderful suburb of Glasgow that was full of grass parks and surrounded by fields and, more importantly, filled with fresh air.

Oh and we even managed to get to Butlin's holiday camp in Ayr six years in a row! Happy days!

Perhaps it's nostalgia, perhaps . . . but the truth is that for me and I'm sure for many others, these were halcyon days, a time that waltzed, shimmied and twisted by to the strains of our heroes and heroines of the studio and stage.

It was always about the music, music that in our house was always in the air and in our hearts: Elvis, Gene Vincent, Eddie Cochrane, Buddy Holly, then the Beatles, the Stones, the Kinks, the Hollies, the Animals, Small Faces, the Supremes, The Who, the Four Tops . . . even the B-sides of their 45s were just as good.

It was a worldly education and the finest of beginnings for a music lover.

Ballroom Bits

For many music fans, myself included, the hard rock and heavy progressive scene was conceived in the late Sixties. In 1966 the Beatles released Revolver, an album that would change the history of writing and recording music forever. When this was followed by Sgt. Pepper's . . . we knew that music would never be the same again.

It was also an era when music was suddenly more accessible. With little airtime afforded to pop on daytime radio, we'd once upon a time relied on the Sunday chart show for our musical fix, or tuned in to pirate radio stations, Caroline or Luxembourg, late night and under the pillow, of course, because our parents were, like, square, man.

In 1967, however, BBC Radio One hit the airwaves for the first time and Dansette record players became ubiquitous. Suddenly, in teenagers' bedrooms, students' bedsits, young couples' flats and bohemian townhouses throughout the Central Belt of Scotland, we were giving it laldy to revolutionary new sounds. Nothing was out of our reach, even if your bag happened to be a trilogy of 45s, 'Hey Joe', 'Purple Haze' and 'The Wind Cries Mary', by a certain James Marshall Hendrix, a young dude who, if you believed the music magazines, played his guitar while it was upside-down, behind his head and occasionally on fire.

Add to this exciting new melting pot of music an embryonic Deep Purple, a fledgling Free and the juggernaut that was waiting to hit the highway, Led Zeppelin and you begin to get the picture.

Glasgow's own musicians would not only embrace the vibe of this brave new world but nurture their own identities and sounds, creating the Glasgow rock scene, an environment that has survived and flourished for more than 50 years.

Central to its growth were the city's ballrooms. East Kilbride's Olympia ballroom, known affectionately by locals as The Big O, was to be a dominant feature in my own musical development in the early Sixties, even if in the very early days I was far too young to gain entry through its hallowed portal. On Saturday afternoons the venue hosted increasingly popular discos, catering specifically for those aged under 18. It was a place kids could safely go to bop away to the latest chart songs.

By night, however, the Big O transformed itself into a different beast entirely, becoming a major concert venue for the grown-ups and attracting star names such as the Kinks, Small Faces and Manfred Mann.

In 1962, the two biggest and most respected local bands playing the Big O and certainly those around with the most relevance to the burgeoning music scene, were the Beatstalkers and the Poets.

Formed that year in the city, the Beatstalkers' original line-up included Davie Lennox on vocals, Eddie Campbell (guitar), Alan Mair (bass) and Tudge Williamson (drums). Within weeks, however, Ronnie Smith had been added to the outfit to play rhythm guitar.

In the space of just two years, the Beatstalkers grew to become a leading attraction in the city's venues, specialising in cover versions of soul and R'n'B songs that hitherto had never been heard live in Glasgow. In fact, such was their popularity, the group were soon being hailed as 'Scotland's Beatles' and, in 1965, an open-air concert in Glasgow's George Square had to be abandoned when police suspected that over-eager fans had begun to riot, fuelled into a frenzy by Stalkermania.

It wasn't surprising then that the Beatstalkers soon secured a recording contract with Decca Records. 'Ev'rybody's Talkin' 'Bout My Baby', 'Left Right Left' and 'A Love Like Yours' were released; certainly worthwhile, they failed to reflect the group's true mettle. The Beatstalkers eventually moved to London in 1967, where they secured a residency at the renowned Marquee Club. However, despite switching to CBS Records, the group were still unable to achieve a major breakthrough and that all-important chart recognition, in part because they relied heavily on material that wasn't their own.

In one final fling for fame and fortune, their new manager Ken Pitt suggested that the Beatstalkers record songs by his best-known charge, a certain David Bowie. Three of his compositions, 'Silver Tree Top School for Boys', 'Everything Is You' and 'When I'm Five', were subsequently released, although only the first was issued as an A-side.

Sadly, the experiment proved to be neither an artistic nor a commercial success. Inevitably, perhaps, the Beatstalkers finally split up in 1969, an ending hastened when all of their live equipment was nicked. Not all was lost with their passing, however, as late-period drummer Jeff Allen would go on to join East of Eden, while bassist Mair would become a member of the critically acclaimed outfit, The Only Ones.

The Poets, meantime, had been ploughing a very different musical furrow and one that was to prove much more fruitful. The free listening post accompanying these musical memories of Glasgow kick off in1964 and that's because this is a track that should be treasured for its historical value: it was the second single from The Poets, recorded with Andrew Loog Oldham at Decca and featuring the six-string bass-playing of one young session player by the name of John Paul Jones . . . and we all know what happened to him!

Even more importantly, however, it features George Gallagher. Three years later, George, by anyone's yardstick one of Glasgow's most charismatic and innovative front men, had left the band he formed in 1961, to be replaced by Andy Mulvey and for that reason I felt it would be a huge injustice not to have a legend such as George represented and given his rightful place in Glasgow's rock history. That's why there are two Poets songs on offer on the download listening post.

Of course, I was only a brat way back when The Poets were formed in Glasgow in 1961 by George, John Dawson, Tony Myles, Hume Paton and Alan Weir. They very quickly became a regular feature in the Glasgow R'n'B scene, decked out in their resplendent fluffy, ruffled shirts, complete with high-collar jackets, mirroring the image of our rascally national poet Rabbie Burns and thus bequeathing themselves the band's moniker: they were the original bard company, you might say.

It is reputed that it was while in Scotland, there to attend his wedding to a bride who was too young to be married in English law, that then Rolling Stones manager Andrew Loog Oldham saw the band in action and at once whisked them away to the Big Smoke down south. There he signed them to Decca and their first single, 'Now We're Thru', was released in October of '64. The track kicked off a six-single career, ending with 'Wooden Spoon'/'In Your Tower' in 1967.

Throughout their spell in the limelight, The Poets enjoyed almost as many changes in their line-up as the Drifters famously did, bringing in such musical luminaries as Fraser Watson, Ian Macmillan, Hughie Nicholson and his wee brother Davie (with whom I'd gone to school in East Kilbride).

There would be a couple more singles, including one for a Strike Cola advert, before the end of the road came in 1970. By then, The Poets had become one of the most important bands of the Sixties. While most of their contemporaries were quite content to cover the pop tracks coming into the UK, emulating their R'n'B, Soul and Motown heroes and heroines from across the Big Pond, The Poets strived very successfully to be original, influencing a new generation of musicians to write and perform their own material.

Indeed, one of the highlights of writing this book was sitting down with a legend such as former Poet Fraser Watson and reminiscing in his cottage and studio complex in Busby, on the edge of Glasgow.

Throughout his professional life, Fraser has worked with some of the biggest names in the biz, playing on a session for George Harrison (alas, that all things must pass) and jamming with legends such as Zoot Money and Peter Frampton.

He also became a part of musical history when he got the call to fly to Amsterdam for John and Yoko's 'bed-in' with his then Apple-signed band White Trash, later shortened to Trash. They'd recorded a Beatles track after a successful stint as a backing band for black soul singer Marsha Hunt.

Over a cup of tea and biccies, Fraser explained: 'Paul McCartney never wanted to release our version of 'Golden Slumbers'/'Carry that Weight' but John Lennon loved it and pushed for its release. And that's why we got the call from John's publicist to get our guitars together and head to Amsterdam for the historical bed-in.'

Fraser, a thoroughly likeable and unassuming man, is now 63 and doesn't have any regrets about eschewing the excesses of fame or fortune of his younger days for the quieter life.

'In our day the music scene was a big hotchpotch of sounds and colours,' he says. 'It was all bubbling under in the late Sixties. I met and played with lots of important people, toured the world and played my music and I loved every minute of it!'

And that, ladies and gentlemen, boys and girls, is just exactly the attitude that this book is all about!

Striking a Chord

IF ever a title of a book represented one person, this tome fits precisely the slightly built but vastly-gifted frame of Glasgow's Jimmy McCulloch for here, indeed, was a minstrel, poet and, yes, a downright musical vagabond.

Jimmy started his musical career in 1964, when he was but 11 years old. He and his older brother, Jack, formed a band in the all-new, all-concrete conurbation of Cumbernauld. They were known as the Jaygars and the full line-up included Jimmy on guitar and vocals, Jack (drums), Robert Ross (vocals), Billy McGowan (vocals, guitar), Norrie Gilligand (guitar) and Frank Quinn (bass, vocals).

Sadly, after releasing just a couple of singles, the band split up. Young guitar prodigy Jimmy, however, had by then attracted the attention of The

Who's guitarist Pete Townsend. Now, at that time The Who had a roadie named John 'Speedy' Keen, who just happened to be a singer-songwriter in his own right and was forming a band.

Townsend recommended Jimmy to Speedy and thus Thunderclap Newman were born and Jimmy, at the tender age of 16, became the youngest ever Glaswegian, indeed the youngest ever Scot, to have a number one single, with their track 'Something in the Air'.

Thunderclap released one album, Hollywood Dream, before a fresh line-up was put together for touring. This was made up of Speedy on vocals, Jimmy (guitar), Jim Avery (bass) andy Newman (keyboards) and Jack McCulloch (drums). They proved to be a rollicking rock act.

After the storm that was Thunderclap Newman and the close of the Sixties, Jimmy's career was as wide and varied as any travelling minstrel and, as we shall see in the next chapter, in the Seventies he would become a Crow and then spread his Wings with Paul McCartney to a worldwide audience.

Another band bubbling under whose various minstrels would play a major part in the grand scheme of all things musical were Dream Police, formed in 1969 by vocalist Davie Bachelor, Ted McKenna, Onnie McIntyre and Hamish Stuart. They were soon signed to Decca and, in early 1970, they released their debut single 'I'll Be Home', produced by none other than Junior Campbell, of Marmalade fame.

As was often the way in those days, after just another couple of singles the band members went their separate ways. Bachelor and McKenna went on to form the inestimable outfit, Tear Gas, while McIntyre and Stuart formed the Berserk Crocodiles . . . on their way to becoming those legendary funk masters, the Average White Band.

All of these bands had blossomed from Glasgow's vibrant live music scene and it wasn't just the Big O that was attracting hot new music. On a Monday, Electric Gardens hosted an 'Underground Night'. There was an 'All-Nighter Club' above Forbes music shop. The Empire café, across from McCormack's music store, was no stranger to impromptu gigs, while the Picasso was a regular hot spot for the Underground/Pink Panther clubs.

One of the city's most underrated bands, The Blues Council, were at that time the resident band at the Bagatelle Club, which was hosted in an old church at the top of Dundas Street, not far from where the statue of our parliament's founding father Donald Dewar now presides in all his melancholy greyness over shoppers and tourists and the odd, banjoed busker.

The Blues Council also played, among many other venues, the Scene club in West Nile Street, having been formed in 1964 by former big band leader and saxophonist from the Plaza, Bill Patrick. He was joined by Fraser Calder on vocals, Leslie Harvey (guitar), Larry Quinn (sax), John McGinnis (keyboards), James Griffen (bass) and Billy Adamson (drums).

Theirs was a mod dance style, a jazzy vibe that fitted so well within the mid-Sixties scene that they were very soon signed to Dick James Music (Dick would also sign Elton John and Bernie Taupin, but famously fall out with Paul McCartney and John Lennon when he sold Northern Songs in 1969 without offering the duo an opportunity to buy control of the publishing company – and hence the rights to their own songs).

With Dick James Music, The Blues Council cut their debut single 'Baby Don't Look Down'. In fact, everything was looking up and the band were looking forward to the single's release on Parlophone when tragedy struck.

Driving home in their van from a gig in Edinburgh, on 12 March 1965, Fraser and James were killed in a crash.

The Council soldiered on for a brief spell with two new musos in the shape of Bobby Patrick and Bobby Wishart but finally disbanded. Les Harvey joined singer Maggie Bell, who had been the in-house singer in music halls such as the Dennistoun Palais and they formed their own band, Power. The line-up incorporated Maggie, Les, Jimmy Dewar, Colin Allen and John McGinnis.

There's a lovely tale told of how this fabulous bunch of musicians ended up playing once a week for nothing, inadvertently setting in motion nearly ten years of undoubtedly the most exciting platform for the most gifted generation of Glasgow musicians.

A somewhat dishevelled and bedraggled youth had been admiring the piano in the Burns Cottage in Paisley Road and soon approached the owner, Old John Watterson and asked if he could play. Old John told him that, regretfully, there was no entertainment put on in the pub. Undaunted, the young lad asked, then, if he and a few of his mates might not come along once a week and play for nothing.

Now this would soon be music to Old John's ears, for the young lad happened to be John McGinnis and his errant friends were none other than Jimmy Dewar, Maggie Bell, Les Harvey and a cast of many, many more.

And so this happenstance meeting was the founding moment of a stage for many aspiring Glasgow musicians, for the Burns Cottage was sold in 1967 and moved lock, stock and barrels to a site in West Regent Street; the legend that was the Burns Howff music venue was born.

Up Close and Personal

It wasn't until 1968 that I was lucky enough to see my first live gig. I was smuggled into the Scotia bar to see a very eccentric trio of gentlemen playing a brand of folk-pop music: Tam Harvey, Gerry Rafferty and a young and rather abrasive lad called Billy Connolly.

Fast forward a year and I was again happily watching the Humblebums, for so they were, only now they had been slimmed down to the deadly duo of Rafferty and Connolly. They were supporting Kenny Rogers and the First Edition in the City Halls in Candleriggs, a venue where AC/DC would make their spectacular Glasgow debut in the mid Seventies.

It was a strange set from these local lads, in as much they sang their own compositions individually. During the gentler, quieter Rafferty number, 'Her Father Didn't Like Me Anyway', Connolly decided to let rip on a couple of latecomers with his impromptu banter. Now, this may have become Connolly's trademark in years to come but in those days it proved to be much to the annoyance of Rafferty, whose piercing, red-eyed glare towards the Big Yin was no less than demonic.

It's perhaps no surprise, then, that their parting of the ways years later made a lot of sense. By the way, Connolly's first solo gig was the Grangemouth Rock and Pop Festival in 1971, an event which had been organised by the actor Stanley Baker and featured Uriah Heep, the Average White Band and the Everly Brothers and was opened, believe it or not, by Chris McClure (I was there, it's true!).

John Peel was the compère but it was Connolly's opening remarks that stay with me and will go down in the annals of history: 'Fer f*ck's sake, I'm shittin' myself. I've never done this before!'

I knew exactly how he felt. My own foray into the big, bad world was when I left school at the age of 15. My dad had secured me an apprenticeship as a pipe-fitter–welder and I think the school no doubt let me leave early because they had decided from the start that I wasn't really in the running to gain any qualifications.

In those days, you see, your allocated school was not worked out geographically by where you lived but rather it was based solely on your perceived IQ. And so, if you were deemed to be an exceptionally bright young thing, you went to Hamilton Academy, while really very clever clogs toddled off to Duncanrig (by the way, in the Sixties the pupils of Duncanrig were given the choice of a swimming pool or a mural in the front hallway and, being the superior beggars that I know they weren't, they chose the mural).

Next, if you were an average kind of Joe with the books you went to Hunter High and, finally, the rest of us were shipped off en masse to The Village Secondary School.

Well, having escaped Village life, one of my first work sites was a special school in Kirkintilloch, where I befriended a young electrical apprentice by the name of Alan Rough, who worked for Scotts. He also happened to be the reserve goalkeeper for Partick Thistle and would one day go on to play for his country in two world cups.

Back then, long before his trademark perm had become a regular headliner in the Scottish newspapers, he always wore a duffel coat and we nicknamed him Paddington.

So along with Paddington, I attended Springburn College of Engineering in Flemington Street and our tea breaks, not surprisingly, soon mirrored the gang culture that was bred within the pub and dance club scene of Glasgow.

I can remember sitting with Paddington, quietly eating our rolls 'n' sausage – I think maybe Paddington had two or three to himself – when a cry went up: 'Tongs, ya bass!' Then came the inevitable rejoinder: 'Cumbie, ya bass!' And then, alas, all hell broke loose.

Tables and chairs were suddenly levitating all around us before being launched into a melée of arms, legs and fists. This, of course, was one of the many reasons that dance halls and live music venues in Glasgow were forcibly closed during the Sixties, as the gang culture grew into a monstrous entity that fed on itself. All it took was a single cry to ignite all-out anarchy.

Thankfully, one of the city's most famous venues, Green's Playhouse, was still happily bubbling under, trouble-free, in the Sixties, though it wouldn't kick in properly as a music star magnet until the Seventies, when it was renamed the Apollo.

The brainchild of the brothers Green, Fred and Bert, the Playhouse was built by the Cinema Building Company in Renfield Street and the grand opening took place on 15 September 1927.

Despite already catering for up to 10,000 movie fans, Fred and Bert also had the grand idea of tapping into the new fashion for dancing. A brand new ballroom, which could hold an astonishing 1,500 dancers, was opened on the top floor of the building. During the 1940s it hosted an array of renowned dance bands, biggies such as Joe Loss and his Orchestra.

Through the years, however, with the advent of big business cinema franchises, the curtains finally closed on the silver screen, but the management had a cunning plan: to put on live rock and pop shows in the main auditorium. It proved to be a winner, attracting huge crowds, who flocked to see their heroes such as Pink Floyd and The Jimi Hendrix Experience.

The Apollo's fame lasted right through those halcyon days of rock, right up until the day it finally closed in 1985.

The Apollo, however, was not the only former cinema to get in on Glasgow's rock scene. One of the biggest venues in the Sixties, also located in Renfield Street, was the Odeon, built in 1934 and originally called the Paramount, after the American film company for whom it was built.

In the 1960s, the cinema famously hosted many live acts, including the Rolling Stones, Johnny Cash, Gene Pitney and several appearances by the Beatles.

Unfortunately, the closest I ever got in those days to the stars of the Odeon was when I was installing a new heating system in an insurance building on nearby West Nile Street.

It was a fine summer's day and so we were up on the roof, taking a fresh-air constitutional. Now, the craze on-site at the time was larking about with a putty gun, which in fact was nothing more than a glorified blow pipe, concocted from a short length of conduit tubing. You put a ball of putty in your gob and spat it through the tube. Yes, boys never do grow up, I'm afraid.

Well, my claim to fame was that from my rooftop sniper's nest I managed to splat the inside leg of Dean Ford, of Marmalade as he stood signing autographs outside the Odeon – no mean feat, by the way, despite his enormous flared trousers that acted as my target area!

Sadly, the Odeon closed on 7 January 2006.

Another venue that was to play a major part in the development of Glasgow's music scene, particularly after the closure of the Apollo, was the Barrowlands. This huge hall in the heart of the famous market area, complete with its extra-bouncy spring-loaded dance floor, would come into its own as a premier music venue in the late Seventies. In the Sixties, however, it hosted only one major gig of (very loud) note, when The Who came to town.

The Barrowlands and coincidentally The Who, are directly linked to another of Glasgow's Sixties stars. A classic beat group who had formed in 1966, Studio Six enjoyed a long residency at the Barrowlands but seemed destined for even bigger things.

Two brothers, Clive and Colin McClure, had been two-thirds of the fabulously named Glasgow band Colin and the Cossacks, when they were persuaded to create a new project: the Studio Six line-up became Clive (on guitar), Colin (vocals), Neil Grimshaw (guitar), Gerry Tedeschi (bass), Ricky Kerr (keyboards) and Ron Milne (drums).

Their manager was the boys' dad, Carl J. McClure. It was a natural choice as McClure senior was already a guiding force behind a successful TV and stage group, the Chris McClure Section.

It wasn't long before Studio Six were sharing an agent with the Bee Gees and our old Barrowlands and Thunderclap friends, The Who. Their first single, written by Neil, 'When I See My Baby' (B-sided by 'Don't Tell Lies') was released on 2 December 1966, by Polydor. It sold 8,000 copies, just failing to make it into the UK charts.

Soon afterwards Ricky and Gerry left and in came keyboardist Douglas Jarvis and bassist Malcolm 'The Grasshopper' Sergeant. On 30 March, Studio Six played the Locarno, sharing a stage with Booker T and the MGs, Eddie Floyd, Sam and Dave and legend of soul, Otis Redding.

They also played all over England and most countries in Europe, on the same bill as hit parade-topping acts such as The Move (who would later become ELO), The Kinks, Jethro Tull, Dave Dee Dozy Beaky Mick and Tich, Manfred Mann and Pink Floyd. Their star was certainly in the ascendant and looked set to shine brighter with news that the Beatles' business guru Brian Epstein was to sign them.

Alas, as is so often the way in the volatile and unpredictable world of rock, just two weeks after the agreement with Epstein, the famous manager died in what then seemed mysterious circumstances. For the band, the promise of worldwide fame would remain unfulfilled.

Drummer Ron retired from the outfit, to be replaced by former Poet, Jim Breakey and, despite the hype that still surrounded Studio Six when they returned to London in October 1967 to record and promote their fourth single, 'Strawberry Window', the major breakthrough would remain elusive.

They embarked on a continental tour and soon afterwards were offered live work in Portugal. This they undertook as the Studio Five, with Colin handling the drumming duties while singing.

The band finally decided to call it a day round about 1970, following a long, hot summer season in Estoril.

Right Side of the Tracks

The year was 1966 and I had become a member of the Life Boys – no, not Glasgow's answer to the Beach Boys, as there was scant facility for surfing on the Clyde. No, this was an organisation much like the Cub Scouts, which young lads would join before going on to the Boys' Brigade.

At one of our weekly meetings in the old Parish Church in the original village heart of East Kilbride, we were shown a film about the plight of lepers living in a nameless village somewhere in the vastness of Africa. Our mission, should we choose to accept it, was to sell 50 crosswords, thereby raising much-needed funds to help these unfortunate souls.

Well, also being an avid member of the local Rangers FC supporters club, I had three busloads of punters to bother and I shifted all 50 crosswords in one outing. Not that it was particularly hard work, but the carrot dangled before me for such enterprise was that, for every 25 sold, I would get a voucher that could be exchanged for a 45rpm single.

Thus it came to pass that a village of poor lepers, working through a bunch of disparate football supporters, earned me my first ever two singles: The Who's 'I'm A Boy' and Small Faces' 'My Mind's Eye'.

You win some, you lose some: despite the beginnings of my own music collection, two years later my musical world came crashing down around me when my big sister Joyce left the family home, taking all of her records. I was devastated.

Mind you, it wouldn't be the last time that Joyce brought musical calamity. In later days she would borrow a barrowload of my cherished LPs for her flat-warming party – by this time she was working in the Bellahouston Hotel in Glasgow. Being too young to merit an invitation to the celebrations, I turned up the next day to discover a scene of utter carnage. Imagine my horror when, reaching the lawn in front of her block of flats, I was met with the sight of all my LPs. Everything from Sgt. Pepper's, to a Four Tops collection . . . lying in the wet grass. Apparently, a party guest, worse for wear on babe-clad cans of Tennent's lager no doubt, had unwittingly invented Frisbee, using my entire album collection for throwing practice.

The covers remained intact; sadly, their contents did not. Joyce, bless her, replaced every one of them and so I ended up with a collection of spare covers. A silver lining on the outside, if you like.

Among those covers, most of which I still treasure to this day, is Disraeli Gears by the world's first supergroup, Cream. And central to the success of that band was a young Scotsman by the name of Jack Bruce.

Jack was born in Bishopbriggs on 14 May 1943. His upbringing was peripatetic, to say the least, with his mum and dad, both musicians, travelling all over Canada and the USA, meaning that Jack attended no fewer than 14 different schools.

After a stint at Glasgow's Bellahouston Academy, the young lad won a scholarship for cello and composition at the prestigious Royal Scottish Academy of Music. It was an auspicious beginning to his musical career, but one that very soon came a cropper. The professors, he felt, were turning a deaf ear to their new student's grand ideas. Disillusioned by their lack of interest and feeling acutely the pains of living in near penury, Jack left the Academy, his city and his country at the age of 17.

He first travelled through Italy and then to England, where he made money playing double bass in dance bands and jazz groups. One such band was Alexis Korner's Blues Incorporated, which he joined in 1962 in

London. Their drummer was none other than Charlie Watts, who would later, of course, find more satisfaction as a Rolling Stone.

Jack left the Blues Inc. the following year and began playing with Graham Bond (keyboards), John McLaughlin (guitar) and Ginger Baker (drums). When John left, saxophonist Dick Heckstall-Smith joined and the outfit became the Graham Bond Organisation. All was right with the world until Ginger decreed that Jack's playing was 'too busy'!

Unperturbed, Jack worked on, even turning down an offer from the legendary Marvin Gaye to join his American-based band because of his impending first marriage. Instead, he briefly played with John Mayall's Blues Breakers. It was here that he first met a guitarist by the name of Eric Clapton.

This was followed by a spell in 1966 with Manfred Mann. Although some considered this move an ill-advised attempt at commercialism, it did earn him a number one single, 'Pretty Flamingo'.

In July the same year, his old sparring partner Ginger Baker asked Jack back to form a trio with Eric Clapton. It was Eric who insisted that Jack be the trio's singer and so Cream were born.

The band were a critical and commercial tour de force, selling an astonishing 35,000,000 albums in just over two years. The trio were awarded the first ever platinum disc for Wheels of Fire. Jack wrote and sang most of the songs, including 'I Feel Free', 'White Room', 'Politician' and, featuring the world's most performed guitar riff, 'Sunshine of Your Love'.

Incredibly, Cream split in November 1968 at the height of their fame and fortune, with Jack explaining that he felt he had strayed too far from his ideals: he wanted to rediscover his musical and social roots.

So began Jack's next career as he began recording solo albums; the first being his influential Songs For A Tailor. From then on he adhered to a strict policy of playing simultaneously in rock, jazz and classical formats, attempting to realise his personal and unique style of performance and recording an amalgam of these three disciplines with a frequent and spicy infusion of new-found world music.

It was during an American tour with one of his own bands, which incorporated guitarist Larry Coryell and Jimi Hendrix's drummer Mitch Mitchell, that Jack was introduced to Tony Williams by old Bond partner

John McLaughlin. He had soon joined Tony's jazz fusion combo Lifetime, along with John and the late, great Larry Young. It was, he said years later, 'the musical time of my life'.

Unfortunately, Lifetime proved to be badly named; when the band broke up, Jack and Tony were in talks with guitar god Jimi Hendrix, but Jimi's sudden and tragic death put paid to their shared ambition of a 'dream band'.

Jack found some solace in returning to his heavy roots, with the formation of West, Bruce and Laing with Leslie West and Corky Laing. Since then, he has fronted many of his own bands, featuring, among others, such sterling sidekicks as Carla Bley, Mick Taylor, Simon Phillips, Tony Hymas, Billy Cobham, David Sancious and Gary Moore.

As well as his numerous solo albums, he has collaborated on special projects and worked as a session man with the likes of Lou Reed and Frank Zappa, with whom Jack co-wrote Apostrophe, which became Frank's biggest selling album.

Jack's influence also came to bear much closer to home. A song written by Jack, called NSU and heard on the Fresh Cream album – dedicated by Jack to Eric Clapton, as the legendary guitarist was allegedly using the same stuff for an unfortunate malady at the time – inspired Glasgow prog rockers NSU. They consisted of John Graham Pettigrew on vocals, Ernest Rea (lead guitar), Peter Grant Nagle (bass and harp) and Alexander Brown (drums).

Little about the band is known in the public domain, except that they played the Royal Albert Hall and then inexplicably chucked rock 'n' roll soon after they entered De Lane Lea studios in February 1969 to record their debut nine-track album, Turn Me On or Turn Me Down, produced by Trevor Walters, who would go on to produce one of Motörhead's Lemmy's first bands, Sam Gopal.

Although they remain one of Glasgow's great musical mysteries, NSU nonetheless left their mark in Glasgow's history with a fine album.

But back to Jack, who in 1993 was inducted into the Rock & Roll Hall of Fame as a member of Cream. It was also the year he celebrated his fiftieth birthday, with a concert that featured many of his old friends, including Dick Heckstall-Smith, Maggie Reilly and Gary Moore. The event was later released as a CD box set, Cities of the Heart.

The gig proved so inspirational that Jack formed BBM with Gary Moore and Ginger Baker, giving the world a top-ten album in Around the Next Dream.

During the late 1990s, Jack toured with several different incarnations of Ringo Starr's All Star Band, with guitarists Peter Frampton, Todd Rundgren and Dave Edmunds, keyboardists Gary Brooker and Eric Carmen, drummer Simon Kirke and horn player Mark Rivera.

The year 2005 was a momentous one. Jack reunited with former bandmates Eric Clapton and Ginger Baker for Cream's first concert tour in 37 years. In May the band played four historic nights at London's Royal Albert Hall, which were recorded and subsequently released on both audio and video. In October the band played three concerts at Madison Square Garden in New York City. That same week Jack was honoured, along with Ron Carter, with the Bass Player Lifetime Achievement Award in recognition of his pioneering musicianship and his outstanding influence on the development of modern bass technique.

It's not been a bad career, then, so far, for the boy from Bishopbriggs. Perhaps we shouldn't be surprised. Jack, after all, is in fine company among the sons and daughters of Glasgow who have come to be acknowledged as musical giants.

And, as the musical trends in Glasgow evolved through the decade, from beat groups to R'n'B to bands offering their own exciting material rather than covers, so the next decade would see set in motion the most exciting chapter for Glasgow's minstrels, poets and vagabonds.

THE SEVENTIES

Into The Fire

WITHOUT doubt 1970 was the seminal, most exciting year of my long life in love with music. It was the year I bought four albums that were to spark my curiosity then ignite a burning passion for rock, a fire that crackles inside me just as fiercely today as it did way back then.

The four LPs were all purchased from a basement record shop in Glasgow's Buchanan Street, called Patterson's - a store that was almost hidden from passers-by under the Picasso club. Here, deep in the city's bowels, I could sit quite happily for hours in a comfy sound booth, cans on the ears, listening to all of the newly released albums in full.

Purchased on the same day were Black Sabbath's self-titled eponymous debut and Deep Purple's In Rock. Together they would shape the way I thought of music, for the sounds made by these new guitar heroes were very loud, very heavy and almost painfully raw. And that suited me just fine.

Also bought that day were two compilations, song collections that would influence me in a big way by opening my ears to a diverse, nay motley, crew of incredible musicians, singers and songwriters. Bumpers, on Island, introduced me to Spooky Tooth, Mott the Hoople, Cat Stevens and, ultimately, Free. The Vertigo album, meanwhile, brought my senses to heady new heights courtesy of Juicy Lucy, Rod Stewart, with his 'Handbags and Glad Rags', Coliseum and a band I would eventually befriend on their first ever Glasgow visit and remain chums with for the next 39 years, Uriah Heep.

It was a Heep anthem which taught me that one day I'd be 'strong enough to fight and win/ The kind of a man/ That he'll understand'. Yes, everyone in life can point to a band or a song that changed their life forever and with me it was 'Gypsy'. For that reason alone, I make no apology for the space given to Uriah Heep and its various members in this book, for they played a major part in my formative youth.

In fact, two of them are my kids' godfathers: my wife Carole and I named our son Lee Michael (who's now 36) after Lee Kerslake and Mick Box and my daughter Cheryl (who's 33) was christened in honour of the wife of the band's sound and lighting engineer, Del Roll.

Del, incidentally, was head of Edwin Shirley Trucking, or EST, a company founded in 1974 to provide transport services for the European tours of stars that Carole and I made a point of seeing: stars such as Heep, Santana, Jethro Tull, Pink Floyd, Journey, Pat Travers, Bob Dylan, the Rolling Stones, AC/DC, Frank Zappa (what a weird gig that was!) and the Moody Blues (the wife fell asleep) and many, many more.

However, it wasn't all galactic tours, stellar venues and meteoric groups in the early days. In fact, the most important venues for me at that time were much more humble, if no less exciting and included the Olympia in East Kilbride and Green's Playhouse and Burns Howff in Glasgow.

Oh and I mustn't forget the Key Youth Club in East Kilbride. This was actually nothing much more than a tiny, sparsely furnished room with a record player where you could take your LPs in for a spin and share your new tunes with your mates: I guess it was the beginning of Podcast culture. My Key Youth membership number was 201, which at the time seemed incredibly auspicious, as it was also the number of the bus I had to catch for Hamilton when I was courting Carole.

Of all these venues, however, it was the Howff in West Regent Street that became the hub of most activity. In the early Seventies you could pop in for the Saturday afternoon sessions, though you'd be put out onto the street at tea time so the bar could be tidied up. But that was just fine because it gave you time to buy a bag of chips and get yourself together for Act Two.

It really was an exciting era. How many pubs can boast aiding and abetting the careers of worldwide names such as Frankie Miller, Tear Gas,

Power featuring Maggie Bell, James Dewar, Les Harvey, Beggars Opera and so many more?

We'll never see the like again and so let's start here.

Heyday At The Howff

Frankie Miller was one of the Howff Mafia in the early days. Truth be told, to this day there can be few pubs on the planet that can boast the array of talent on show in the Howff in the Seventies. So let's start with Frankie – The Don.

David Arthur is a lifelong fan of Frankie and has been given the task of compiling an authorised biography and so it seems quite fitting, as Frankie's number one fan, that he should tell us the great man's story:

'When a young Frankie Miller penned the lyrics to 'Bridgeton', a song all about leaving behind his life in Glasgow, little did he know that his outstanding talent would lead him to be associated with the some of the biggest names in the music business, from legendary producers such as Elliot Mazer and Allen Toussaint to musicians in the class of Joe Walsh and Nicky Hopkins and receive accolades from Otis Redding's wife . . . even have one of his songs recorded by Ray Charles.

'Born on 2 November 1949, in the east end of Glasgow, it was his mum's record collection that inspired Frankie's love of music. While his mum had a fondness for Ray Charles, his older sisters introduced him to Little Richard and Elvis Presley. He identified instinctively with Little Richard's flamboyant aggression. He recalls: 'The music was alive, exciting, I loved it. I realised later that I could get my own aggression out through music. R&B and soul music, I just knew, was what I really loved.

'With a guitar bought by Mum and Dad, the nine-year-old from the east end began writing songs. The first, a song called 'But I Do' caused tears of laughter amongst his family members but Frankie was to remain undeterred.

'He remembers: 'You know, I realised that I could sing and it would make me feel better. It was better than thumping someone on the head, which is what most people were into. I didn't realise until after I'd left Glasgow that singing was a way out. An escape from all that.'

'This natural escape through his music and a natural vocal talent took a positive form in the shape of a succession of early groups. At school there were The Deljacks, West Farm Cottage and a soul outfit called Sock It To 'Em JB, an outfit which featured his good friend Jimmy Dewar.

'Frankie eventually joined the Stoics, who were signed by Chrysalis in early 1970. A German tour supporting Ten Years After was followed by an appearance at the Isle of Wight Festival under the moniker Howl, but, as is the way, the band would split up before completing any recordings.

'Frankie then met up with former Procol Harum guitarist Robin Trower, Jethro Tull's former drummer Clive Bunker and, once again, bassist Jimmy Dewar, who had just left Stone the Crows. Together they formed a group, called Jude. Despite a number of college gigs in the London gig circuit, Jude never made it to the recording studio and also, sadly, split.

'After the demise of Jude, Frankie signed a solo contract with Chrysalis in 1972 and recorded his debut album Once in a Blue Moon, using pub rockers Brinsley Schwarz as his backing band. Material-wise the album showcased Frankie's skills as a well above average songwriter and 'I Can't Change It' was accorded what must have been, for Frankie, the ultimate compliment when Ray Charles covered it on his album Brother Ray Is At It Again.

'The Brinsleys ended up backing Frankie when he was given the support slot on the Ten Years After UK tour, bringing him back to Scotland to perform for the first time since the Stoics days. They also cut a four-song BBC session for the Bob Harris Show, which would finally be released in 2002 on Hux Records.

'Frankie's career really took off after that first album. On hearing it, legendary producer Allen Toussaint, he of Lee Dorsey 'Working in the Coal Mine' fame, took him to New Orleans to record 'Highlife', with Frankie's soulful leanings allowed a free rein. Released in January 1974, the critics' reception was good, though without the sales to match the plaudits it was clear the collaboration would be a one-off.

'During this period, without a band or hit record to his name, Frankie helped his good friend Phil Lynott to write, perform and record a track for Thin Lizzy's Night Life album. The track turned out to be a classic. 'Still in Love with You' became one of the highlights of Thin Lizzy's shows for years to come.

'A brief collaboration with progressive rockers Procol Harum saw

Frankie front the band at the London Rainbow Farewell Show, during which he featured songs from Highlife, including 'Shoo Rah Shoo Rah', 'Brickyard Blues' and 'The Devil Gun'.

'Many people had compared Frankie's soulful style with that of Paul Rodgers and, when former Free bass player Andy Fraser was looking for a new band, he clearly saw in Frankie a similar vocal talent. The two wrote and recorded together, though nothing permanent came of their collaboration.

'However, their search for a permanent lead guitarist led them to ex-Grease member Henry McCullough, with whom Frankie would form the Frankie Miller Band. The Rock, released in September 1975, marked the band's debut, with bassist Chrissie Stewart, drummer Stu Perry and keyboard player Mick Weaver completing the line-up.

'The Rock was produced by Elliot Mazer, who was also at the reins for Neil Young's Harvest and recorded in San Francisco in sight of the famous Alcatraz Prison. Frankie once commented that it was only music that had saved him from a similar kind of fate in the pokey and dedicated the album's title song to 'prisoners everywhere'.

'The album also featured the legendary Memphis Horns and the Edwin Hawkins Singers, who supplied vocal backing on classic songs like 'A Fool in Love', which enjoyed a lot of airplay on both sides of the Atlantic and was a sizeable hit in the US. 'Ain't Got No Money' became the album's most covered song, with notable versions from Cher, Chris Farlowe and Bob Seger.

'When the band returned to the UK, Henry left to record a solo album and Frankie put together his new Full House band, with Procol Harem lyricist Keith Reid taking on a management role. The result was a year of hard graft on the road, beginning with a 50-date UK tour, kicking off in May 1976 and finishing with a triumphant show at London's Victoria Palace on 27 June. Frankie had added Ray Minhinnett on lead guitar, Jim Hall on keyboards, former Entwhistle's Ox, Graham Deacon on drums, with Chrissie Stewart completing the solid backing band.

'Recordings for the Full House album began in November 1976 and combined Miller originals with choice covers including John Lennon's 'Jealous Guy', which Frankie sings with great feeling and a first ever UK chart single, Andy Fraser's 'Be Good To Yourself'.

'Full House disbanded after a long American tour and Frankie returned to the States for a third time to work with Aerosmith producer Jack Douglas on Double Trouble.

'The Record Plant in New York was where Double Trouble took shape in April 1978 and Frankie brought yet another impressive line-up with him, including legendary drummer BJ Wilson from Procol Harum, Chrissie Stewart on bass, highly rated session player Ray Russell on guitar, a two-man horn section of Chris Mercer and Martin Drover and, perhaps the most impressive recruit, keyboardist and vocalist Paul Carrack, who would co-write five of the songs with Frankie.

'Stephen Tyler from Aerosmith made a guest appearance as backing vocalist and the album contains some powerful playing and singing, but in the opinion of their opening act, guitarist Steve Simpson from Meal Ticket, both band and songs were even better live.

'Later in 1978 Frankie went on to have his first Top Ten single. 'Darlin', a song written by Q Tips brass player Stuart 'Oscar' Blandamer. 'Darlin' was included on the Falling in Love album and featured Frankie's new touring band of drummer Fran Byrne, bassist Tex Comer and Paul Carrack on keyboards, that trio forming the backbone of 'How Long' hitmakers, Ace, plus Steve Simpson and Ed Deane on guitars. They toured Europe extensively and supported Rory Gallagher on the German leg before returning triumphantly to the UK.

'In 1979 Frankie decided it was time to diversify and made a move towards acting. He starred in Peter McDougall's TV film Just A Boys' Game, winning rave reviews for his performance. He also wrote and performed 'Rules of the Game' for the soundtrack.

'The early Eighties found Frankie in the capital of country music, Nashville and with some of the finest sidemen that city could offer, he cut Easy Money, an album that merged rock, country and R 'n' B. Frankie co-wrote five songs with Troy Seals, a respected country songwriter whose work has been covered by Lonnie Mack, Rod Stewart and Percy Sledge. Heartbreak Radio, written by Frankie, has in turn been covered by a diverse selection of artistes, including Kim Carnes, Roy Orbison and the Osmonds.

'The release of Easy Money in July 1980 would effectively end Frankie Miller's link with Chrysalis Records, but the connections and impact he made in Nashville would prove deep and long-lasting – within the decade he would become one of Country's most sought-after songwriters.

'Frankie returned to the States yet again with a record deal from Capitol Records and, in June 1982, released his eighth album. Standing on the Edge was recorded at Muscle Shoals Sound Studio in Alabama, with the backbone of the music being supplied by part of the legendary Muscle Shoals Rhythm section, who had worked on such classics as 'Respect' by Aretha Franklin and 'Mustang Sally' by Wilson Pickett. While the recording location and musicians involved were undoubtedly American, the material was self-penned and pure and simple Frankie.

'Songs such as 'Danger Danger', 'To Dream the Dream' and, particularly, 'Jealousy' would be highlights of Frankie's live shows for years to come. From the early to mid Eighties and onwards, the live performances were moving back to a rockier side with former Free/Bad Company drummer Simon Kirke and Brian Robertson from Thin Lizzy joining Chrissie Stewart to form a powerful backing band to complement Frankie's voice.

'Together, they cut Dancing in the Rain in New York and the album was released in the spring of 1986. It contained several collaborative compositions with Jeff Barry, whom Frankie had met when a plan to re-record the Crystals' 'Da Doo Ron Ron' was mooted.

'Instead they came up with a batch of new songs that feature on the album. The band did a tour of major cities in the US with Bob Seger later that year and toured extensively throughout Europe into the early Nineties, when Frankie had a number one hit in Scotland with 'Caledonia', a soundtrack from a television advert that was released by public demand.

'Frankie continued to become an in-demand writer on the country music scene and had started on a new project to record with Joe Walsh and Nicky Hopkins when he suffered a massive brain haemorrhage in New York on 25 August 1994. It should have killed him but he has shown remarkable courage to fight his way slowly back to health, after spending 15 months in hospital.

'With massive support from his partner Annette, Frankie is learning to walk and talk again and has even written a new song with lyricist Will Jennings called 'The Sun Goes Up, The Sun Comes Down'.

'The 2002 tribute album of Frankie Miller covers, featuring artists such as Lulu and Rod Stewart and a charity concert for the Drake Music Trust which featured more than 20 live acts at the Barrowlands in Glasgow, including Joe Walsh and Nazareth, show the depth of feeling and respect the music business has for Frankie Miller today.

'March 2006 saw the release of Frankie's first album since 1986, Long Way Home, on Jerkin' Crocus Records. One reviewer, Doug Collette, wrote: 'Long Way Home is a testament to the living, breathing quality of music at its most inspirational. While on the one hand it's a tragedy that we may never see Miller perform the wrenching confessional that is 'The Rose', we must consider ourselves blessed to have this collection of songs to savour. It might be selfish to want more of the same, but that hope for something more is simply a reflection of the very foundation of Frankie Miller's personal and artistic ethos.'

'The album has recently been described in Classic Rock as the album Rod Stewart 'should have released' and with a series of re-releases and another new album on the cards, our deepest, most selfish wishes may yet come true.'

Bands-A-Loud

In the earliest days of the early Seventies, one of the bands to make a deep, ear-ringing impression on me and everyone else, were Tear Gas. Now, Tear Gas were loud. I mean really LOUD!

I'd listened to the band's previous incarnation, Dream Police, in the Big O in East Kilbride, but Tear Gas were just like a canister of the stuff to my senses: I was, quite literally, blown away by the energy, excitement and heavy sound they created. They were exactly what our local rock scene needed at that time – okay they were not Deep Purple, Uriah Heep or Black Sabbath, all of whom were making huge noises nationally, but they were our very own local heroes.

Formed in Glasgow as Mustard in the late Sixties by former Bo Weevil members Zal Cleminson on guitar and Chris Glen (bass) and augmented by Andy Mulvey (vocals), Wullie Munro (drums) and Eddie Campbell (keyboards), they built their reputation by playing loud, heavy, aggressive rock. In 1970, when Davie Batchelor joined on vocals and Gilson Lavis took over on drums, Tear Gas were ready to record their debut album, Piggy Go Get Her, on Tony Calder's Famous G label. There would be yet more changes on the way to their second album, Tear Gas, on the Regal Zonophone label in 1971, in the shape of Hugh and Ted McKenna on keyboards and drums.

In truth, neither studio album particularly enhanced the band's reputation. In fact, it was as a LIVE and very LOUD band that they attracted the attention of one Alex Harvey, late in 1971. In joining forces with the legendary Glasgow R 'n' B veteran one of the greatest ever Glasgow rock bands was forged, but much more of that later.

Right then, one of my other favourite bands at the time were Northwind. They were, if you like, a blast of fresh air and, like many of the bands I talk about in my book, they are musicians I'm lucky enough to know personally. Guitarist and vocalist Brian Young I know very well and I was chuffed when he kindly gave permission for Northwind song 'Castanets' to be among the songs on the listening post that comes with the book. Many a night I had in the Howff heid-bangin' to that song!

Northwind formed in Glasgow from the remnants of Power of Music, who in their day had supported big bands such as the Move and the Pathfinders at the Maryland (where in 1970 I would meet Uriah Heep). The founder members were songwriters Brian and Hugh Barr (also on guitar and vocals), Tam Brannan (bass and vocals), Colin Somerville (keyboards) and Dave Scott (drums) – who was in the Elastic Band briefly with Andy Scott before Sweet.

Northwind recorded only one album, Sister, Brother, Lover for Regal Zonophone through EMI. In the early Seventies, successful producers Denny Cordell and Tony Visconti both had companies releasing records through the label. During this period, too, the label had album and single success with artists such as The Move, Jo Cocker, Tyrannosaurus Rex and Procol Harum.

During the mid Seventies many of these production deals ended and, despite a few sporadic releases by Blue Mink, Geordie (featuring Brian Johnson, the future star of AC/DC) and Dave Edmunds, eventually EMI ceased to use the imprint as a major pop label, with many of the label's artists moving to Fly Records or to the EMI imprint.

Northwind's album was, by any standard, excellent and Brian has now secured all rights for it – it's hoped this gem will be released very shortly, but for now you and I, dear reader, must content ourselves to listening to 'Castanets' with the headphones on, the volume turned to LOUD and a can of the amber nectar in hand . . . all in the comfort of our own living rooms (come to think of it, mine is the same size as the Howff's tiny interior, so I should feel perfectly at home).

Someone who found success way beyond the realms of local rockdom was Dougie Thomson, whose musical career began in August 1969, when he joined local Glaswegian band The Beings.

In September 1971 Dougie joined the Alan Bown Set, where he briefly worked with a lad by the name of John Helliwell. In February 1972, Dougie successfully auditioned for Supertramp, playing several gigs as a temporary stand-in. A year later, he became a permanent member, also lending a hand to Dave Margereson in managing the band's business deals. He also persuaded his former bandmate John to join the group.

He played with Supertramp on some of their most commercial albums: Crime of the Century, Crisis? What Crisis?, Even in the Quietest Moments, Breakfast in America, Paris, . . . Famous Last Words . . ., Brother Where You Bound and Free as a Bird.

When Supertramp initially disbanded in 1988, Thomson became a publisher in the music business, creating Trinity Publishing and worked with a Chicago management company, also working with JBM Management, managing bands such as New Sense, Disturbed, The Fags and Dark New Day.

Far removed geographically and financially from the commercial success enjoyed by groups such as Supertramp were the days of the nascent bands back in the 'burbs of Glasgow.

Jamie Barnes and his band Cochise started out in the east end of Glasgow in the early Seventies. The first time I saw them was in the Big O in East Kilbride and I wouldn't renew my acquaintance until last year, when I was researching this book, in the Glasgow bar Rockers. Jamie has a residency in this great pub and, every time I've had the pleasure of visiting, there has been a sell-out crowd. Indeed, there are always a few well-kent faces among the regulars, who go along to participate in a set that is an embarrassment of riches: soul, rock and blues numbers, as well as original material, all of which has enabled Cochise to build a massive following all over Scotland.

This should come as no surprise. The band's reputation has turned it into something of a cult over the years, with many of Scotland's big names dropping into a Cochise gig to jam with the band, including luminaries such as the aforementioned Frankie Miller, who would always make a point of joining Jamie onstage whenever he was in town.

Relentless gigging (sometimes up to six shows every week) fine-tuned the band and gave them a reputation that is still well respected today. The current line-up comprises Jamie on vocals, Nod Kerr (drums), Ped Reilly (bass), Gordon Campbell (guitar) and Stevie Flynn (guitar).

Despite major record company interest, a profile in a TV documentary, a stint on Glasgow's detective show Taggart and a million great live performances, Jamie has managed to avoid fame, evading the inevitable record and publishing deals due more to the fact he is his own man and has never liked to be told what to do, where to go and, most importantly, what to sing. In all of these virtues, he has been compared with New Jersey legend, South Side Johnny.

A bona fide Glasgow legend, Jamie never made the step up from singing in pubs and clubs to the huge concert arenas, though I and many, many others believe that it's a step he and his voice could have handled with ease. However, his career choices were all his own and that is what Jamie is all about . . . get along on a Saturday to Rockers and witness one of the true Glasgow vagabonds, a fellow who inspired me to write this book, along with all of the unsung heroes.

Red Bull

Makeovers? Everyone's at it these days. But, of course, our own personal transmogrifications have always been part of who we are, or at least who we'd like to be seen as. Around this time, my big sister Joyce decided that I needed my own makeover.

The first step was to take me in the bus into the heart of Glasgow. There she bought me a bright red skinny-rib jumper and a pair of cherry red, crushed velvet Wrangler flares. Was I the bee's knees?

I wore my new get-up for the first time at the Big O in East Kilbride for a band night. I thought I looked very muso. Rock lived and so did I in my rock god outfit.

Joyce was waiting outside. She happened to ask a few females leaving did they happen to notice her wee brother in the hall? What did wee Robert look like, quoth they. When the laughter subsided, one wee lass piped up: 'Aye, it's just as well there were no any bulls in tonight!'

Rock god? Suffice it to say, my face matched the clobber. But the band were excellent and, just like the guys in their stage gear and despite the girls' giggles, I felt proud, a feeling born of an affinity for loud music and the wish to break free, to be different. The band? Oh, aye, they were Beggars Opera.

What had begun as a jumped-up school band called System, formed in Glasgow in 1969 by songwriter and guitarist Ricky Gardiner, this outfit played their first gig on 3 December that year. Martin Griffiths (singer) and Marshall Erskine (bass) had played with Ricky Gardiner in System and had worked with him through that blistering hot summer of the moon landings on the M40 Beaconsfield Bypass, to earn some cash. With their hard-gotten gains – not to mention the small sum of £1,000, a loan from Ricky's uncle, John Spence – they fitted themselves out with what was to become a famous backdrop of ice-white Marshall stacks.

To complement the new equipment would come three new members: keyboard player Alan Park, who had been resident organist at the Locarno and drummer Raymond Wilson, formerly of the Beings, who successfully auditioned after responding to the band's newspaper ad. In 1970, last, but certainly not least, joined Virginia Scott, who had been studying piano in Italy.

With their shiny new equipment and a repertoire of progressive rock covers they quickly landed the Saturday morning spot at the Burns Howff in Glasgow, thanks to John Waterson, then proprietor.

Alan was a qualified pianist and quickly showed a real talent for arranging the popular classics. Thus tracks such as 'Raymond's Road', a real favourite of the Beggars fans, came quickly into our consciousness. Never one to rest on his laurels, Alan forged on. Next came his 'Poet and Peasant' and 'Light Cavalry', his own arrangements of the famous overtures by Franz Von Suppe, into which he and Martin Griffiths cleverly inserted new tunes and lyrics.

By this time Virginia, too, was contributing original material and tracks such as 'Time Machine', 'Passacaglia', 'Memory', 'The Fox' and 'Sarabande' were created.

The band's identity was evolving and the emerging and thoroughly progressive, rock label Vertigo offered Beggars Opera an album deal. Less than a year after the formation of the band came Act One, the first of a quartet of albums and the first single, 'Sarabande'.

Between 1970 and 1974 Beggars Opera toured throughout the UK and Europe. Following their incredibly successful live gig to a crowd of more than 100,000 at the Great British Rock Meeting at Speyer, Germany, in August, 1971, their single 'Time Machine' from second album Waters of Change, hit gold in the German charts.

The band's phenomenal success also meant a gruelling tour schedule and, finally, in 1972 Martin Griffiths would leave the band. Auditions were held in London for his replacement and Savoy Brown's Pete Scott so impressed the band with his fantastic ability to improvise and his classical training, it, erm, beggared belief. Indeed, such was his charisma and his blues-tinged influence, that, on average, Pete can be blamed for eliciting five encores every night from audiences.

It's shocking to think, then, that after a series of verbal scuffles following the recording of their Get Your Dog Off Me sessions for Phonogram Studios in 1973, with Pete on vocals, he felt he had to leave the band.

The late Linnie Paterson, of Writing on the Wall, was asked to step into the breach – he would continue to perform live with the band until 1974.

In 1975 Ricky Gardiner was approached by German label Jupiter Records to produce two more Beggars Opera albums. To his eternal credit, on a budget of beans and tin cans, he brought together Pete on vocals, Virginia on keyboards and with session drummers Mike Travis, formerly of Gilgamesh and the outstanding Clem Cattini, brought forth Sagittary and Beggars Can't Be Choosers.

In 1981 the Beggars re-formed under Gordon Sellar to produce the album Lifeline, an aptly named album which was released on Vertigo in Germany.

To this very day Beggars Opera are still making amazing music and so the journey continues. I thank Ricky and Virginia from the bottom of my heart for their correspondence when I was tracking their history. And here's a wee trivia question from the boys themselves. Who in the early Seventies was Beggars Opera's wee 17-year-old van driver (without a licence)? Answers on a postcard to a Mr Rab Andrews, c/o Park Lane Studios, Glasgow.

Tearaways

By the year 1971 I was in the fourth year of my apprenticeship at Springburn College and I had begun to meet some interesting characters.

Let us consider one Osmond O'Donnell, or the Big O and a man responsible for getting me into more than a few adolescent scrapes – yes, even my mum finally told me to stop running about with him. These exploits included being barred from the local boating pond after he'd sunk his paddle boat playing pirates and culminated in an incident in the Howff where we were chased by a raging mob baying for blood (his, not mine, though I'm sure they'd have taken me as a donor).

Imagine the scene. We've just bunked off college (again) and popped into the Howff for a wee beer. The place is mobbed and Alex Paton, the larger-than-life and extremely popular barman, is serving and not paying any attention to us at all, as is his wont. Well, doesn't the bold Big O, who's having none of it, shout at the top of his voice: 'Hoi, barman - two pints of f*ckin' lager!'

It was nothing less than downright rude and as everyone in the bar seemed to stop what they were doing and stare daggers at us, I bolted out the door, followed by Alex. I turned left at the Odeon, the Big O right and though a sizeable posse all followed him, they caught neither of us.

The Big O had met a wee lassie from Hamilton, called Sheena Haughton and said she had a friend, Carole who she thought would like me. We met a week later on a blind date at the Lunar Seven, off Buchanan Street.

I fell in love with Carole right there and then. We were married on 18 November 1972 and here we are all these years later with two grown-up children and three grandchildren. And still snogging the faces off each other.

Whatever happened to Osmond, the Big O? I have no idea. Though, come to think of it, he was a big Leonard Cohen fan, so either he's a bankrupt Buddhist touring Europe or living in Siberia writing bloody miserable poetry. I'm sure Alex would appreciate the Schadenfreude.

But back to the music. One of our first dates was at the Trocadera in Hamilton. Now Carole, her brothers Norman and Tommy and her big sister Irene, were raised in Burnbank by their mum Doris, who had been tragically widowed early in her life and was a superwoman, made entirely of love and determination.

I considered Doris to be my second mum and so asked permission to take her wee lassie out for a night of jiggin' and we headed off to see a band called the Bay City Rollers.

But these were not the Rollers who would make it mega in the mid Seventies. This was the tartan troubadours' earliest incarnation, promoting their single 'Keep on Dancing'. Nobby Clarke was on vocals with the Longmuir brothers, Billy Lyall on keys and a lad called David Paton on bass guitar, both of whom would one day turn up in an outfit called Pilot.

Ah, David. Many years after that early show in the Trocadera, as manager of the Glasgow club the Cathouse, I put on two sell-out shows with Fish, former frontman of bestselling rock outfit Marillion.

Fish, gent that he is, introduced me to his band and to David.

'I saw you in your first band.'

'You saw Pilot?' said David.

'No, the Bay City Rollers!'

Fish burst out laughing, completely lost it. When he could, he finally turned to David, said: 'You never f'n told me that!'

'It was only for two weeks,' our poor ex-Roller protested, before turning to me and saying: 'Christ, you have an f'n good memory!'

Well, I guess that's why, of all people, I'm writing this book and, believe me, there's plenty more surprises to come . . . not all so well plaid, as it were.

Power To The People

The year 1972 was a good one for my mum and dad as, finally, all of the Fields brood were hitched. My elder sister Ruby had married Danny in the mid Sixties and made me an uncle at the tender age of 13, with Kim.

This is the same Kim who made her Apollo debut in the Eighties, going to see Toyah Willcox. When the big day came my lovely niece badgered her mum to buy her a new jacket for the gig . . . when Toyah took to the stage Kim ran to the front and flung her jacket for the blonde munchkin to wear for one song. After wearing it, the punk pixie tossed it back down to my unsuspecting wee niece who suddenly had around 500 screaming fans on top of her. The only part of the jacket she came home with, you couldn't have blown your nose on.

Big sister Joyce had just married her lovely big bloke Chris Watson and my wee brother Gordon left the house to marry Heather and live with his in-laws, which left Carole and me an empty double room and the space to get married and live with my mum and dad.

I may have still been at my folks' but I felt liberated, empowered even. And the music that was emerging in Glasgow was even more empowering.

'Stone the crows!' exclaimed the very portly Led Zeppelin manager Peter Grant, as he witnessed the raw force that was Power. Maggie Bell had formed the band with Les Harvey (on guitar), Jimmy Dewar (bass) and John McGinnis (keyboards).

Maggie had a raw, rasping, sandpapery voice that surpassed in tone and timbre the sound of any of her contemporaries. Sharing the vocal duties with Jimmy, her Power was a band of progressive soul that may have been a prescient nod to future rock, but who paid their dues in the pubs and clubs and toilets of Glasgow.

It was while they were gigging as the house band at the Howff that Zeppelin's Peter Grant signed them up. In 1970, they changed their name to Stone the Crows, adding to the line-up drummer Colin Allen, formerly of Zoot Money's Big Roll Band and John Mayall's Blues Breakers.

Jimmy Dewar, of course, was an excellent bass player and Les a gifted guitarist who had spent some time across the Big Pond, touring with Cartoone. He had acquired a feel for heavy rock and the band's tight rhythm section made them an excellent live attraction.

Les, moreover, was determined to get members of the band to write their own material. Their studio work was produced by Peter Grant. Their albums met critical approval but failed to sell in large numbers. Nevertheless, Stone the Crows were a powerful blues-based rock band and always a popular live act, touring university campuses, dance halls and festivals. They also toured the States and played alongside Frank Zappa, Edgar Winter and the MC5.

Finally, in 1971, understandably disappointed at the lack of real commercial success, Jimmy and John decided to quit the band. They were replaced by Ronnie Leahy and Steve Thompson.

The following year Les was tragically electrocuted on stage during a gig at Swansea University. Despite their obvious grief, the group battled on. Peter Green, formerly of Fleetwood Mac, was first choice for the replacement member, but he pulled out and Steve Howe, of Yes, helped out the band until the young lead guitarist was invited to join – it was our old friend from Thunderclap Newman, Jimmy McCulloch.

Despite making another album, it soon became evident that the heart of the band had gone with Jimmy's departure and the tragic loss of Les. Stone the Crows broke up in June 1973.

After the split, Peter Grant stayed on as Maggie's manager, organising her first solo album, Queen of the Night. In 1974, Maggie, along with Bad Company and the Pretty Things, became one of the first signings to new label Swan Song Records.

In fact, Jimmy Page contributed to Maggie's first album Suicide Sal; strangely, its sales were less than stellar. Maggie next tried to recapture blues-rock glories by fronting Midnight Flyer, a phenomenal live act, but whose sole album, in 1981, was not a success. Returning to her solo career, Maggie had her biggest hit in the UK in 1981, duetting with B.A. Robertson on a cover version of 'Hold Me', which reached number 11 in the UK singles chart. Such was the strength of her live shows, she was also asked to perform at many charity gigs and cabaret shows.

Nobody move, there's been a hit single! Maggie's song 'No Mean City', written by Mike Moran, was the theme music to the TV crime drama Taggart. Maggie herself appeared in the show in 1990, playing the character of Effie Lambie in a one-off episode called 'Evil Eye'.

After living in Holland for the best part of 20 years, Maggie returned to the UK in early 2006 and joined the British Blues Quintet, sharing lead vocal duties with the veteran blues singer and keyboard player Zoot Money and Maggie's old Crows bandmate, drummer Colin Allen.

The band quickly have become established on the UK and European live blues circuit. Their debut CD, Live in Glasgow, was recorded at one of their first gigs, on Glasgow's Renfrew Ferry, in 2006 and released in 2008. In addition, Bell has toured with the Manfreds and Chris Farlowe – they even played my big sister's pub in Ipswich. Yes, it's a small world indeed.

See You, Jimmy

But let's go back to Jimmy Dewar. Now, in today's era of reality pop pap, where a love of music and hard-earned skills have been replaced by a hankering for nothing more than 15 minutes of fame, Jimmy had what is sometimes referred to as the full package. Possessed of a slim, diminutive frame, which he regularly clad in leopardskin breeks and cowboy boots and topped off with a wild afro and fronted with a preposterous handle bar moustache, he looked like a bona fide rock star.

Add to the image a voice that you would die for, that quite often could break your heart with its deep pathos – as Big George, who worked with him near the end of his career, told me one night: 'He's the voice that would bring a tear to a glass eye!' And that's all before we even begin to talk about his phenomenal bass playing, a mean, moody sound, with a style for every moment of the song's beat. Suffice it to say that all those years ago in the Howff, it was obvious to everyone that we were witnessing something special and unique, a talent that, quite frankly, we will never see again.

It's nice to know, however, that the legend of Jimmy Dewar lives on among us. One night, not so long ago, I was watching Paolo Nutini on telly when his interviewer launched into a skewed critique of Paisley's musical heritage, slagging off its singers and citing Kelly Marie as an example. Let me tell you that young Paulo turned round quite proudly and said two words: 'Jimmy Dewar.'

Well done, young man and, if our paths ever cross, I promise to buy you a well-deserved pint!

Jimmy's career began in the early Sixties, when he sang and played bass in a local outfit named the Gleneagles, playing alongside Alec Bell (on guitar), Ross Nelson (guitar), Jimmy Smith (saxophone) and David Miller (drums). In 1963 they were the resident band at Glasgow's Lindella Ballroom and it was here one night that they were joined on stage by an abrasive young raw talent who went by the name of Marie Lawrie, from Dennistoun. (my cousin Tommy Kelly remembers her from his schooldays) Fired up by the entrance of this 15-year-old brat, they changed their name to Lulu and the Luvvers, relocating to Le Phonograph, where they'd blagged a residency.

The club was owned by Tony Gordon, who had major contacts in London and, by February 1964, he had negotiated a recording deal for the group with Decca. The result of this union was the debut 45 'Shout', one of the cult singles of the Sixties era and, notwithstanding its rebirth as a duet with Take That, still filling the dance floor in its original form at any function I officiate or DJ to this day.

43

'Shout' reached the UK top ten and, as is ever the way throughout the history of rock and pop, the attention quickly shifted to the lead singer. The Luvvers, in effect, became a backing band, with the usual revolving door of session musicians assembled for touring and recording purposes.

It's no big surprise that, understandably feeling alienated and disillusioned, Jimmy chose to return to Glasgow in 1965. Such was his talent, not to mention the strength of his character, that just two years later he was forging a brand new career in a brand new band called Sock 'Em JB, covering soul and blues classics and fronted by the godlike voice that was ex-Del-Jack Frankie Miller, accompanied by pianist John McGinnis.

Rock being the truly fickle mistress that she is, Sock 'Em JB would be together for only a matter of months, ending when Frankie left to form a new group, Westfarm Cottage, before forming the Stoics.

Jimmy and John, however, stayed together and, by the following year, had formed a new outfit which focused on blues and heavy rock, a move that was more in line with the musical vibe of the day.

As we've seen, Power was born with Leslie Harvey and Maggie Bell, later becoming Stone the Crows, but, once again, Jimmy grew disillusioned with his role in the band; while it's true that his bass-playing was second to none, his voice was slowly being pushed into the background. Both he and John McGinnis moved on in February 1971.

Jimmy's next career move was to team up with old friend Frankie Miller and Jude were formed in July 1971. Frankie had quit the Stoics, but Chrysalis, with whom he had a publishing deal, suggested he pair with guitarist Robin Trower, who had recently left Procol Harum.

With Jimmy on bass and Clive Bunker (ex-Jethro Tull) on drums, Jude seemed like a major concern, but it was not to be. Frankie suggested to Jimmy and Robin the idea of forming a power trio and in 1972 a new group, dubbed Robin Trower, made its debut in Vienna with a line-up completed by drummer Reg Isadore.

Two enthralling albums, Twice Removed from Yesterday and Bridge of Sighs, followed, on which Trower's searing but melodic guitar work perfectly complemented Jimmy's soulful voice, fully free at last to express all of its incredible emotion and human empathy.

By 1974 Robin Trower were established on the American gig circuit and, when former Sly Stone drummer Bill Lordan replaced Reg, it could be argued that a more rhythmic texture came to the fore.

A series of wonderful recordings were made – Earth Below (1975), Live and Long Misty Days (both 1976) – before another former Sly member, Rusty Allen, took over on bass to allow Jimmy to concentrate more fully on vocals.

City Dreams (1977) and Caravan to Midnight (1978) were completed before Rusty decided to quit and the group reverted to a trio for Victims of the Fury (1980). This was the last Robin Trower album to feature Jimmy. Robin formed a new band, BLT, with ex-Cream bassist Jack Bruce, while Jimmy hooked up with Big George and formed Adults Only. One of their best songs was 'My Father' and you can hear it among the songs on the free online listening post with this book.

In 1997, thanks largely to Jimmy's commercial success with Robin Trower, Chrysalis commissioned him to put together a solo to showcase his unique vocal prowess. Stumbledown Romancer, created with various mega musicians – among whom were Matthew Fisher producing and adding organ, piano and synthesisers andy McMasters, formerly of Motors, who wrote or co-wrote some of the material, John Platania and David Hayes from Van Morrison's Caledonia Soul Orchestra and Fairport Convention drummer Dave Mattacks.

This was to be Jimmy's last ever recording and showed what a unique and gifted and truly special person he was. Sadly, he was forced to stop shortly afterwards and passed away in 16 May 2002. Big George provided a fitting memorial to one of Glasgow's rock legends:

'The man who many have called 'The Pavarotti of Rock 'n' Roll' died peacefully in his sleep on Thursday, 16 May 2002 after a long illness . . .

'Among James Dewar's biggest fans were Frankie Miller, Billy Connolly, Donny Hathaway, Rod Stewart, not forgetting Maggie Bell and Lulu herself. The famous Scottish screenwriter, Peter McDougall, still talks of his first experience of meeting Jimmy. When having a drink with Frankie, Peter noticed that the man standing next to him was clothed in snakeskin trousers, cowboy boots and not much else.

'Who's that?' Peter asked.

'Frankie replied: 'That's James Dewar.'

'Peter howled: 'Well, I want to be one of them!'

'It says it all. Everyone from Metallica to the Stereophonics was influenced by the voice of the Scotsman. The man the music industry recognised as the voice from heaven has finally gone home. We will all miss you, James.

'The little guy with the big voice.'

The Trouble With Some Folk

'I was only seventeen when I fell in love with a gypsy queen!' Ah, those lyrics, the heavy riff of the Hammond organ blasting through the twin Les Pauls, the strangely melodious banshee wail of wahwah pedal and the concrete block harmonies . . . it could only be Uriah Heep.

I just couldn't get their song out of my head and heart and here they were, coming to Glasgow. The venue was the Maryland club in Scott Street, perhaps one of the most neglected venues in Glasgow's rock 'n' roll history, despite hosting such luminaries as Pink Floyd, Eric Clapton, John Mayall, Jack Bruce, John McLaughlin, Muddy Waters and Geno Washington, to name but a few.

Then, on 25 September 1970, my life changed forever. First on at the Maryland were the support band – Mollsmyre – whose bass player burst a string playing Black Sabbath's eponymous anthem, a song called Black Sabbath.

And then it was the main event. Uriah Heep may have played countless bigger and better gigs in the years to come – and I'm happy to say that I've been lucky enough to see every Scottish show they played since – but that night was my epiphany, such was the raw power of the music, the intensity of the band's lyricism, the overall nape-tingling, heart-blasting strength of the Heep's sound.

Immediately after the gig my brother Gordon and I got chatting to Mick Box and co. and I have been chatting to him through the years ever since. Two more of their motley crew, Del Roll and Johnny Allan, keep in touch, too and remain great friends to this day.

We still share tales of their earliest Scottish gigs, in the Picasso in Buchanan Street, the Olympia in East Kilbride – once with Sha Na Na and Paladin and the other with Amazing Blondel - who were a folk band with one of their number playing a nose flute (ahh the idiosyncrasies of the Seventies, when anything went) – and the Electric Gardens, this time supported by the JSD Band.

Now, let us wander off on a wee diversion at this point, for the JSD band are well worth consideration. They first got together when they were school friends in the Sixties in Rutherglen. Originally influenced by the seminal groups of that period, including the Beatles, the Kinks and the Animals, in 1968 they moved towards an acoustic line-up and so the JSD Band was born. The name was derived from the three original members of Jim Divers, Sean O'Rourke and Des Coffield.

Those early JSD days became more and more influenced by the members' Celtic background, a rich mix of Scottish and Irish and inspired by recordings of the Clancy Brothers and the Dubliners. They were also influenced by vinyl gems found in the Barras (sadly no more a rich mine of music and tat), records by people such as the Doc Watson Family and Michael Gorman & Margaret Barry, whose style of traditional Irish songs and instrumentals formed the JSD backbone.

A more contemporary influence on JSD came from the Incredible String Band and String Driven Thing, an outfit I can remember seeing in the Disco Viva in Union Street. Come to think of it, I also recall there was a parrot in a cage on the Viva staircase and we used to feed it chewing gum while we were queuing up – it was the only way to get the feathered fiend to shut up!

String Driven Thing formed as a three-part harmony folk band in 1967 with the Adamses and guitarist John Mannion and put out a self-titled album on the small independent Concord label (copies of which are collectable and difficult to find).

The group moved from Scotland to London and Chris Adams decided to try to take the band away from its folk roots into the folk rock genre. He met up with classically-trained violinist Graham Smith and folk guitarist Colin Wilson, who moved to bass, but soon afterwards lost John Mannion, who did not think the new direction suited him.

They secured a deal with Tony Stratton-Smith's famous Charisma label and another self-titled album came out, produced by Shel Talmy. The band toured with other Charisma artists such as Genesis and this helped raise their profile and included some TV appearances, an American tour and a second album, The Machine That Cried, which was recorded with the addition of a drummer, Billy the Kid Fairley, was a bleaker and rockier offering and a forgotten classic. Recorded while Chris Adams was suffering health problems, including a collapsed lung and depression, the album did not sell particularly well. This is the era of the band I remember most, however and the track on the listening post is from this time. Following numerous line-up changes, the band are still in existence today, with me ol' mucker Ronnie Garrity on bass.

But I digress . . . One of the first places JSD played was a pub called the New Inn in Halfway, Cambuslang, where they took on a short-lived residency before deciding their next career step should be to try to get a booking in their local Folk Club at the Burnside Hotel. What was called for was a recce and so along they trooped to check out what might be expected of them.

That night it was none other than the Humblebums performing, made up of Billy Connolly, Tam Harvey and brand new member Gerry Rafferty. Not surprisingly, JSD were impressed with the mixture of Americana, original folk compositions and generous sprinklings of jokes and laughter. There and then, they decided they'd need a wide variety of sounds.

They succeeded in convincing the club organisers to let them do a floor spot the following week. It was a strong start and from this foundation they began the slow process of building up a large collection of folk clubs across Scotland by the same method of turning up, doing a floor spot and securing a return booking.

The next stage in their development came when they introduced Colin Finn. As career moves go it was an astute manouevre. Colin, you see, had that precious luxury, a car and since he was already running them around to gigs, they thought he might as well join in musically. Initially, he played bass drum and set of skulls (picked up, where else but at the Barras) and then picked up the spoons for the jigs and reels.

When the band ventured further afield, all the way to Newcastle, they met up with fiddler Chuck Fleming. Chuck was living in Durham at the time, where he shared a house with Dave Richardson of the Boys of the Lough. They immediately gelled and Chuck suggested they form a folk rock band along the lines of Fairport Convention. So now the band was a five-piece.

They entered and won a competition called the Scottish Folk Group Championship 1970. Part of the winning prize was a recording contract with EMI on the Regal Zonophone label. This debut album was a mixture of Irish, American, String Band and original material by Sean and Des.

Theirs was still mainly an acoustic sound, although a full drum kit made its first appearance.

The early Seventies saw the band make a foray into brand new musical territory, playing folk rock with a more electrified sound. Of course, this came as a downright shock, an affront even, to many traditional folk club members. My God, they bellowed over their ales, what's this? This, dear reader, was a sound and attitude more related to punk. You could argue, in fact, that here was a sound that in years to come would be taken up and made famous by the Pogues.

The JSD line-up changed with the departure of Chuck, to be replaced by fiddler Lyndsey Scott from Hawick. Lyndsey was the grandson of well-known Borders folk singer Willie Scott and a very talented player.

By now the band was being managed by Brian Adams, of Intercity Entertainments Glasgow, who also handled Beggars Opera. Brian was securing bookings outwith the constraints of the usual folk club circuit, moving the lads into the dance hall venues that in the Seventies were springing up all over Scotland, before pushing south to cover the rest of Britain.

The band built up a strong following nationwide, performing mainly in the university circuit with a reputation for supplying a rip-roaring night's entertainment. After getting a spot in Kingston Polytechnic in London, supporting a warm-up gig for David Bowie's Spiders from Mars Tour, the band were invited to be the support act for the whole tour. JSD's star was most assuredly in the ascendant.

It was at this time the band recorded their second album the JSD Band 1972. During the tour it was interesting to see how Bowie operated, starting the circuit by playing to quite small crowds before progressing to sell-out venues, aided all the way by some very well-organised PR coverage and, of course, by the timely release of his great hit single 'Starman'.

The JSD Band got on very well with the Spiders from Mars team during the tour -- Lyndsey was asked to record the fiddle part to complement Mick Ronson's lead guitar on Bowie's single 'John, I'm Only Dancing'.

The following years saw the band tour hard in France, Belgium and Germany, as well as embark on extensive gigging schedules of Britain and Ireland.

As is the way in all bands, big or small, on the road pressures inevitably saw personnel changes. Lyndsey left, which meant the return of Chucky. A third album, Travelling Days was followed by a short tour of the US of A. The far-ranging circuit, taking in destinations such as Newport, Rhode Island, Washington, New York, Cleveland, Boulder, Denver and Boston, was more than a headache for poor Chuck, who had a phobia of flying.

The band managed to get their fiddler to fly from the UK to New York, but after the first flight Chuck steadfastly refused to board any more planes and had to travel the rest of the tour by Greyhound bus. A late arrival meant that he missed a gig in Boulder, Colorado, while it took a six-day round trip by bus to get to an outdoor festival at Coyote Ridge near Denver before heading straight back east to meet the rest of the band in New York.

Thankfully, after all the to-ing and fro-ing, when the tour finally finished an exhausted Chuck was able to pack up his fiddle and head back home in the luxury of the QE2.

After their experience in the US, the band began to pull in different directions, with Chuck and Sean favouring the folk approach, while Des, Jim and Colin were eager to pursue something more contemporary, along the lines of the Eagles and the Nitty Gritty Dirt Band. Sadly, this friction resulted in the band splitting up in 1974. Des, Jim and Colin went on to be involved briefly with the New JSD Band (the title was at their management's insistence, they wanted a fresh name).

This incarnation saw the inclusion of a guitarist, Ian Lyons, who hailed from Buckie. And whom they'd first met years before when he played with the band My Dear Watson. With Ian on board, they tried to capture a more American sound, even introducing two girl backing singers for the occasional gig, such as Glasgow City Halls.

Unfortunately, they soon found that they were struggling to win over audiences, who were for the most part made up of fans who came expecting to hear the old sound. Commercially, it just didn't work out for them.

Thankfully, however, the JSD still exist today and, with every gig, sound just as potent as ever.

Colin, who has become a great mate, runs the Village Music Shop in the East Kilbride, while the next generation forges ahead – Colin's son Jamie is a great wee drummer and is playing with the much talked about local band Kobai, whose debut album has just been released in Japan.

Satisfaction

Just like the first kiss, it's a feeling you never forget. Nor would I want to. My first visit to Green's Playhouse on 5 June 1970 was a momentous occasion, the beginning of a long love affair. It was my first major rock gig – it doesn't get much bigger than front row seats for Black Sabbath, Family and Chicken Shack.

Just stepping into the place would set the hairs on the back of the neck tingling, the butterflies would be partying in the belly and, as the place filled with excited fans, the buzz could have powered the whole of Glasgow.

The Playhouse wasn't just a venue, it was the hub for a way of life, a forum where rock fans' dreams came true as long-held fantasies were lived out under the spotlights and amid the clamour and camaraderie of hundreds of rock brothers and sisters.

As a veteran of 85 gigs there, I never once lost that frisson of excitement stepping through the doors and seeing THAT stage and being on THAT balcony. To this day, more than 20 years after it closed its doors for the last time, I refuse to go down Renfield Street, never mind have a drink in the gargantuan bar that has long since taken its hallowed spot.

Thankfully, my memories of each and every gig remain fresh and alive in my mind. On my debutant night, not even the fact that Sabbath never turned up, citing their habitual van problems as an excuse, could put me off enjoying the show. Both Family and Chicken Shack more than made up for the loss of the headline act, with extended sets. I still cherish an image of Stan Webb with a ten-mile long guitar lead strolling up and down the aisle as he enthralled us with an extended version of 'Tears in the Wind'. I was mesmerised.

It was a trance-like state that was to be visited upon me many a night at Greens, for this was a venue that attracted the great and the good. One of history's biggest bands was among its many visitors, although it was only by the skin of my teeth that I managed to be among the hordes who were lucky enough to be there to see them.

The main culprit was timekeeping, or rather its entire absence in my psychological make-up. The virtue of being anywhere on time simply seemed to elude me throughout my college days. In the depths of winter I could blame the fact that East Kilbride was often snowbound for not making it to classes, though this was a more difficult line of defence to put to my teachers in July and August.

I'd been booted out once before for late-shows and no-shows, a situation only temporarily remedied by the late intervention of the union and soon found myself on my last – no really, Fields, this is the last! – warning.

Well, the last warning, somewhat inevitably, was soon followed by my last day in further education. I met my college friend Brian Green, a truly gifted guitarist with whom I'd form my only band, Crisis Point, on the same bus and, guess what, we were late. With a flash of inspiration I recalled one of our lecturers once confiding that, better than turning up late on a final warning, it might be prudent to phone in sick instead.

Eureka. So, there we were, out and about in town, kicking our heels until the record stores opened, when we spied a disorderly queue all ages outside an electrical shop in Sauchiehall Street. Curious, we wandered over only to discover this was a queue for tickets for a gig at Green's in a few weeks' time. And who was playing? A band called the Rolling Stones.

I thought Brian, budding guitarist and number one Stones fan, was going to faint, such was the whiteout pallour of his spotty young face. I was more of a Beatles man myself, but of course, we immediately joined the end of a miraculously short line.

It was only after half an hour of shuffling along in the queue that it dawned on me I didn't have a ha'penny piece on me. The tickets cost from 14 shillings right up to a whopping £2.20.

I told Brian not to move, unless it was forward very slowly, made my apologies to everyone behind and made for the Ivanhoe Hotel in Buchanan Street where my sister was head honcho. Joyce, may the gods of all things rock 'n' roll bless her, gave me £5, instructing me to buy two £2.20 tickets for her and her boyfriend. Now timekeeping may not have been my great virtue, but nascent accountancy skills, not to mention a Machiavellian streak, told me I could tell big sis all the £2.20 tickets had sold out, leaving me no option but to buy four at 14 shillings.

I raced back to the shop only to find that, by now, the queue was the length of the street. Undeterred, ignoring the great wall of angry heckling from the back of the line, I settled back in next to Brian.

It was a lovely summer's day, I had the necessary funds for the golden tickets in my back pocket and the Rolling Stones were coming to town. I have to say I was feeling pretty happy with how my day was turning out.

That was until the film crew turned up. Now, I know Brian didn't mean any harm and, after all, he wasn't the one on his final warning at college, but giving an interview to the STV news team about how he and his mate – the one who was somewhat bizarrely trying to hide from the camera under his pulled-up jacket – were huge Stones fans who had been camping out all night to get tickets – camping! Where did that come from? – wasn't really the brightest of ideas.

Brian's moment of television history over, the tickets finally in our pockets, we headed off to our favourite wee record shop in Buchanan Street to listen to some albums, as this perfect day softened into a haze of music, sunshine and the afterglow of a sneaky wee bottle of Mr Merrydown's finest vintage cider.

Next day, of course, head still buzzing, I was hauled immediately into the Big Office at college. I don't think there was a student or staff member who hadn't enjoyed Brian's moment of Rolling Stones mania on the evening news. Unfortunately for yours truly, it had also been patently obvious who the figure skulking inside a pulled-up jacket next to him was. My college education was at an end. Who was it said you can't always get what you want, but sometimes you get what you need?

Brain didn't get off entirely scot-free either, though the come-uppance came months later on the day of the big gig. The first thing I noticed was the fact it was Groundhogs' drum kit and backline that was set up, but Tony S. McPhee missed the train for the afternoon shows (they played the night one) and, instead, we were treated to local outfit Merlin. Magically, they just happened to be sitting in the Howff when an emergency call came through that a band were needed to support the Rolling Stones and, like the proverbial rats up a drain pipe, Merlin were off to Green's – which just goes to show you that some good can come from sitting in the pub all day.

Queue lights, queue curtain and on prances Mick Jagger in a pink satin suit, waving a basket of flowers, up rises the audience as one in adulation, up jumps the bold Brian on top of his seat and is promptly slung oot by Big Willie, the door surgeon.

It was as quick and decisive a piece of non-elective surgery as I've ever seen and, though Brian pleaded with the big man that his friends were inside, we gracefully declined Big Willie's chance to be reunited out front.

To this day Big Willie remembers Brian, utterly inconsolable, standing in tears outside listening to the show. To his eternal credit, Willie finally gave in and let Brian in for the end of the encore (big softie that you are, Willie!). And so Brian, now living in Canada, can boast that, if only for a few minutes, he saw the Stones and his hero Mick.

Drummed Out

I've very briefly mentioned Crisis Point. Truth be told, our career was almost as long as the mention. Brian was on guitar and I was the singer. For the life of me, I can't remember the drummer's name but I do recall he had only a snare, bass drum and pedal and a single hi hat. Jim Clark was our bass player, feeding his axe through a mono record player.

Despite everything, even the record player, we got gigs. The first was in Cambuslang, in a bar called the Wooden Cask. It was not the kind of hostelry you are used to seeing in Glasgow, not least because of the peculiar architecture that saw it built on stilts. The Cask's owner knew, first hand, that Brian was incredibly good and, fair play to the poor man, assumed we must be too.

Anyway, we were to fill in the gaps during a talent competition, entertaining the audience while the judges were deliberating the various merits of local talent. As I stood there in my stage gear – where would I be without my red skinny-ribbed jumper and matching crushed velvet Wrangler flares? – belting out the Kinks' 'Lola', I noticed the owner waving at me so I waved back. Strangely, this seemed to infuriate him immensely. Actually, he was waving at us to get the f**k off the stage as we were crap and had only one song all the way through.

Rock 'n' roll stars that we thought we were, we remained undeterred and things improved slightly at our next gig when some of the band's dads became involved in a sing-along. One set of our new backing band was in the Hibernians, the other in the Orange Lodge and, with their new-found talents employed on a regular basis, we soon found one week we'd be heachin' and hochin', the very next it was hochin' and heachin'. But the set remained the same, with numbers from Free, Sabbath, Cream, the Kinks and, for no rational explanation, Kenny Rogers.

We lived up to our name when things came to an abrupt and sticky end: we were murdering innocent music at the Miners Welfare club in Cambuslang when someone launched a pie at me, messing up the clobber and entirely deflating the rock god persona. Things must have been bad, because according to my mate Billy Forsyth, the pies in that club were renowned for being the best in Lanarkshire.

First the drummer walked out, with his entire kit under one arm. Brian had soon talked me into talking my mum into buying me a drum kit. The proviso was that I had to have my hair cut – no small price to pay, let me tell you. But the deed was done, my hard-grown locks shorn and off we trooped to Patersons Music shop at the top of Buchanan Street. I picked out an amazing Ajax kit that, despite bearing art work that closely resembled a pair of Y-fronts covered in pizza sauce and skid marks, was all mine.

Next day Brian came to the house to jam and, after a drop or two of Mr Merrydown's bubbly, I managed to put one of my sticks through the snare.

Now, as anyone will tell you, for that particular kit the snare had to be taken away to be sorted. Apparently, it involved heating the skin then stretching it over the frame and clamping it before it ran away. All of this malarkey took a month to complete.

I'd only played the kit once and when, four weeks later, I collected the mended snare we headed off to Howff with a new determination.

Northwind were playing that night. Unfortunately, so were Rangers against Everton in a friendly at Ibrox and my mate had a spare ticket. So off the three of us went: himself, myself and the fully fit snare drum. How any of us survived the whole game intact I don't know, as everyone wanted a shot of leading off the football chorus ubiquitous the world over: 'Dadadadada dadadada!'

What was even more daunting was that I still had the Howff and Northwind to contend with. By the time we arrived at the Howff, I was well gone and chose a prime seat, with the drum held between my legs giving it laldy. When the lads struck up 'Casanettes' I joined in with my snare and was unceremoniously flung out by Auld John for drowning out the band.

All was not lost. On the number 70 bus, with snare and some dignity still intact, I was nearing my stop in East Kilbride. Crisis Point Number Two. As I made to get off, the bus suddenly lurched, I slipped forward and, in an effort to save my face from kissing the tarmac, dropped the snare drum and put my foot right through it.

I sold the kit two days later and let my hair grow again.

So, where were we? Oh, aye, the Seventies. That means Alex Harvey.

Alex: A Personal Tribute

Alex Harvey. What can Robert Fields say about a man who, more than anyone, became the focus of Glasgow's burgeoning rock scene? In all honesty, my own experience of his genius is not as rich as I'd have liked, or as it should be. But many's the Glaswegian, indeed many's the music lover the world over, who has a tale to tell of Alex, cherishes a fond memory of a gig or, indeed, is a living encyclopedia to the man's way-too-short career. One such fan is Martin Kielty, the official voice of the Sensational Alex Harvey Band, the man who to this day manages their final incarnation and who has written their definitive biography. I therefore humbly and gratefully, hand you over to Martin, who has kindly agreed to introduce you to the legend that was the truly sensational Alex Harvey.

Martin says: 'Glasgow likes a good fight. Not always the fists-and-teeth type either – a good wee argument over a pint will do fine. And Glasgow rock fans enjoy nothing more than a good big argument over lots of pints about the best and worst of the city's hard 'n' heavy heritage.

'But there's one man no one can dispute was the king of it all. The one person who embodied everything about the city and what it stands for, falls for and wants to be remembered for. Good evening boys and girls – I'd like to take this opportunity to introduce Alex Harvey. The Sensational Alex Harvey.

'The story goes just the way you like it. Alex was born in the 1930s in the hard working class environment of the Gorbals. He discovered rock 'n' roll when he was 20, just as it was growing out of the bastard concoction of American white folk music and black blues music. In those days the exciting new sounds travelled from the States to Scotland and then to the rest of the UK, so Alex was front line. He started his first band by asking his mates, 'How would you like to get into debt?'

'As blues led to skiffle then soul, the Alex Harvey Soul Band became the nation's first real rock stars. In 1964, after (Alex claims) 35 jobs including lion-tamer and six years as a professional musician, the Soul Band followed the beat trail to Hamburg, where the following year Alex recorded the acclaimed and valuable Alex Harvey and his Soul Band. Only it wasn't his band – it was Kingsize Taylor's backers, for contractual reasons.

'Back in London the music machine tried to launch him as a pop crooner, something like Cliff Richard – but the mask wouldn't fit. After a trad blues album with some desperately deep vibes, Alex jacked in the gigging gig and joined the pit band for the hippy musical Hair, where it's said he enjoyed the happiest, most stable five years of his life.

'It wasn't exactly stunning stuff, mind – and when he was introduced to Jimi Hendrix by Animals bassist (and Jimi's manager) Chas Chandler, Alex knew he had more to do. And if his Glaswegian work ethic wasn't woken straight away, it had the rudest of awakenings when his younger brother Les died by electrocution on stage with his band Stone the Crows.

'That was May 1972, by which time Alex had been in the game more than 15 years. By the standards that said rock 'n' roll was a young man's game, he was already in breach of the rules. But that kind of thing had never bothered him.

'So it was that bingo millionaire Bill Fehilly – who'd always had a soft spot for Alex and was known as the only man who could control that determined character – went into the music industry with the sole intention of making Alex a star.

'The first job was to recruit a band and eyes turned to home, where prog-rockers Tear Gas were being called Fear Gas by audiences because of the sheer volume they generated. Already known for killer live shows and mooning from venue and van windows, the four-piece act was imploding because, quite simply, they were too big for the nation's circuit to support.

'Guitarist Zal Cleminson, bassist Chris Glen, keyboardist Hugh McKenna and his cousin, drummer Ted, were made an offer – double wages, debts paid off and let this old man Harvey sing with you.

'Needless to say there were doubts. But all were dispersed after 20 minutes in a rehearsal room, where Alex taught them the riff to 'Midnight Moses' – it seemed simple, they thought, but soon realised that a widdly-widdly band trying to remain that solid for that length of time held its own challenges. And out of that rock-solid tension came an almost terrifying energy . . . encrusted when Alex moved up to the mike and abandoned the spoof-American soul voice he'd been using, relying instead on the honesty and power of a good Glaswegian grunt to sell the story.

'Sensational, he called them: the Sensational Alex Harvey Band. It gave them something to live up to, because everyone would want them to fail. They were all up for the challenge.

'Almost immediately they threw themselves into an agonising pace of gig-gig-gig. In their first year they played over 200 shows with no more than a fortnight off for Christmas and their first album, Framed, set the scene for what was to come. It was more of an Alex solo album, with the rest of SAHB replacing the suspects Alex would have rounded up, but it had something that promised everything. When they played 'Framed', they played it so slow, a silence fell against the tension of a thunderstorm waiting to burst. Night after night the band left the stage to no applause whatsoever – because it took people half a minute to recover from what they'd experienced. After that they didn't stop cheering.

'Without doubt Alex was seen as a father-figure. He was an average of 17 years older than anyone who came to see him. But he was a pretty cool dad, even though he made it obvious he was in charge. His message was stern but full of love: 'Don't make any bullets, don't buy any bullets, don't shoot any bullets . . . because when you do, you only make a rich man richer. And don't p*sh in the water supply.'

'In 1973 they broke big by supporting Slade while the glamsters were at the top of their game. No one wanted the gig because Slade's fans didn't want to tolerate a support act. But SAHB loved the challenge – Alex stood between Zal and Chris and they marched, slowly, painfully slowly, one chord, then one step, towards the audience. And the audience moved back and considered doing a runner. Slade supporters arrived as enemies and left as fans.

'The albums did well – Next, The Impossible Dream, Tomorrow Belongs to Me. But SAHB couldn't get a hit single, principally because it was so tough to summarise what they were in a three-minute one-shot. By 1975 they were the biggest-grossing live act in the UK, with tens of thousands of people mesmerised as Alex played the hand-placing 'Faith Healer', the wide boy in 'Runaway', the two-bit 'tec in 'Man in the Jar' and of course Hitler in 'Framed'.

'One May night the band recorded a live show to test out their new sound system. They headed to the States still looking for that hit – and flew home in a hurry after the management released 'Delilah' from the live recording without their knowledge.

'Naturally, it was a mixed blessing. Anyone who's had a hit will tell you, there's no stopping or back-patting . . . the priority is to get another hit right away. But SAHB were labelled a novelty act – they'd only ever done 'Delilah' because they were looking for a song with a comedy dance opportunity. And as a result the pressure was on for another novelty hit.

'Anyone who has only experienced SAHB via 'Delilah' has totally, utterly, missed the magic. This was a big band in every sense, in every direction. All of human life was in their Vaudeville-inspired show. There was a deeply intelligent and important message in a SAHB performance, borne out of hard Glasgow living and the knowledge that things needed to change, people needed to get better and the kids were the future and needed to believe. But it's tough to explain if you never felt Alex telling 50,000 people he loved them – and KNOWING he was really only talking to you.

'In 1976 the wheels came off. After masterminding another top-ten hit, 'Boston Tea Party', which bode well for the future, manager Bill Fehilly died in a plane crash. Alex was inconsolable – he'd lived with death all his career, but it seems that this was the last straw.

'He began taking too much medication and too much liquid medication and took most of the year off, leaving the band to record and tour in an interesting but ultimately lacking SAHB (Without Alex) project.

'They gathered again for Rock Drill, in which Alex embraced the now-massive punk ethic, encouraging the band to abandon their concept of musical sense in favour of raw animal feeling, while still using their talent and experience to out-play the punks and out-express them too.

'It's truly a masterpiece album, certainly my favourite SAHB disc and the Pistols and co. loved Alex, who was known as 'the world's oldest punk', so it would have done well even though it flew in the face of what people were meant to like.

'But during final rehearsals for the tour Alex decided he couldn't go on, got in a taxi and turned his back on SAHB. (As a wee aside you may be interested to know AC/DC got their big break in the UK because, at short notice, they were dragged in to replace SAHB on a BBC music show they'd been meant to headline.)

'One year later he was back with the New Alex Harvey Band and released two more albums; but he never got near that SAHB magic again and indeed seemed something of a spent force, trying to recapture old glories when his mantra had always been 'They do that, so we'll do something different.'

'In 1982 he suffered a heart attack while heading home from a disappointing European tour. He died on 4 February, one day before his forty-seventh birthday.

'In the Nineties and then again this century, the remaining members of the band have re-formed to acknowledge the spirit of the man who led them, as well as giving a display of what we're missing. They've released two live albums and enjoyed heroes' welcomes at festivals across Europe. Zal Cleminson has left the fold and the line-up is now Glen and the McKenna cousins, along with Mad Max Maxwell (vocals) and Julian Saxby (guitar). It would be unfair to call them a tribute act, although any label that gets you along for a listen will do for me. Because you need to hear them and ask yourself this: if SAHB can sound as good as they do now and entertain as fully as they do now, without the man who provided most of the sound and entertainment . . . just how sensational were they at full strength?

'It's hard to quantify, but there's a clue coming. In 1974 an album was abandoned after completion because the band felt producer Shel Talmy hadn't made them sound the way they wanted. Then, it was to be called Can't Get Enough. In 2009 it's called Hot City and represents a slightly more mainstream, but still massively powerful, music force. Importantly, it's got Alex right up front in the mix, which is where perhaps we'd all have liked him to be, but he and the band disagreed. And it's an incredibly powerful performance from Mr Harvey.

'Remember what I said about Alex talking to you and you alone? I never felt that myself. I was born the day SAHB played their first gig and I was nine when Alex died. But I wrote a book about them and managed the rest of the band for a few years and I like to think we did one or two things right. But what I learned was, it was only so much to do with the band, or the fans, or me.

'You look into the night sky and you see the light from a star that died millions of years ago. Well, that's the light that shone around me and the SAHBsters. If Alex Harvey was even just a little brighter than the 25-year-old afterglow he left us in, then I can say with every confidence that he was the best, the very best, of Glasgow rock 'n' roll. And I'll argue with you over a lot of beer about it.'

Another man well qualified to comment on the phenomenon who was Alex Harvey is lifelong fan and aficionado Douglas McMahon. Here he relates his fondest memories, ignited by the recollection of seeing the man at Glasgow's Apollo on 4 May 1975, then again at the renowned Christmas Concerts later the same year.

'Good evening, boys and girls, it is a gas to be here. I would like to take this opportunity to introduce you to my band, the Sensational Alex Harvey Band.'

'Three and a half thousand fans roared their approval as SAHB launched into 'Faith Healer'.

'Let me put my hands on you,' sang Alex, as Zal, Chris, Ted and Hugh menacingly surveyed the three tiers of the Apollo before assaulting the audience with their own brand of rock.

'A SAHB gig was never just five guys getting up on stage and playing their basic set. Alex wanted to communicate with his audience, to do more than just entertain. He wanted to grab you by the balls and seriously get your attention, but more especially he needed your input. It was early days, but an interactive experience was probably the best way to describe a SAHB gig.

'Alex's adventures in Hamburg in the Sixties had delicately led up to 'Action Strasse'. This was closely followed by a song inspired by the writing of Robert Louis Stevenson, 'The Tomahawk Kid'. Alex by now was beginning to prowl the stage, assisted by the Mackenna cousins on drums and keyboards.

'In front of Ted stood the impressive figure of Chris Glen on bass, looking like Elvis's lovechild in a fetching blue catsuit and an enormous codpiece – an appliance he swore was merely to support the massive bass guitar and prevent him from some serious hernia problems.

'Completing the line-up was the charismatic Zal Cleminson, looking for all the world like an escapee from Chipperfield's circus, dressed in what could only be described as some sort of designer clown's outfit and wearing face make-up to accentuate the faces he pulled . . . but what a guitarist!

'Give My Compliments To the Chef' continued the onslaught and this was followed by SAHB at their best.

'Hugh struck the opening chords and 'Delilah' was upon us. Alex conducted the choir at the chorus but the best was yet to come as Chris and Zal performed their well choreographed dance routine, which drew frenzied appreciation from the fans.

'With Alex flanked by Zal and Chris, one foot balanced on the monitors, book in hand, he began 'The Tale of the Giant Stone Eater'.

'Two large torches that Alex had taped together shone out from above the monitors as he described the character who had developed into Vambo. 'Vambo Rools' was adopted by the legions of fans throughout the world and many a wall has had those words spray-painted on them – copied from Alex who during Vambo would spray a brick wall with 'Vambo Rools' in white paint.

'Midnight Moses' followed, one of Alex's pre-SAHB compositions and one of the earlier collaborations between Alex and Tear Gas.

'Dance to the Music was Alex paying homage to the music of the Sixties, but Tomorrow Belongs to Me had courted controversy, coming from the film Cabaret. Alex was a pacifist, but many thought he was promoting the Nazi ideal by playing this song: 'Don't make any bullets, don't buy any bullets and don't fire any bullets; a Fender Telecaster has more penetration than an AK-47'. These are words that still stick in my mind.

'On to another singalong from the Next album and 'Gang Bang' had the fans in fine voice. Singing it along with 3,500 other fans was surreal.

'Alex thanked everyone for their support as he and the band left the stage.

'After a brief break SAHB reappeared and finished off the night's entertainment with 'Framed'. Wearing a leather biker's jacket and a stocking over the head, he told the story of how he was framed and how he never did nothing. 'Do you believe me?' Alex pleaded with the audience for their support throughout the song.

'Alex disappeared backstage while Zal let rip with a solo that had the hairs on the back of your neck stand up. Alex reappeared by breaking his way through the Vambo wall and convincing the fans to back him and not the band.

'The gig was over as Alex and the guys took the applause from the front of the stage . . .

'The Christmas concerts in December '75 have gone down in folklore as being some of the most memorable nights in the Apollo's history.

'Having released Live and Tomorrow Belongs to Me earlier in the year, SAHB were conquering all before them. The gigs were the hottest tickets in town: it was £1.75 for a seat in the stalls, seats which, by the way, were seldom used.

'With new material and confidence high, SAHB produced one of those 'I was there that night' gigs.

'Who else but Alex would stop the gig mid-song and announce: 'We're gonnae have a talent contest'? Alex would be the compère, with the band competing in a sort of Opportunity Knocks-type contest. Each member had to entertain the audience with a party piece performed on stage. Whoever got the biggest cheer from the audience, won the contest.

'Zal played an acoustic number while perched on the edge of the stage. Not a wise position to be in, as everyone knows the Apollo stage was kind of high.

'Hugh won hands down when he produced an accordion and had the whole Apollo dancing to some traditional Scottish music.

'Alex's portrayal of a private detective during 'Man in the Jar' would have put Humphrey Bogart to shame. Wrapped in an old Macintosh raincoat and standing under a street light, he flipped open a pack of cigarettes, while telling the story of how he was left as the patsy.

'The gig continued and Delilah went down a storm. Dancing Cheek to Cheek was one of those strange songs for a band to play but it seemed to work. The three pretty dancing girls helped considerably, but the moment they turned their backs on the audience to reveal bottomless dresses, the place erupted.

'When the pipers come on stage during Anthem the hairs on the back of your neck stood to attention, while the audience as one swayed side to side, conducted, as always, by Alex.

'The concert finished with a sensational version of 'Framed' with Alex, as always, trying to convince the audience that he was good and that the band were bad. We had to believe him that he was Framed or he would take the huff.

'Treasured memories, indeed, of a night that still brings a wry smile to my face to this day.'

The Captain's Finale

Once upon a time, a nineteenth-century novelist and renowned mariner inspired the name of a fine Glasgow band, even though the closest the merry swashbucklers ever came to life on the high seas themselves was a gig at the Bay Hotel in Gourock.

Captain Marryat, who formed in 1970, were singer Tommy Hendry, Ian McEleny (guitar), Allan Bryce (keyboards and vocals), Hugh Finnegan (bass and vocals) and Jimmy Rorrison (drums).

Frustrated by rock 'n' roll gigs in west-coast working men's clubs, where they played between the OAPs' bingo sessions, they sought to widen their audience by playing music inspired by such Uriah Heep, Deep Purple, Beggars Opera, Cream, Neil Young and the James Gang.

The culmination of paying homage to artists past and present were two original songs, penned by Allan and recorded in Thor Studios in St Vincent Street. Later that same week the studio phoned the lads and asked if they'd like to record a full album. This was a bit of a problem, as they still only had the two songs.

After a few weeks' hard graft with instruments and pen and paper, they returned to the studio and produced an album, limited to 200 copies.

The recording was followed by hard gigging, with Tuesday night stints in the Burns Howff. By all accounts this hallowed slot may have come too early in their careers, for the place was deid. Practice made perfect, however and with a bonus Saturday slot secured the band were off and running; other gigs included the Watermill Hotel in Paisley, Gourock's Bay Hotel, the Olympia in East Kilbride and the Terminal One Club in Glasgow.

The band split up in 1975 but since one of their albums popped up on eBay nearly 34 years later, selling for 3,000 quid, they have suddenly found themselves back in the spotlight once again – and they fully deserve their place in this history of the Glasgow rock scene.

Through Thick And Thin

When, at the tender age of 18, Glaswegian guitarist Brian 'Robbo' Robertson joined Thin Lizzy, he became, along with Scott Gorham, one half of the group's twin-guitar sonic attack that helped to establish them as one of the world's top rock acts in the Seventies.

Robbo had spent eight years learning classical piano as a youngster before switching to the guitar. Just as he entered his teenage years, he began playing in several different local Glasgow bands, one of which, Dream Police, would later evolve into Tear Gas.

He also served me on many occasions in Gloria's Records in East Kilbride where, if you went in with a bun, he would make you a wee cuppa and you could shoot the breeze on the rock scene while playing in full the albums you wanted to hear.

I met Robbo again a few years ago in the Underworld in Camden when he came to see the Heavy Metal Kids/Blue Sugar line-up I was putting on. He looked amazing, having been sober and clean for a few years. When I reminded him of Gloria's he asked: 'Did I used to make you tea and biscuits and play your albums? Well, it was because of people like you I got the f'n sack!'

Lizzy were auditioning for a new guitarist in June of 1974, a man to fill the boots of original founder member guitarist Eric Bell. An audition was eventually set up for Robbo when a friend of his, who also happened to be a roadie for Lizzy, put a word in for him.

The auditions were being held in London and Robbo left Glasgow as skinny and skint as a council park rabbit, with just his guitar and a pair of drumsticks. He figured that, if he didn't land the gig, perhaps he could try out for a drumming position in another band.

As it happened, he sailed through the audition. Not long afterwards, Lizzy welcomed Scott into the fold, a move that sparked the birth of one of the band's musical trademarks, twin guitar harmonies: a sound that would be copied by numerous future groups, among them Iron Maiden, Def Leppard and Heavy Pettin'.

Led by bassist/singer/poet Phil Lynott, the Robertson-Gorham version of the group would become the most popular among fans, but it took the new line-up a couple of releases to get used to one another: 1974's Nightlife and 1975's Fighting. By 1976, Lizzy had solidified their style, focused their approach and built a rock-solid reputation, scoring a breakthrough hit with 'The Boys Are Back in Town' and a gold-certified album, Jailbreak.

With the seventh album Johnny the Fox flying off the shelves in 1976, Lizzy landed a lucrative tour of American arenas, opening for Queen. But on the eve of the tour's launch, Robbo was involved in a bar-room brawl, in which a broken bottle severed the nerve and artery of one of his hands. Unable to hold a pint glass, never mind play his axe, Robbo's future with Lizzy was suddenly thrust into doubt, with Gary Moore assuming his role on stage for the upcoming tour with Queen.

With the tour over, Robbo was asked to rejoin on a temporary basis to lay down tracks for their next studio album, 1977's Bad Reputation. Despite Robbo's face being omitted from the album's cover, he was eventually welcomed back into the group as a fully-fledged member once more. His inimitable guitar talents came to the fore the next year on the classic double 1978 in-concert set, Live and Dangerous, especially on the slow-burning blues of 'Still In Love With You', a song that was co-written by Lynott and Frankie Miller and his guitar dogfight with Gorham on 'Emerald'.

Although Thin Lizzy were, by now, enjoying massive worldwide success, relations between Robbo and the band had deteriorated rapidly, a situation which finally led to his ousting from the group in mid 1978 when, once again, he was replaced by Gary Moore.

Wild horses couldn't drag Robbo from his love of live music, however and when Wild Horses were getting together he joined bassist Jimmy Bain, a fellow refugee from another big-name band, this time Rainbow. Although Wild Horses initially enjoyed some moderate success in the UK, their gallop slowed to a trot after just a pair of forgotten releases, 1980's The First Album and 1981's Stand Your Ground.

Thankfully, Robbo didn't have to wait long before his next secondment. At that time Motörhead, who were enjoying the biggest commercial success of their career, had just parted company with longtime guitarist Fast Eddie Clarke and Robbo was invited to come on board. Although the move must have looked like the perfect symbiosis on paper, it simply didn't work on vinyl. Robbo and Motörhead stayed together for just one studio album, 1983's Another Perfect Day.

Diehard Motörhead fans simply refused to accept our lad from Glasgow and the guitarist was sent packing once the album's supporting tour wrapped up. A live recording of their ill-fated liaison would be released years later in 1997: King Biscuit Flower Hour Presents Motörhead is now regarded as a classic. I think it's fair to say that their line-up had a similarity to Deep Purple's Come Taste the Band era, with Tommy Bolin replacing Blackmore.

Robbo rejoined Lizzy on stage for a night during the group's final tour in 1983, along with most of the group's other guitarists past and present, which was documented on a double disc set the same year, entitled Life. Little was heard from Robertson subsequently in the Eighties, during which time a rumoured Lizzy reunion featuring the Live and Dangerous line-up proved to be false and would ultimately never come to pass, as frontman Lynott passed away in January of 1986.

Robertson magically reappeared during the Nineties, however, guesting in a Thin Lizzy tribute band called Limehouse Lizzy. They were, still are, regarded as the world's top Lizzy act and, it was for this reason that in 1992 I put them on in the Cathouse – the club I was by then managing.

In Glasgow we also had our own Lizzy tribute, Fat Betty, featuring the splendid guitarist David Brocket and his mates from the Sound Control store.

The deal was that Fat Betty would play a two-hour set, followed by a set featuring Robbo. The main problem was both parties agreeing on which material to use, as both, understandably, wanted to play all of the classic songs.

Finally, an agreement was reached and the songs and boundaries agreed – this meant only a few songs being duplicated. One was 'Still in Love With You'. Bassist and lead singer Wayne, being the gentleman and scholar that he is, thanked Fat Betty for supporting them and announced this was a wee song Betty had played earlier.

At this point the bold Robbo stepped forward and cried into the mic: 'Aye, but no half as f'kn good as this version!' Priceless.

Also part of the deal was two nights' accommodation for Robbo. As the promoter for the Bruce Hotel, in East Kilbride at the time, I managed to get him two nights' bed and breakfast and, as he had at that time what we might call a penchant for the odd and the even, tipple, I was also to be his official babysitter.

My two-day tour of duty started off so well. I met him at the hotel and he took me down to meet his mum and dad in Cathkin, a lovely couple who were obviously proud of their son. They saw all the major Lizzy shows in London and across the UK and were keen to come to the Cathouse the following night. At one point, Brian excused himself and went to the loo and that's when his mum leaned over to me, looking very concerned and whispered in my ear: 'Listen, son, whatever you do, don't mention Jimmy Bain or Wild Horses in front of Brian.' I didn't. So far, so good.

Later that night, prior to setting foot in the Cathouse for a quick recce, Robbo out of nowhere informed me I wasn't allowed to use his name or picture on the posters for the gig (which I had done, of course) and, if he saw any, he'd 'crack up'.

In a panic, I phoned ahead and got the gang – Kim, Remo and Sandro – to do their rounds and take down all the posters. They managed to remove all except one – the one, of course, plastered to the wall of the bar Robbo and I chose to take a constitutional.

He turned to me and said simply: 'That'll cost you.'

I replied in four words: 'Free bar all night.'

We shook hands and we both laughed and, to this day, I still can't recall how we got home that night, never mind how Robbo managed to play the gig the next night. I can only guess it was down to the fact we both shared the globally infamous Glaswegian constitution.

Robbo returned to the Cathouse a few months later with his new band The Clan and would go on to record albums with Swedish rockers, Lotus: Quartet Conspiracy and A Taster for the Big One. In 1995 he issued his first ever solo release, a six-track EP called The Clan.

Through the years, Robbo has also guested on other artists' recordings, including Pat Travers' Makin' Magic, Roy Sundholm's The Chinese Method and then joined the live band for Frankie Miller's Dancing in the Rain.

It can be a cruel, dog-eat-dog world, this business of rock 'n' roll and, more than any, Brian 'Robbo' Robertson should know that. But there's a born survivor in the boy who once made me tea and biscuits.

Births, Deaths & Marriages

By 1972 Green's Playhouse was kicking in as the major gig in Glasgow. I eventually got to see Black Sabbath, as well as Deep Purple, Groundhogs, The Faces, Humble Pie with Peter Frampton's Camel and Alice Cooper, before he washed off his make-up to play golf with presidents.

The first half of the following year was to be the last throw of the dice for Green's and I attended the first of nine shows there by Uriah Heep. By this time, they had emerged as one of the top touring rock bands in the world.

The line-up had settled down, recovering from a regularly defunct drummer situation straight out of Spinal Tap. Now at their mighty thumping heart was Lee Kerslake and joining him in the rhythm section was Gary Thain, one of the best bass players I've ever seen – and I've seen a few.

The nucleus of Heep consisted of founder member Mick Box on guitar, David Byron (vocals) and Ken Hensley (keyboards). Heep had grown special to me and my family in those three short years in which they had evolved from the Maryland gig and graduated to the Grand Old Lady and, as we shall see later, would go on to even bigger conquests in Europe and the States.

In fact, in the summer prior to our marriage in November 1972, Carole and I had followed the full itinerary of British tour dates with Heep. The lads looked after us really well, through the many nights we spent sleeping in dodgy B & Bs or on hotel floors and one best-forgotten night in a bath.

One of the most diverse shows they were booked to play was the Grangemouth Rock and Pop Festival on 29 September 1972. Held in the full-on glare of BP's oil refinery flares, this was Scotland's first major outdoor showcase for an eclectic mix of international rock, pop and folk music.

Promoted by Great Western Festivals, whose directors included the star of the movie Zulu, Stanley Baker, it was opened by Glasgow's Chris McClure and boasted barnstorming sets from Status Quo, Lindisfarne, an explosive funk set from the anything-but Average White Band, English folk-rock from Steeleye Span and a long, labyrinthine excursion into Scottish prog-rock madness from Beggars Opera.

What made Grangemouth different were the one-off appearances by the Everly Brothers, replete with their soar-away harmonies, ideal for a sunny afternoon and the mighty, rumbling rock power trio Beck, Bogert and Appice, who played a chaotic set in a rain- and beer-sodden finale.

And let's not forget appearances by Billy Connolly, in his first ever solo gig, John Peel, who was inexplicably stationed up in a high tower and Marsha Hunt.

I did say Heep were booked to play. The huge disappointment was they were never able to take the stage. They arrived on time, along with Carole and myself of course and were scheduled to play second last. The hitch was that they had to catch a plane to get back down to London sharpish to do some pre-production for their next album, Sweet Freedom. They asked the Everlys to swap slots, they asked everyone to swap slots. No one would do it and Heep had no option but to leave.

Thankfully, they were back in Scotland and playing Glasgow the very next year – although there would be two major events before then. The first was a happy day, for on 10 May 1973, Carole presented me with a baby boy. We named him Lee Michael, after Lee and Mick from Heep. I remember we sent wee birth cards to the lads and for fear of offending either, on Mick's we put Michael Lee and on Lee's we put Lee Michael. Of course, they laughed about it when they found out the truth.

The second event was not so cheerful as, on 30 June 1973, Green's Playhouse closed its doors for the last time. Its demise was truly the end of an era. They do say, however, that for every tragedy there is born something wonderful and good. Along with wee Lee Michael, there was another birth that year. On 5 September, Unicorn Leisure relaunched Green's as a concert venue that would become legendary across the world: it was the Apollo.

The very first gig was by the Man in Black, the one and only Johnny Cash, but on 7 November it was Heep's turn. Without a moment's hesitation. Carole, Lee Michael, barely six months old and I were off to the show. I still cherish the photographs of us on that stage, positioned conspicuously behind big Lee's drums and a cool pic of Lee and Mick loitering without any semblance of musical intent outside their dressing room.

Careering Out Of Control

In fact, 1973 turned out to be a big year in my own career. My five-year apprenticeship was at an end, or so I thought. When the union man went in to negotiate my papers he was informed that Mr Fields would have to work an extra six months. I was gobsmacked. Why the six months? They told me it was to make up for all the time I'd wasted following that Uriah Heep band around the country. Looking back, in fairness, we had done two UK tours back to back.

'Wasted?' I screamed. 'It was the best bloody time of my life!'

So I left and joined a wee boiler-makers' called Hawkhead Bray, who gave me the necessary papers for the last six months. I'd end up staying there for a few years and this is where I met John Toal. We became inseparable friends from that day on until he sadly passed away early in 2009, for we very quickly discovered that we shared the same passion for music. He liked the humble side, I the heavy stuff and we were resident guests in the Apollo, each of us buying tickets for the bands we wanted to see, while the other happily tagged along, never knowing who was playing.

One such gig, with John the ticket buyer, turned out to be Mott the Hoople. Now, as the Apollo had no bar of its own, John was in the habit of staying in Lauders Bar while the support band were playing. I badgered him, pleaded with him, promised him the support were excellent but he wouldn't budge. And so he missed a night at the Apollo with Queen.

Poor John should have been a millipede for the amount of leg-pulling he would get for that one through the years, though, in his defence, he did redeem himself slightly the following year when we saw Queen at Glasgow University's Queen Margaret Union. Freddie and the boys came on late after a big dressing-room fight over make-up and then overloaded the Union's power circuit after playing only a few songs: a hilarious, if unintentional, premonition of Spinal Tap and The Darkness in years to come.

I wasn't the only one who was experiencing career changes. That year a phone call would come that would change forever the life of a young Jimmy McCulloch. As we've seen, Jimmy was a founder-member of Thunderclap Newman, who went on to work with various artists before getting the nod to replace Les Harvey in Stone the Crows.

In late 1973, Paul McCartney, his wife Linda and Denny Laine were recording Linda's solo album, under the name of Susie & the Red Stripes. They were selecting musicians who subsequently were billed for Wings and Jimmy got the call.

He joined them in May the next year and stayed with them until

September 1977. From those album sessions, there is only one single available, 'Seaside Woman' (finally released in June 1977) with Paul (on vocals, bass, guitar and piano), Linda (keyboards), Denny (guitar, vocals, bass), Jimmy (guitar, vocals) and Geoff Britton (drums).

This line-up made their debut with single 'Junior's Farm'. But soon after, in February 1975, they changed the drummer, in the middle of the recording for a new album, Venus and Mars and Joe English took over on drums. A horn section was assembled for their British tour in September that year, comprising Tony Dorsey (on trombone), Howie Casey (saxophone), Steve Howard (trumpet and flugelhorn) and Thaddeus Richard (saxophone, clarinet and flute).

On the CD reissue of Venus and Mars there is an anti-drugs song composed by Jimmy and former Stone the Crows bandmate Colin Allen called 'Medicine Jar', leaving Jimmy with the legacy of having one of his own compositions on a Wings album. Incidentally, the album also includes short contributions from Geoff Britton, who would appear later in Rough Diamond with ex-Heep singer David Byron, Dave Mason of Traffic and lately in Fleetwood Mac, Allen Toussaint and sax player Tom Scott, of The L.A. Express.

Jimmy's writing contribution doesn't end there. On Wings at the Speed of Sound, there's another track composed by Jimmy, again with Colin Allen, called 'Wino Junko'.

While he was still flying high with Wings, Jimmy also formed Jimmy McCulloch's White Line with his brother Jack on drums and Dave Clarke on bass and vocals. The trio released a single in 1976, 'Call My Name/Too Many Miles' and even appeared on Twiggy's Jukebox TV show to perform the A-side, sung by Dave (Jimmy sang 'Too Many Miles').

In July the same year, Jimmy had some fun too, playing with friends and bandmates of keyboardist Tim Hinkley, under the moniker Hinkley's Heroes. Only together for two months, without releasing any records, they did, however, offer some spectacular concerts with stellar line-ups: consider the two shows Jimmy played alongside Maggie Bell (vocals), our old friend Brian Robertson (guitar), Boz Burrell (bass), Tim Hinkley (keyboards) and the legendary Mitch Mitchell (drums).

When he left Wings, in September 1977, Jimmy joined the great Steve Marriott for a short one-month tour. It wasn't a complete reunion, because original member Ronnie Lane didn't rejoin the band, being replaced by Rick Wills. The line-up was Steve Marriott (guitar, vocals), Jimmy McCulloch (guitar), Rick Wills (bass), Ian McLagan (keyboards) and Kenny Jones (drums). They recorded the album 78 in the Shade, which also included the collaboration of Ronnie Lane, Sam Brown and Madeline Bell.

In 1978, in a period of relative obscurity, certainly to me, Jimmy was for a very short time a part of Wild Horses with Robbo and Jimmy Bain (from Rainbow). Despite rehearsing together for a while, Jimmy was replaced by Neil Carter in early 1979.

The same year Jimmy went on to join The Dukes, an outfit that comprised Jimmy, Miller Anderson on guitar and vocals, Charles Tumahai (bass, vocals) and Ronnie Leahy (keyboards). Although they employed the inestimable talents of guest drummers in the studio, Stuart Elliott and Barry DeSouza, it was Nick Trevisick who beat the skins at live concerts. They toured supporting Wishbone Ash.

The Dukes would be Jimmy's last band, his last recorded song, 'Heartbreaker', taken off their first and only eponymous album.

That year Jimmy's life ended in his West London flat, cut short at the heartbreakingly young age of 26 by a heroin overdose. Another of Glasgow's greats was gone.

Bitter Sweet

Glam Rock was all the rage in the early Seventies and Glasgow had its own star of the genre in none other than Sweet's Brian Connolly. I remember the night his name was first brought, quite forcibly, to my attention. I was DJing the Rock Club in the Bruce Hotel in East Kilbride and I had Sweet on full blast when this big, hairy, bearded biker came up to me and told me that, if I didn't turn it off, he would take me outside and kill me. Turns out he was related to Mr Connolly and hated him big style for the way he had treated his family. Gentle gent that I was, I apologised profusely, informed him I didn't do domestics and put on Motörhead.

So who was the Sweet man who could invoke such a bitter reaction?

Well, Brian Connolly was born in 1945 in Govanhill, Glasgow (though some early Sweet biographies will try to persuade you he was born in 1949). While the true identity of Brian's father was never made public, his mother was a teenage waitress named Frances Connolly. He was left in a Glasgow hospital by his mother as an infant, possibly suffering the effects of meningitis.

Fostered at the age of two by Jim and Helen McManus, of Blantyre, it was only when he reached the age of eighteen that he inadvertently discovered his true parentage and reverted to the name Connolly. His brother was not the late actor Mark McManus, who found fame in the title role of detective series Taggart, as is occasionally claimed. True, Mark's father and Brian's foster father, Jim, were brothers, but the confusion is largely due to the fact that Jim McManus also had a son named Mark and he and Brian grew up together.

At the age of 12, Brian moved to Harefield in Middlesex, where he played in a number of local bands before eventually replacing singer Ian Gillan, later of Deep Purple and Black Sabbath fame, in a band called Wainwright's Gentlemen, an outfit that included drummer Mick Tucker. Although the band split up in 1968 without releasing any recordings, Brian and Mick stayed together, taking on board guitarist Frank Torpey and bassist Steve Priest. They named their new band Sweetshop.

The group recorded several singles, eventually shortening their name to Sweet. Andy Scott joined the line-up in late 1970, just before the release of their first hit single 'Funny, Funny'.

Over the next eight years Brian sang on many internationally successful singles and six albums. Life was, indeed, sweet . . . that is until his drinking caused ructions in the band and forced his exit in late 1978, though the announcement of his departure was not made public until March the next year.

After leaving Sweet, Brian launched a solo career that met with little success. Over the next three years he released a handful of singles – 'Take Away the Music', 'Don't You Know A Lady' and 'Hypnotised' – under his name but these made little or no impact on the charts. He also recorded a dozen or so new tracks but most never got past the demo stage. One, never officially released, was called 'Magic Circle' and was a potent reminder of Brian's wonderfully melodic voice.

In late 1982 Brian suffered multiple heart attacks in a single night. Although he survived, his health was permanently affected.

At the start of 1983 he supported Pat Benatar at the Hammersmith Odeon in London with Connolly's Encore, a band that included most of the members of Verity, which was fronted by former Argent guitarist John Verity. Also in the line-up that night was Terry Uttley, bass player from Smokie. Their set included 'Windy City', 'Fox on the Run', 'Hypnotised' and new numbers, 'Sick and Tired', 'Red Rage' and 'The Candle'.

Despite his continuing ill-health, Brian continued to tour with his backing bands, New Sweet and Brian Connolly's Sweet, from 1984, then, in 1988, he was reunited in Los Angeles with former bandmates Scott, Priest and Tucker to rework studio versions of 'Action' and 'The Ballroom Blitz'.

This Mike Chapman-produced reunion floundered all too quickly and Brian was quickly back performing with his unknown and often changing backing band. One of these was a band called Ninja, an outfit I put on in the Bruce Hotel in the early Nineties. They performed some Sweet songs and I still have a treasured demo of them; in fact, just listening to them as I write reminds me that when Sweet rocked, they really, really rocked.

I'm not alone in my appreciation: check out Sweet F.A., an album that inspired so many rock bands and is still namechecked by Aerosmith and Mötley Crüe, both of whom cite Sweet as one of their first influences.

Sweet reunited again in 1990 for the promotion of a music video documentary and again there were rumours of a full reunion. Ultimately, this came to nothing and, by the late Nineties, Brian's drinking had taken a toll on his body. He died of liver failure on 9 February 1997.

I can't say if that big hairy biker was right or wrong, but I tell you this: I'll never take off another Sweet album.

Heep's More Where They Came From

I've mentioned Lee Michael's debut at the Apollo, there in November 1974, at the age of six months, to witness Uriah Heep promote their Wonderworld album. This would be the final one with bass player Gary Thain. Gary was a really quiet and likeable lad, who also had an all-engulfing heroin addiction, an affliction that was slowly, inexorably consuming his life and musical talent: only a few months after leaving the band he died of an overdose.

His place was taken by John Wetton, formerly of Family and Roxy

Music. Again, he was a really nice bloke and an ace bass player but, somehow, I always felt he didn't sit very well musically with the band. On joining, he was reputed to have said to singer Dave Byron that he always wanted to sing lead vocals in a band – to which Dave answered: 'Maybe, mate, but not in this f'n one!'

After just two albums, Return to Fantasy (1975) and High and Mighty (1976), John would leave to fulfil his dream of lead vocal stardom with Asia. At the same time Dave Byron himself was replaced for much the same reasons as Gary Thain had gone – although David's poison of choice was alcohol. David had always made Carole and me feel welcome, always had time for a chat and it was sad to see him go, even sadder when he passed away from drink-related problems in 1985. Rock 'n' roll can be such a wilfully cruel mistress. What a waste of life, love and talent!

Well, rock 'n' roll goes on and John and David's places were taken by Trevor Tufty Bolder, formerly of Bowie's Spiders from Mars and John Lawton, once the voice of Lucifer's Friend. They would record three albums together: Firefly (in 1977, when Cheryl Carole Fields made her Apollo debut, having joined the Fields clan on 18 November two years earlier), Innocent Victim (1977) and Fallen Angel (1978), before limping into their tenth anniversary tour . . . but that's for the next chapter, kiddies.

In the meantime, there would be another mega-gig taking place in Glasgow, perhaps one of the most important for two native-born sons, since leaving their homeland for the land of Kylie and Jason.

Yes, we've come at last to AC/DC, to their guitarists Angus and Malcolm Young and to their triumphant concert in the City Halls in Glasgow's Candleriggs in 1976.

Angus, one of eight children born to William and Margaret Young, was brought forth into the world in Glasgow, before moving with his immediate clan members to Sydney, Australia, in 1963 – including older brothers Malcolm, George and Alex, who all became musicians and sister Margaret, who offered the inspiration for AC/DC's name by virtue of having spied the letters on a sewing machine.

Angus, would you believe it, was not in the land of Skippy five minutes when he took up the axe: it was a neighbour's guitar and five-year-old Angus couldn't keep his hands off it every time he visited. He was finally given his own, an acoustic mind you, by his big brother George.

As a teenager Angus played in a band called Kantuckee. He was 18 when he and his 20-year-old brother Malcolm formed AC/DC in 1973. Angus, of course, played lead guitar, with Malcolm on rhythm, Colin Burgess (drums), Larry Van Kriedt (bass) and Dave Evans on vocals.

Their first single was 'Can I Sit Next to You Girl', a song the band would later re-record with another Scot and ex-roadie, Bon Scott, from Kirriemuir, as their vocalist.

Now we all know Angus as the Peter Pan of rock, forever dressed in his schoolboy uniform, with bare knees shining as he shimmied across the stage with his axe. In fact, he'd tried a number of stage costumes before settling for shirt and shorts; let's draw a veil of charity over Spiderman, Zorro, a gorilla – yes, I kid you not – a gorilla and Super-Ang.

Who could have predicted that Scotland's finest would come together in a land so far removed from their roots, yet the lads went on to become legends. Much has been made of the fact that Cliff Williams was English and, of course, an Englishman replaced Bon when he so tragically died in 1980. Yet the impact of AC/DC on me and thousands just like me, growing up in Glasgow, was immeasurable.

From humble beginnings – ah, but aren't all the true rock gods born of the rag and bone shop, just like the rest of us? – AC/DC would become mega-stars and record their live magnus opus If You Want Blood at none other than the Apollo – just like Status Quo and, if you listen really hard, you can hear Robert Fields clapping on both albums.

Of course, in their choice of the Apollo they were in fine company, for the Glasgow venue that was a phoenix rising from the Green's, also held the same attraction for luminaries such as Judas Priest, Sabbath, Purple, Gillan, the Stranglers, Humble Pie, Roxy Music, U.F.O., Whitesnake, Journey and Bad Company . . . to name but a few.

One must-mention, before leaving Down Under, goes to Jimmy Barnes. Born James Dixon Swan on 28 April 1956, in Glasgow, his dad was the renowned prizefighter Jim Swan and his older brother rock singer John.

Jimmy's career, both as a solo performer and as lead vocalist with rock outfit Cold Chisel, has made him one of the most popular and best-selling Australian music artists of all time. The combination of 14 Australian Top 40 albums for Cold Chisel and 12 charting solo albums gives this Glaswegian troubadour the highest number of hit albums of any Oz artist . . . but he has never forgotten his Glasgow roots and, for that reason alone among many, he earns his place in this wee book.

A Few For The Road

Such was the fertile state of the musical scene in Glasgow throughout the Seventies that numberless venues sprang up across the city, enhancing its well-earned reputation as the place to play and savour rock music. The Elgin Bar, the Amphora, Shuffles, His Nibs, the Griffin, Tiffanys, the White Elephant, Satellite City . . . they were all magnets that attracted metal of the finest kind, for the bands just kept coming.

One such moth to the flame were Underhand Jones. Formed in the mid Seventies, they comprised Billy Fairbairn on vocals, Campbell (Cammy) Forbes (guitar/vocals/keyboards), Brian Coyle (guitar/vocals), Eddie Walton Jnr (guitar), Billy McLeish (bass) and Stevie Irvine (vocals).

While many of their contemporaries and truth be told, wannabes, were quite content to wow the bar crowds with sets jammed full of covers, Underhand Jones won a huge following on the strength of their original songs. Playing their fist gig in the Charing Cross Hotel in 1977, they rapidly established themselves as one of Glasgow's finest rock outfits, securing a residency in the Amphora on a Thursday night, augmented by gigs in the Victorian Carriage, Greenock and Davy Jones Locker, Gourock.

In May 1978 they played at the first Kelvingrove Rock and Pop Festival, wowing the several thousand-strong crowd from the park's bandstand.

Both of the Billys left shortly afterwards and were replaced by Roger Cameron on bass and the soon-to-be-legendary Stevie Doherty on vocals. Sounding better than ever, they appeared at the Loch Lomond Rock Festival, alongside the Buzzcocks and the Boomtown Rats. Securing a publishing deal with Rondor Music in London they cut their wonderfully titled debut LP, Jammy But Nice.

Sadly, despite their virtuoso live performances and the calibre of this recording, Jammy failed to stick in the charts and unlucky Underhand Jones split up not long afterwards. Cammy would go on to form the Dolphins, while Stevie, of course, went on to superstardom . . . but for that you'll have to wait for the next chapter.

Meantime, let's not forget a few more bands who made the Seventies such a wonderland for rock fans in Glasgow. High among these were Red Ellis, a bunch of like-minded mates from around South Lanarkshire who got together with the sole purpose of making a noise, their great excuse being that they had been inspired by the likes of Led Zeppelin, Bad Company, Deep Purple and Jimi Hendrix.

Formed by vocalist Joe Cochrane, Dave Sweet (bass), Joe James (drums) and Chick McSherry (guitar), they were lucky enough to rehearse in the scene's latest state-of-the-art practice studio: Thornliewood United's changing hut!

Ignoring the smell of the kits – or maybe even high on the adrenaline-infused socks, who knows? – they soon knocked a set into shape and made their debut at Holly Cross School in Hamilton in 1977, just as punk was reaching its zenith.

Gigs followed at Glasgow University, where they supported the Henry Gorman Band, then in the Victorian Carriage, Greenock, Davie Jones Locker, Gourock, the Queen's Hall, Dunoon, the Royal Hotel, Wick, the Dial Inn, Glasgow and even the Royal Navy bases in Dunoon and Edzel.

I can't forget, of course, the couple of gigs when I was lucky enough to see them in my home town of East Kilbride: the Salmon Leap and the Tower Bar, the same where Frankie Miller used to exercise his tonsils.

In 1980 they opened the second day of the Loch Lomond Rock Festival, a bill that included the Henry Gorman Band, Ian Gillan, Denny Laine, Saxon, Lindisfarne, Wild Horses, Krokus and Wishbone Ash. Later they would tour with Frankie Miller and Thin Lizzy. Chic left to form a new band called La Paz with ex-Tryxter vocalist Doogie White and was replaced by guitarists Ian Harris and Jim McClelland.

After calling it a day, Joe James joined one of the finest melodic rock bands ever produced from these fine shores, Zero Zero. Hero to sublime Zero. Who said there was no irony in rock 'n' roll?

Another bunch of high-fliers seeking airtime around now were Flying Squad. The group was formed by guitarists Monty Monagle and Alex Calder, both of whom hailed from Milton in Glasgow. The first line-up was called Rogue and featured singer Joe Keogh, Jim Anderson (drums) and Davey Gilmore (bass). By the time they were ready to record their first album, the line-up had evolved into Monty, Alex, Jimmy Kelly, George Crossan and Ian Muir.

The lads had become popular on the live circuit throughout the UK, before a CBS scout spied them and three songs were soon put down on vinyl for a single. The record company was so impressed, however, that an album, Flying Squad, was recorded at IBC Studio in London, Threshold Studio London and, finally, at the Visilord Phonogram Studio in Hilversum, Holland, produced by Francis Rossi, of Status Quo and engineered by John Eden.

The first single was 'Drive On' and the follow-up was 'Backroom Boys'. Although the singles and album received some very good reviews, punk was breaking big-time in the UK and the record company's focus was elsewhere.

Following management difficulties, the band split and did not record a second album – much to Rossi's surprise. Ian 'Finn' Muir would go on to form Waysted, while Monty and George Crossan formed a band called The Difference and released three albums on the Big Ideas private label between 1979 and 1982.

Last, but in no way least and finishing the Seventies off with a flourish, are Sneeky Pete. This was one of the first and best-known bands to emerge from the Seventies Glasgow pub rock scene, setting up gigs and paving the way for others to follow.

The original band was formed in late 1971 by the three Cameron brothers, Wallace on vocals and guitar, Duncan (vocals and bass guitar) and Johnny (vocals and lead guitar) and were later joined by John McGinlay on keyboards and John Ward on drums.

They established a strong local following by initially setting up a regular Saturday morning session in Glasgow's Dial Inn, playing a set of original songs mixed with their own arrangements of classics. As the band's popularity grew, the covers gave way to whole sets of original material.

Sneeky Pete were soon playing bigger pubs, pulling bigger crowds and, finally, playing a pivotal role in the emergence of the Glasgow's rock scene. The Saturday session moved to Saints and Sinners, now King Tut's and Pete underwent a change of line-up – and a subsequent change of direction. Keyboardist Robert McQillian, from TF Mutch Band and drummer Sandy Brown, formerly of Chico, joined the brothers, constantly gigging and establishing themselves nationally on the university circuit and London pub scene, headlining venues such as the Marquee, Dingwalls and many others.

The band also attracted industry interest and were finally signed by L.C. Promotions and publishing giants Chappells, recording for Phonogram. However, Sneeky Pete very much followed their own minds and hearts when it came to music –the original Indie Kids, if you like – and soon set up their own record label, releasing their records themselves and self-promoting their wares.

Their first double A-side single 'Nighttime in the City/Getting Out Today' was released on their NOW (North of Watford) Records, with manager Leon Catani. They went on to release a live album, Live and Kicking, on their own SPR label. This was a compilation performances taken from a tour of their favourite Scottish venues.

Another change of line-up followed, with Gary Groves replacing Robert on drums and Donny Finlay replacing Sandy on keyboards, later replaced himself by Nicky Woolfson. A new management deal with London-based Handle Artists saw the band join forces with Glam Rocker Andy Scott, ex of Sweet, to produce what was to become their first major album.

The band also toured extensively during this period, forming a strong gigging partnership with fellow former pub rockers Dr Feelgood, with whom they later shared the stage at the first Loch Lomond Rock Festival.

The band owed a great debt of gratitude to their strong Scottish fan base and the Glasgow gig scene, in particular – so much so, that their first single was packaged with a guide to Glasgow pub rock and the many venues they played: hubs of all that is good and great in Seventies rock 'n' roll, such as the Dial Inn, Saints and Sinners, the Amphora, Speakers Corner, Nico's, the Maggie, Burns Howff, the Mars Bar, the Glen Douglas, the Brothers, the Bungalow Bar, the Mayfair, the Pavilion, the Apollo, the White Elephant, the Plaza, City Halls . . .

When Sneeky Pete disbanded, Duncan, Johnny and Robert continued to perform as the Force, exploring new frontiers and forever seeking new horizons . . . oh and blagging a major recording deal with Atlantic Records in New York.

Duncan and Johnny are still actively involved in the Glasgow music scene as working musicians and engineer/producers and partners in Riverside Studios, in their hometown, a city that is lucky to have them.

New Buddies

In any musical history of Glasgow, there are bound to be many geographical overlaps, with our minstrels wandering at will all through, from the suburbs and satellite towns. Findo Gask, who formed in 1968 but came into their own in the Seventies, were one such band of itinerants and hailed from Paisley.

Now, throughout the years, Paisley has always been a successful nursery for new talent. Home of the Watermill Hotel and the Burns Cottage – which was owned by John Waterson and moved into Glasgow to become the hallowed Burns Howff, Paisley has also been home to Jimmy Dewar, Buddah Grass Harbour and, most recently, Paolo Nutini.

Findo Gask, not to be confused with the band of the same name currently doing the rounds, were a country rock band, would take shape slowly, first from the bones of a band called Sunday, the core of which included vocalist Davie Pattison and bass player Bert Downie.

As its resident band, they were almost single-handedly responsible for turning the Watermill Hotel into a rock gig, opening the doors for the likes of Beggars Opera, Northwind and Tear Gas.

Playing the place five nights a week, plus Sunday afternoons, they honed their act to perfection and were regularly joined on stage by musicians such as Jimmy Dewar, Maggie Bell and Les Harvey.

Sunday petered out around 1970, due to the most commonly cited reasons: being skint, having wives and weans, but the next year Davie and Bert formed a new band called Newday. The line-up included Jim 'Frosty' Forrest (keyboards, also from Sunday) and Jim Breakey (drums, from The Poets and Studio Six).

After just a short while 'Frosty' headed south and was replaced by an old friend of Bert's, Davie Colquhoun, who caught the bug again and came out of retirement. Things were looking rosy at last when, all of a sudden, Jim Breakey decided he was leaving. As luck would have it, another old friend of Bert's (Bert had a lot of old friends in those days), Tam Doyle, had come along to watch the band and was persuaded to join as tub thumper.

By this time the band were called Findo Gask and all the hard work gigging seemed to have paid off when they signed a production deal in London with Hush. This company was run by Shel Talmy and Hugh Murphy - the duo would go on to win the Producer of the Year award in 1978 with Baker Street by another Paisley son, Gerry Rafferty.

The deal with Hush led to their one-and-only 45er. It was a catchy number written by Pattison and Colquhoun, called Dr Phinn's Elixir with a B-side of Pay Your Respects, penned by the same duo. It was released in Holland and Belgium on the Pink Elephant label and you can hear the track on the listening post.

This led to Findo Gask being signed to EMI by Nick Mobs - who many years later would infamously sign the Sex Pistols to his label. With the firm promise from Nick that he wouldn't change the band, the deal was done.

More than in any other business, however, in music the goalposts can be shifted without warning and Findo Gask suddenly found their sound being nudged in a new direction. A song written by Australian-born songwriter, Harry Vanda and Glaswegian, George Young - who were both original members of the Sixties combo the Easy Beats - was foisted on the band. George just also happened to be a brother of AC/DC's Angus and Malcolm Young.

Yesterday's Hero was to live up to its name, hitting the final nail into Findo's coffin. Before the single was released Davie Colquhoun left to pursue a solo career – he felt he had been badly represented at A&R level. His position was filled very briefly by Des Coffield, of JSD fame, but the chemistry wasn't right and the band split up.

Over in the States, meanwhile, Jimmy Dewar and Robin Trower bumped into fellow stablemate Ronnie Montrose at a management meeting. Ronnie was looking for a singer and Jimmy recommended former Findo, Davie Pattison. Sent for posthaste, our man Davie never came back, going on to sing with Ronnie Montrose in Gamma and work with Michael Schenker and Robin Trower.

Another outfit following the Paisley pattern of success in the late Seventies, however short-lived it might prove, were Snapshots, whose line-up comprised of Stephen Reid (vocals, guitar), Glenn Sissons (bass; Alan McAuley played bass before the creation of their album), Bobby Evans (drums) and Davey Eckford (guitar).

Having formed in 1978, they were brought on to the ill-fated Coma Records label, which was owned by Bill Martin and Phil Coulter – Martin signed them after a tip off from a Glasgow band called Scotch.

The next year they set about recording an album at Rockfield Studios in Monmouth, Wales, with Pete Gage producing, slotted in after supergroup-in-the-making Simple Minds had recorded Reel to Reel

Cacophony. The album was due for release in early 1980, but Martin and Coulter ran into difficulties with their parent company and the label was dropped, along with all the artists signed to Coma.

The worst part of all this was that Stephen Reid was tied up in a publishing deal with Martin and Coulter and prevented, therefore, from looking for a new deal for the next five years.

Snapshots called it a day in 1980 and it would be almost 10 years before Stephen would re-emerge in a band called Buddha Grass Harbour. He was joined then by Billy Love (bass), Scott Donaldson (guitar), George Lundy (drums) and then later by Dave Watson (drums) and Jack Webb (keyboards).

They rehearsed at Sunset Studios before playing extensively around the UK, finally recording an album at Palladium studios near Edinburgh. Instead of releasing the album they went to Los Angeles to try their hand with the major labels. One of the first appointments was with Atlantic Records, where the head of A&R, Kevin Williamson, was blown away by the six tracks.

When word got out of the buzz in LA, EMI got involved in the race to sign Harbour and, along with Atlantic and Warners, they came to Glasgow to see the band live. It's reputed that extravagant advances were bandied about by the bigwigs.

And so it's all the more perplexing that Paisley's Harbour never were signed to a major. Instead, they hooked up with an indie label, Motion Records, who released a single, 'Soul Sister'. Although this met with a measure of critical acclaim, it all came to naught and Buddha Grass Harbour called it a day in 1992. They got back together again in 1994 as Italian artist Umberto Marzotto's backing band, recording an album in Glasgow's Park Lane Studios that did well in Italy.

Another album was recorded before the Italian label ran out of money and couldn't afford to pay to get the masters released from the studio. Sadly, they are no doubt still there, gathering dust on a shelf.

Which is how I often felt about myself by the close of the Seventies. My own career in music was having its own ups and downs and in 1979 I joined Gray Tool Co, where I was employed as a fitter-welder. I hated it. My God, they were American-owned and had us exercising first thing in the morning! I hadn't even realised Americans knew anything about exercise beyond a questionable taste in Spandex leisure suits!

Most of my colleagues lived their lives scared of losing their jobs. I think you know me by now: yes, my days were numbered. Despite having to leave behind many good friends, I lasted a year before joining a refrigeration conmpany, Craig Nicol.

I'd have ten great years there before taking the plunge into a full-time career in the music business in 1990. But more, much more, of that later.

THE EIGHTIES

Rock Of Ages

MOST rock historians, not without good cause, will opine that 1980 was the greatest year in rock metal's history. Much happened this year, after all. Following the death of their legendary frontman Bon Scott, AC/DC re-electrified themselves with their darkest and biggest selling album to date, Back in Black. This magnus opus was a work whose mettle in our psyche was tempered by the indestructible alloy of British Steel by Judas Priest, The Blizzard of Ozz (Ozzy Osbourne), Heaven and Hell (Black Sabbath), Wheels of Steel (Saxon) and stunning debuts by Iron Maiden and Def Leppard.

This so-called New Wave of British Heavy Metal barely ripples the surface of what was really going on, however. More than any other era, the Eighties would once and for all smash through musical boundaries and herald a new age, a movement led by Aerosmith and Run DMC, who created the metal/hip hop/rap anthem 'Walk this Way', a track that blasted open the doors into the mega-arena for the likes of NWA and Public Enemy.

Finally, the barriers were being pushed to their limit. The Goth scene blossomed with the Cult, the Sisters of Mercy and the Mission. Thrash had evolved in the shape of Metallica, Slayer, Megadeath and Anthrax, who also crossed over with Public Enemy for the thrash/hip hop classic 'Bring the Noise'.

The funk movement, too, was gathering pace, whipped along in a battle-bassed frenzy by the flea circus that was Red Hot Chilli Peppers and the first all-black metal funk band Living Color.

And let's not forget Fishbone, Primus, 24–7, Spyz and Faith No More, who brought us the truly awesome album The Real Thing, standard bearers for the heavier-armoured troops.

Oh and, of course, there was no getting away from the slap in the rouged visage that was the glam scene: Mötley Crüe, Poison, Hanoi Rocks, Warrant, Cinderella, Tigertailz and the beast that became Guns N' Roses and their seminal album Appetite for Destruction.

This decade would also see the emergence of the industrial scene, with Ministry and Nine Inch Nails as their blitzkriegin' vanguard.

Finally, as the Nineties fast approached, a young man whose mum was forever hounding him about 'joining that stupid club', would release his band's debut album. Bleach and the entire Grunge movement was born, slapped into life, mewing and spewing wonderful urban poetry out into the wide world beyond Seattle.

In those ten years Glasgow enjoyed a live music scene that was as vibrant, cutting-edge and cosmopolitan as any other city on the planet. We could choose from a wide and varied range of hot spots: the Venue, Shadows, the Ampora, Wipers, the Heathery Bar, the Bruce Hotel, the Dial Inn, Saints & Sinners, the Muscular Arms and, in 1987, the pub that saved everyone's life, the Solid Rock Café in Hope Street.

The local bands, meanwhile, were busy strutting their stuff on stages and in the corners of bars: Heavy Pettin', Glasgow, Underhand Jones, Scheme, La Paz, Zero Zero, Sneeky Pete, the Dolphins, Gun, Big George and the Business, Lyin Rampant, Danger, Metro, Trident, Anaconda, Centurion, Cannes and so on . . . and on.

Radio Clyde introduced Tom Russell's Friday Night Rock Show, which meant that, even you if were skint and forced to stay in, as was too often the case, you could tune in to Tommy Vance, ten till midnight, then Tom's own show until 2 a.m. Four glorious hours of rock. Turn it up!

It seemed, too, that even science was on the side of rock. The CD format was introduced and, with the advent of MTV, we now had a television station pumping music videos into our living rooms 24 hours a day, bringing all the new releases at the touch of a remote control.

In 1980 we were treated, too, to the first Castle Donnington event. At long last, rock was recognised nationally, by the people for the people, instead of being chewed over in esoteric reviews and interviews in the likes of NME and Sounds, which soon had its own monthly (now weekly) rock magazine Kerrang!.

Sadly, not everyone made it through this decade of phenomenal changes. We lost John Lennon, Alex Harvey, Cliff Burton, David Byron, Randy Rhodes, Razzle, Phil Lynott, Sid Vicious, the Big O, the Howff and the legend that was the Apollo.

And so, while it may have been, as that Dickens of a man once said, the best of times and the worst times, it would forever be our rock of ages.

Swan Songs

The Eighties were a massive decade for Glasgow-based bands, for they witnessed the birth of some truly great talents. By now, I was working in the Craig Nicol Refrigeration Company, such a cool job, where I had some great mates: Billy Forsyth, the two Ronnies, McLachlan and Sanderson, Peter Spence and Bob Cameron, to name but a handful. However, the most musical of them all was Davie Swan.

Davie was in a band called Heaven and he was forever accosting me with new demos to listen to. To be honest, I minded not a jot, for they were brilliant.

Now this Heaven outfit had actually started out in 1978 as Street Fighter, before changing their name to Wildcat. The original line-up consisted of Brian Clark and Joe Kilna, from the Rez Band, Steven Hayman, Lawdy Mama, Archie Dickson and Neil Russell. Michael Boyle, from the Downtown Flyers joined after Steven left to join Heavy Pettin', while Neil left to later join Heaven.

Neil was replaced by George Caldwell on bass, also ex of the Downtown Flyers and the line-up that most people would come to recognise as Wildcat were Brian Clark on lead guitar and vocals, Archie Dickson (also on lead guitar and vocals), Joe Kilna (drums and percussion), George Caldwell (bass) and Michael Boyle (lead vocal).

A hard rock act, they gigged extensively throughout Scotland, becoming the resident band at the Burns Howff on Saturdays. Their progressive, metal style of rock featured tracks such as 'Woman of the

Tower', 'House of Indecision', 'She' and 'Hot Sister' and they were viewed by punters and musical peers alike as one of the best up-and-coming rock acts on the scene.

They produced several demos and just missed out on a deal with Mountain Records. Ray Stark, of Mountain, had requested a meeting immediately after hearing a demo tape but finally had to decline as the label had just invested in another new act called Marseille. Before Wildcat got round to recording more material and following up on interest that was being shown by Stuart Hornal, of music publisher Rondor Music, they split up.

They had been together for just over a year. Their influence, however, lasted longer, with many young acts in the Glasgow area, such as a very young up-and-coming pub band called Weeper, citing Wildcat as their very first paws for thought in music.

Internal differences and external commitments were cited as the cause of Wildcat's own demise – is there ever any other? Brian went on to play in a variety of club acts, the main one being Vegas, before moving to Spain, while Steven had, of course, gone on to enjoy international success with Heavy Pettin' and is now living in America and still actively writing and performing.

Archie, Mick and George, meanwhile, formed our new act called Heaven. Bassist George, however, soon decided to work on other projects and would go on to play for several bands. As well as being a keen graphic designer, he played in many sessions when he moved to London to work with former guitarist Jim Ward, from the Downtown Flyers. In the next 20 years George would travel across the world and is now working on his PhD, looking at how music affects the brain.

And so in 1980, Heaven were made up of Archie, Mick, Neil Russell, Tony Macaulay (drums) and a vocalist and keyboardist by the name of Davie Swan. My super-cool refrigeration mate, which is where I think we came in.

Davie's vocals and keyboard skills added an inspirational new sound to Heaven, a vibe that was more suited to the American market and more accessible to radio. Songs such as 'Background News', 'Why Do You Play the Charade?' and 'The Storm' allowed Heaven to use to the max the strong guitar riffs written by Archie, while the powerful harmonies Davie and Mick provided helped shape the direction and sound of the band, appealing to a much wider audience.

The band were noticed by Jay Crawford, of Scotland's Radio Forth, who recognised the talent in Heaven and a strong working relationship evolved, with Jay supporting the band whenever he could.

The lads played only a few live gigs, as the master plan was to develop their material, focus on recording good demos and thereby secure a recording/publishing contract. Although there was a lot of interest, particularly from Robin Godfrey Cass at Warner Chappell Publishing, the band lasted just over a year, unable to secure the contracts to sustain themselves.

Heaven's celestial status was acknowledged by their musical peers – Nazareth guitarist Manny Charlton, who worked on several of their recordings, heaping praise on the lead vocals and songs the band were producing.

Michael is now a successful folk songwriter in Glasgow, while Davie became a piano teacher and continues to both teach and perform. And I still listen to those demos.

Glasgow By Name

The other erstwhile members of Wildcat and Heaven became involved in a band that took their name from the members' native city. Glasgow were put together in 1983 by Archie Dickson (on lead guitar), Mike Boyle (vocals) and Neil Russell (bass). Autumn of the same year saw another former Wildcat – believe me, these guys had many more than nine musical lives – join the line-up, with the addition of Joe Kilna on drums.

In the years since, Glasgow have often been referred to as being at the forefront of British Heavy Metal's new wave. Certainly, for the best part of 16 years their music and influence were a strong refrain in a burgeoning scene.

Although there were several changes to the line-up during Glasgow's long existence, the band's nucleus remained Archie and Mick.

Glasgow very quickly gained a hardcore and enthusiastic following based on the strength of their songs and sheer force of their live performances, with the fans naming themselves the Battalion. Archie recalls: 'These guys followed as all over the UK and often helped promote the band through fanclubs and fanzines at their own cost. Remember this was all pre-internet. These fans were incredibly loyal and will always be remembered by us.'

The band continued to grow and became a must-see act on the city scene, gaining resident slots in the Burns Howff and Dial Inn before embarking on live tours throughout the UK.

It was during the early months that they came to the attention of Alex Dickson, Richard Park and Tom Russell – then of Radio Clyde, now of Rock Radio, who found himself inundated with requests to play the new band. They approached the band with a one-off deal, the result of which was a three-track EP called Under the Lights.

This first offering certainly put them under the spotlight. It was heard by Radio 1's Tommy Vance, who invited the band to record a session for his famous Friday Night Rock Show. This session led directly to an approach by Russ Conway, of the Eighties cult rock label Neat Records, which was based in Newcastle. The end product was Glasgow's first single 'Stranded' b/w 'Heat of the Night'.

Following a favourable response, Neat Records immediately launched into talks with the boys about putting out an album, but Glasgow had bigger plans, choosing instead to hunt for a major label.

Glasgow stayed together for another three years, supporting many huge artists on tour, including Kiss, Bon Jovi, Uriah Heep, Frankie Miller, Alaska, Nazareth and Phil Lynott's Grand Slam, to name but a handful.

It was certainly an incredibly productive and enjoyable period for the band, reflected in their increasingly theatrical live performances and ever-stronger songwriting skills, a talent no doubt nurtured by hanging with so many successful artists.

Towards the end of 1986 a new management team was put in place and Glasgow continued to tour, write and record, eventually securing a production deal with Sonnet Records in the autumn of 1988.

With a new drummer, Paul McManus, replacing Joe, who had chosen to bow out, in January 1989 the band began pre-production for their debut album and Zero Four One was released in the autumn of that year to national acclaim from the music press.

Four singles were released through Sonnet: 'Secrets in the Dark' (written by Chris Thompson of Manfred Mann), 'Under the Lights', 'Meet Me

Halfway' and 'Will You Be Mine' – a song that Alan 'Fluff' Freeman described as 'the song that I believe will break the band in the UK'.

Although there was certainly a flurry of interest and flapping of chequebooks from major labels within the UK and even further afield in America and Japan, no new deal was ever secured. Inevitably, this led to more changes in Glasgow's personnel and some major detours in their musical direction.

Without the hint of a real deal to chew over, Glasgow finally split with their management and Sonnet. It would be a whole two years before Archie and Mick appeared on the scene again as Glasgow, this time with a new line-up, new material and an arguably much more commercial AOR sound, augmented by the introduction of Stuart Clyde on keyboards, Brian Galloway on bass and David Halley (formerly of Passionate Friends) on drums.

With their fresh new sound, great new material and brand new management in place, the band were soon being hailed once more as 'the next big thing'.

Attracting a whole new audience and with three albums of material written and ready to be recorded, Glasgow set off on an arduous circuit of live gigs, while their new manager, Richard Gibbons, set about building new relationships with big labels in America.

All of their work proved successful, with co-writing partnerships established and a deal finally struck to record a new album in Nashville. Then, disaster. On the very day they were due to fly out to the US of A, the deal collapsed.

Valiantly, Glasgow continued to write but finally disintegrated in the spring of 1996.

What remains is a reputation for huge personalities and powerful rock performances and few rock fans of the last 20–25 years will forget the great times that were had at a Glasgow gig. The band influenced many of the rock acts that would follow them in this decade and the next. However, although they have been asked to re-form many times in recent years, they continue to work in the biz under their own individual steam.

Today Michael still works in the music business, while Archie teaches at Stow College in Glasgow in the Creative Industries Department, plays guitar with local band Salon Society and is promoting singer-songwriters through the Artbox gig in Glasgow.

Joe wrote movie scores and formed Clannad Drumma, but passed away this year. One of the city's most respected drummers, he will be sadly missed by all.

Neil moved to Holland, where he is actively involved in management.

Paul, a successful businessman, still plays drums and manages bands.

Brian, one of the nicest and most patient guys you could ever meet, plays bass and has his own business as a freelance sound engineer.

David went on to play and record with several artists, while Stuart worked with Abel Ganz and has enjoyed a successful career as a music teacher.

It seems you can take the boys out of Glasgow, but you can't take Glasgow out of the boys!

When Davie Swan asked me to take some photographs of Heaven in 1980 it was the catalyst for a chain of events that would see me befriend the various band members. In Archie, Mick and Big Davy, I have enjoyed a friendship that has lasted over the subsequent 29 years.

This was great when I was Robert Fields, the rock fan, but as my own career in the music business took off, it was perfect, as I was able to arrange lots of gigs for the band in the Bruce Hotel in East Kilbride and Glasgow's Videodrome.

I can remember that most nights I would be down in the front row of a gig in the Venue, singing along with all the songs. However, as the Eighties motored on and the musical changes were rung in, bringing new bands with brand new sounds, I had to take off my friend's bunnet and put on my promoter's hat and there was a problem: Grunge was slowly but surely taking over, the kids were wearing baggy jumpers with sleeves that hid their hands and Glasgow, as with many of the melodic rock bands that had defined an era, were overlooked. Crowds were beginning to dwindle. Finally, there came a point when I was forced to stop giving the band work and inevitably this proved a difficult time for friendships.

I remember an irate Mick on the phone, giving me dog's abuse for turning my back on the boys. Later, when they made it big in Japan, I wouldn't get a sniff at them.

Fast forward nearly seven years and I'm opening the street hatch in my Glasgow club, Strawberry Fields, to take a beer delivery from Scottish and

Newcastle. My eyes meet the driver's and I realise it's Mick, when suddenly a keg of lager comes barrelling towards me and thuds on to the mat just inches away.

'What the f**k are you trying to do, Mick?' I scream.

'Oh, it's you,' is his reply. 'If I'd known that, I'd have hit you with it!'

We met later, in 2007, at a Journey concert in the Armadillo and he gave me a big hug, so I'm hoping we're okay now.

When it came to compiling the listening post to complement this book, Glasgow's name was one of the first names on the list – they were always special and I can pay them no higher compliment than to pass on their music to you.

Poetic Injustice

A Glasgow outfit whose music reflected the far-left politics of the era, moving from the Seventies and through the early Eighties, were the Dead Loss Band. Heavy rockers, they were very loud and ever-so-slightly self-indulgent. Formed after the demise of the Poets, the line-up incorporated Fraser Watson, George Gallagher and Dougie Henderson. Their track, 'Free from the Party' is on this book's online listening post and is a pretty good example of their material of the time.

In fact, the lads also played for a fun band called the Dansettes, whom I saw many a times in the Torrance Hotel in East Kilbride – the Dansettes played traditional rock 'n' roll and Sixties classics, a pursuit which paid the bills and allowed Fraser and co. the luxury of continuing with the Dead Loss Band. The Dansettes' bass player was a guy called Gordon Pitcairn, who was eventually replaced by Jackson Clarkin, with whom I'd gone to school.

Once that project had run its course, George formed the Blues Poets in 1991, essentially the Dead Loss Band with the addition of a brilliant young blues player by the name of Scott McGowan. One of George's friends was a guy called James Kelman – you may have read one or two of his little books, which seem to be mighty popular among our Scottish intelligentsia.

Now, there had been some interest emanating from the Hollywood Hills in one of Kelman's novels, with the intention of making it into a film.

Being a fan of the Blues Poets, who had already appeared in a play he'd written based on their musical exploits, he had asked if the band's music could be used on the soundtrack should the film go ahead.

Alas, the Hollywood dream never came true, the movie never materialised and another historic band went their separate ways.

Abel And Willing

The year 1980 saw the birth of prog rockers Abel Ganz. I must admit I only saw them once myself, in Shadows, I think it was. I wasn't into their sound, or that of Genesis, Yes, Marillion and the like, being a much more basic rock animal, but they were braw all the same and deserve their place in Glasgow's rock history.

They were formed by keyboard player Hew Montgomery and multi-instrumentalist Hugh Carter. Although both had played in various bands over the years, it was a shared interest in progressive rock and a need for a songwriting platform that brought them together, with the line-up completed by guitarist Malky McNiven and drummer Ken Weir.

The band played regularly in the Glasgow area and, as their popularity grew, it was decided they should recruit a new vocalist. Small of stature but huge of voice, Alan Reed came on board from Stirling band Trance Macabre and Abel Ganz recorded their first album, Gratuitous Flash, in 1983.

With regular gigs and airplay on Scottish radio, Abel Ganz were building up a solid following, a fan base that was bolstered by an appearance at Glasgow's Kelvingrove Festival, an event with a fine reputation for launching the careers of many Scottish bands. However, the gig was a double-edged sword: wee Alan's performance that day brought him to the attention of Pallas, who were searching for a replacement for their recently departed Euan Laurson. One audition later, Alan was off on a free transfer to Aberdeen and 20 years on is still belting out the songs for Pallas.

Malky, too, would leave, to pursue a career in horticulture, of all things, to be replaced by Paul Kelly on guitar and vocals. This move was swiftly followed by Gordon Mackie taking up duties on bass, when Hugh Carter stepped out of the spotlight to concentrate instead on managing the band. This new line-up heralded the band's most productive era, with constant gigging throughout Scotland and the north of England and the recording of a second album, Gullible's Travels.

In 1985 there was a third album, The Dangers of Strangers, with Denis Smith on drums and guest appearances from former Ganzers Alan and Paul. This year also saw the popularity of Abel Ganz spread across Europe, thanks to a contract with the French record label M.S.I.

The next decade, however, proved to be difficult for the band and the writing was on the wall when co-founder Hew, the creator of the Wall of Ganz keyboard sound left to be replaced by Stuart Clyde, who would later pop up in the band, Glasgow. By this time the band was slipping into the murky waters of AOR rock. A fourth album, The Deafening Silence, left just that, for Hugh Carter split the band rather than allow Abel Ganz to turn into the mute monster it was threatening to become.

There then followed some years of inactivity as Hew went to ground and Hugh continued to write and record in his studio in Glasgow. However, a chance meeting of the two in 2001 saw Abel Ganz back on track again. With the Hugh and Hew duo at the helm again and Dangers of Strangers drummer Denis Smith back on board, joined by his long-term collaborators Davie Mitchell (guitar) and Steven Donnelly (bass), the band now has a settled line-up and is sure to be around for a long time to come.

Meet The Osbournes

The call arrived just a few days before the gig from my old mate, big Lee Kerslake, who had left Uriah Heep, that he would be up in Glasgow at the Apollo with Ozzy Osbourne. Not only this, but he would leave four passes on the front door and was looking forward to seeing us all again.

This was to be Ozzy's first gig without Sabbath. His debut album, The Blizzard of Ozz, had already met critical acclaim and his line-up – who played on Blizzard and the next album, Diary of a Madman – was Lee on drums, Bob Daisley on bass and Randy Rhoads on guitar. Incidentally, both albums were co-written and produced by Ozzy, Bob, Lee and Randy. And so, on 12 September 1980, with the kids and big Davie Swan in hand, we were off to see the Blizzard, the wonderful Blizzard of Ozz.

To be honest, meeting the Double O was a dream come true for me, as I was a massive Black Sabbath fan and meeting Lee at the front door then climbing the stairs to the dressing room, I was incredibly nervous. So was big Davie, who unbeknown to me had secreted a big bottle of plonk inside his leather coat to calm himself down!

Before reaching the tune-up room and entering the dressing room, there was the eldritch noise of the life being strangled out of a guitar and the hairs on the back of my neck stood to attention. I looked at Lee and a huge grin split his face.

'That's Randy,' he said. 'You'll meet him later.'

We entered the dressing room and there in front of me was the man himself. Lee introduced us as his family and my kids as his Godchildren and straight away Ozzy came over and shook everyone's hand and started playing with the kids. Despite his manic stage persona, he was, up close and personal, very warm and genuine and a charming host. He was, if anything, as nervous as we were and not at all the madman I'd been expecting.

All went well as he posed with us for pictures. Randy came in, looking rather sheepish and shook hands, as did Bob and keyboard player, Lindsay Buckingham who would play on stage behind the curtains.

Explaining that we'd be leaving straight after the gig to get the weans off to bed and asking Big Lee to keep in touch, we popped into support act, Budgie's dressing room to say hi before settling down for a classic gig from the Double O.

That night reaffirmed, if affirmation were ever needed, that all of the worry and doubts that had plagued Ozzy all day and night before this solo gig, were for naught. All fear of failure was blown away big style, as the man bestrode the stage like the Colossus he was and blasted us with his rock anthems. We knew there and then that here, indeed, was a true rock legend, with or without his beloved Black Sabbath.

Pick A Perfect Peck Of Punk

Formed in Glasgow at the tail end of 1979 were a bunch of wannabes led by the flamboyant and dynamic vocalist Ross Allison. Alongside him were guitarist Donald Macleod, formerly of the Clan, Caroline Simpson on bass, Gavin Murray (lead guitar) and Paul Dill (drums).

Heavily influenced by the emergence of punk, if in the more mellifluous form espoused by Siouxsie and the Banshees and the Slits, First Priority were unleashed on an unsuspecting Glasgow audience. After blagging a support slot with the Clash at the Apollo, lucky blighters, they built up a large local following in and around Glasgow and became a regular attraction at such venues as the Mars Bar, the Doune Castle and the Key Youth Centre in East Kilbride.

Soon they were an intrinsic part of a Glasgow scene that incorporated acts such as Johnny and the Self Abusers (later to become Simple Minds), the Berlin Blondes, Aztec Camera and Altered Images.

Like moths to the flame, they soon relocated to London but, after just a short while, they returned home with a vastly new and improved act and sound and continued where they left off prior to their wee tea break in the Big Smoke.

The year 1984 brought another big blagging coup in the form of a major recording and publishing contract with MCA, which saw them endure the ignominy of appearing on numerous occasions on Peter Powell's Oxford Road Show.

First Priority's first single was 'Lady Christabelle'. Studio crafted by Cure and Banshees producer Mike Hedges, it was released to coincide with the band's first UK-wide tour, on which they supported John Lydon's Public Image. This was the punk prince's first tour since splitting with the Sex Pistols and must surely have been a real eye opener for our wee band of vagabonds from Glasgow.

The band's touring continued relentlessly through the decade and a second single, 'Pillow Talk', was released. They also toured with New Model Army in 1985, but major commercial success eluded them and, in 1986, they disbanded, with Ross and Donald flying again in the late Eighties under the guise of The Crows.

Snakes On A Different Plane

Another of one of the hardest-working pub bands at the kickstart of the decade were Anaconda, which history records as the last band to play the legendary Burns Howff.

Formed in 1979, their original line-up consisted of Ian Crockert on lead vocals and rhythm guitar, Derek Hall (lead guitar), Billy Russell (bass) and

Laurie Kennedy (drums).

At the end of that year Kenny McKay joined to play second lead guitar, in a move that allowed Ian to concentrate more fully on the singing. This line-up held for a couple of years, mostly as the resident band in the Burns Howff with the odd additional gig in the Dial Inn and Doune Castle in Shawlands. Their set consisted of covers of AC/DC, Ted Nugent, Deep Purple, Led Zeppelin and Neil Young, with a few of their original tunes peppered throughout the mix to add a little seasoning.

While Anaconda squeezed every ounce of energy from their instruments, their grip on personnel was not so tight. First, Laurie left and was replaced for a short spell on drums by Tony Gavigan, then by Billy Drennan. Bassist Billy Russell also departed and so Ian took over additional duties on bass. This line-up lasted two more years, until Billy Drennan was ousted from behind the kit.

The year was 1985, Anaconda were auditioning for a new drummer and did none other than Tommy Vance invite them on to his radio show? The DJ wanted the boys to do a Tommy Vance Rock Show session on Radio 1 (though for some reason, this is often now listed as a Peel Session).

In the early Eighties, you see, when we couldn't get a regular fix of live rock music, we tuned in first and foremost to radio host Tommy Vance. After Tommy it was Tom Russell on a Friday night, as he blitzed the airwaves for four hours from 10 p.m. And for the times when the radio was playing all that pop pap, whether it was a biker reading in the bar over his pint, or a teenager hiding at midnight under the covers with a torch, we could still keep up on all that was really fresh betwixt live gig and radio shows, for we were blessed with the bible that was Kerrang!

The magazine started out as a monthly publication, went fortnightly, then weekly and offered to use bands', promoters' and venues' free gig guides etc to catch up on all the latest news, views and reviews . God bless Kerrang!, yes, the sound of a smashing guitar, for coming into our lives!

During the Eighties and well into the early Nineties the mag, which was first published on 6 June 1981 and edited by Geoff Barton, awarded the front-cover billing to many thrash and glam metal acts: outfits such as Mötley Crüe, Slayer, Bon Jovi, Metallica, Poison, Testament Venom. However, the usual suspects would soon be pushed aside when usurper Grunge acts such as Nirvana began their meteoric rise to fame.

Kerrang! remains as original and pertinent today as it did way back in the day and I still buy it, whenever I remember. But so much for my glossy aside . . . let's get back to business.

Anaconda hurriedly recruited a drummer called Dave McRoberts for the Tommy Vance session. Although their turn was well received and repeated on the show, the band were not convinced by the drumming and, by mutual consent, parted company with Dave. Enter stage right, Greg Orr.

This last all-together is often considered the classic Anaconda line-up and is the one that made up the last band ever to play the Howff. After the closure of that hallowed music hub, Anaconda were regularly found gigging in Shadows.

Derek Hall left just before the band were asked to play Kelvingrove's 10th Anniversary Festival in 1987 and, once again, the boys found themselves hastily recruiting.

Raymie Wilson was their new man. Shortly afterwards, Shadows closed too and they became resident in the Doune, which many readers might know better as formerly Leon's Waterfront on Clydeside.

Next up to leave was newcomer Raymie. It was around this time yours truly put Anaconda on for the one and only time in the Bruce Hotel in East Kilbride, when they drafted in Mark Polo Barrett for his only gig. After that, John Carr was taken on as second lead.

Several years of gigging saw Anaconda move from a closed Doune (get it?) to Platini's, formerly the basement in Furlong's and now known as the Iron Horse. They were also one of the first bands to play in the Solid Rock Cafe basement.

The band reformed with a 'reunion' line-up that saw Derek Hall, Kenny McKay and John Carr present a three-guitar sound. When Kenny moved down to London, the band continued with Derek and John on guitar duties.

By 2000 Anaconda had changed its skin so many times that it actually no longer existed. Derek, Ian, Greg and Polo had formed Gratis Quo, a tribute to Status Quo circa 1970–76 and I kid you not, Polo would later be replaced by Rab Baird, formerly of the Smokey Bears, Fresh Air Fortnight and Rose's Home, with Big George.

In 2002 the so-called classic Anaconda line-up re-formed for what turned out to be a one-off gig at Macsorley's, in Glasgow. Derek then left

Gratis Quo, confusingly to be replaced by none other than one Kenny McKay. Seriously, lads, this is getting incestuous!

In September 2008, Ian quit Gratis, finally bringing to an end Anaconda's rock family tree. In all, for a pub band with no great pretensions, these lads always offered a great night out, with inventive playing and an intuitive choice and blend of covers and originals.

Check out their track on the free online listening post – I'm sure you'll agree certainly they rocked, pure and simple, which is as good a reason as any for their place in the pages of this book.

Dolphins In The Park

It's a scenario that anyone who works in the music business, or who simply loves live music, has faced more than once. You're in a venue, watching an amazing band and at the end of the show, perhaps slightly out of kilter betwixt head and feet on the heady mix of rock music and Tennent's lager, you get to talk to one of the band members. You say how wonderfully, terribly braw you thought they were and indeed you enquire whether there might be a single in the offing, or perhaps even an album on the way, what you might purchase and, to the constant shaking of the head, finally ask, well what label are you on then?

And the answer comes back: 'You're kiddin' aren't you, chief? We're no' even signed!'

Well, the venue this night was the Dial Inn and the musician answering Mr Fields' irrepressible line of questioning was the genius that was Cammy Forbes and his band - one of Glasgow's finest, the Dolphins.

Formed from the ashes of Underhand Jones in 1981, the Dolphins – Campbell Forbes on lead vocals, guitar and keyboards, with Brian Coyle (lead guitar, vocals and harmonica), Drew Phillips (keyboards), George Dunnachie (bass), Davie Edgar (drums, 1981/82) and Harry Denmark (drums, 1982/84) – soon carved out a reputation as being one of Glasgow's most talked-about and refreshing young bands.

Certainly, they deserved the plaudits: their standard of musicianship, songwriting and live playing was second to none. Their sets featured the intro to 'The Baseball Furies Chase' from the film The Warriors, quickly followed by self-penned tunes such as 'Running'.

They really were an outstanding band and their repertoire of all-encompassing musical styles ranged from rock and reggae to pop and the odd classic instrumental, there to give Cammy's delicate wee tonsils a well-deserved break.

Every once in a while, the boys would even throw in a ragtime number, 'Inspiration', to add a bit of levity and diversity to the set. But the full-on rock anthems 'Shock Horror' and 'Light up the Sky' would bring the set to a rousing close.

As the popularity of the Dolphins grew, they began to attract a loyal local following, who would turn up regularly at gigs such as the Mayfair, the Dial Inn and the Lincoln. They then had the audacity to book the Kelvingrove bandstand and pull more than 4,000 punters for an evening concert. Now how many young, up-and-coming bands could pull that off?

At one point in the evening, Cammy looks out into the crowd, or rather where the crowd should be, for by this time, they are in pitch darkness.

'This is like a scene from my favourite movie,' shouts Cammy and the band immediately launch into 'Light up the Sky', played to the explosive backdrop of a massive fireworks display.

This impromptu, if inspired, gig resulted in immediate TV exposure, with an interview with news reporter Louise Batchelor in which Cammy managed to get across the message that there is a very healthy music scene happening in Glasgow, thank you very much, it's just that the mainstream media, record labels and assorted bigwigs seemed oblivious or simply chose to ignore its existence.

Cammy was making a fair point – notwithstanding the Eighties success of pop bands such as H2O (oh, no I can't believe I've given them a mention in my book: now I'll 'dream to sleep, sleep to have nightmares'!) who, while never in the same league or musical vein as the Dolphins, did go some way to highlighting a flourishing Glasgow scene.

The Dolphins' second TV appearance was in BBC Scotland's The Untied Shoelaces Show, hosted by radio DJ and presenter Tiger Tim Stevens. They played three songs: 'Tonight', 'Chelsea Mornings' and 'Slow Down'.

By the by, my old pal big Davie Swan once told me once that, before joining Heaven, he was in a band with a certain chap by the name of Tim

Stevens, a lead vocalist who was yet to gain his famous feline growl.

Well, after a British tour supporting Chris Rea, signing a publishing deal with Rondor Music and securing a management deal with Checkmount, Cammy headed over to the United States of America, armed with Dolphin demos. There he met people from RCA, Warner Bros and Geffen, but all to no avail. No deal was ever done.

The Dolphins did, however, get to play in front of Charles and Diana in 1983 at the King's Theatre in London at an event staged for the Prince's Trust.

Cammy, who cites his musical influences as Uriah Heep (what a delectable taste in music, young man!), Alice Cooper and Bruce Springsteen, then went solo under the nom de plume of one David Forbes yet, as for so many heroes in this book, still the elusive big break proved elusive.

Cammy is a really nice bloke and I've had the pleasure of working with him at the Cathouse club in Glasgow on many of the shows I do in there for young local bands. He's an incredibly talented sound engineer and I thank him immensely for some great nights we've had. He's still a Dolphin in my eyes and will always be a star.

The Original Tea In The Park

You may have noticed that a great many of the artists and bands I've written about so far have featured at the Radio Clyde Kelvingrove Rock and Pop Festival. Certainly, Kelvingrove was to be a prominent and important milestone in the career of up-and-coming stars.

Kicking off in 1978, it was a legendary gig throughout the Eighties and would last well into the Nineties, only coming to an end when the west end park's famous bandstand was finally condemned as unsafe by the Glasgow patricians.

The idea of the festival was Radio Clyde's answer to the major and strongly warranted criticism aimed at them for having lost touch with the younger generation in their programme of live music. In his programme notes, recorded in 1983, Jimmy Gordon wrote:

'In 1976 Radio Clyde launched the first of a series of festivals of which Clyde '83 is now the eighth. It seemed to us that everyone enjoyed the

Glasgow 80 celebrations in 1975 and that we shouldn't have to wait another 100 years for the next party.

'Our aim has been to provide something for everyone. We have produced concerts for all tastes in music and for all ages. Each year Joe Loss returns to Glasgow [dear God, see what I mean about having lost touch!] to play for dancers, many of whose memory goes back to when he was a regular in the old Green's Playhouse.

'Another annual event is the senior citizens concert in the Kelvin Hall [yes, you can see there's a theme here] and each year we co-operate with the city's cleansing department in a schools clean-up campaign.

'Another major feature is our recently new free Rock and Pop concert in the Kelvingrove bandstand.'

Well, he got there in the end!

In the same festival programme John McCalman, the festival director and the man originally responsible for the legendary event, wrote:

'Over the years there has been a tradition of free entertainment in the Kelvingrove Bandstand in Kelvingrove Park.

'In 1978 Jammy Music approached Radio Cyde's Jimmy Gordon with a view to obtaining finance to run a free outdoor music festival as part of the annual Clyde festival. The aim of the festival was to provide a platform for local musicians to perform original material in front of a large outdoor audience.

'While the entertainment was to be provided free of charge to the public, all the musicians' fees, PA costs and security were to be met by Radio Clyde. So with Radio Clyde's backing the first Kelvingrove Free Music Festival took place on Sunday, 21 May 1978 and was an astounding success with both musicians and punters alike.'

And so say all of us!

John goes on to say: 'While the first festivals were essentially for rock and pop bands, with some solo acts sneaking in, it was decided in 1981 to run a folk festival in Glasgow's Queens Park to complement Kelvingrove. Last year we switched the folk event to Kelvingrove and made the Free Festival a two-day event. This paid off with a cumulative attendance of more than 10,000 revellers over the two days.

'The selection of the acts is never an easy task. There are many acts who merit a place on the bill but there is no space for everybody. The idea of the final selection is to mirror the cross-section of the talent we have here in the West of Scotland so that the many months of preparation and organisation and planning that go into the event are rewarded and on the day there will be something for everyone to enjoy.'

And not a truer word was ever said, for Kelvingrove has been one of those, admittedly small-scale, events that has nevertheless attracted an incredible range and variety of top-notch bands. Outfits of all shapes and sizes and musical backgrounds have appeared in that grassy oasis over the space of 20-odd years and here's an abbreviated list of some of the true highlights. How many did you see and have I missed any favourites?

Sneeky Pete, the Jets, Woza (an early form of Deacon Blue), Hue & Cry, Underhand Jones, One O'Clock Gang, Real Politique, Charley Browne, the Soft Cloks, Young Things West, Gentlemen of Leisure, Chou Pahrot, Those French Girls, Abel Ganz, Dick Broad and the Fallen Goats, the Petted Lips, PS, 30 Bob Suits, Amanda's Tapes, Zero Zero, Bite the Pillow, Rubber Yahoo, The Force, Henry Gorman Band, Pretty Boy Floyd, Mean Street, Trident (oh, yes, they really did!), La Paz, Big George + Fraser Speirs, Anaconda, Centurion, Conduct of Pigeons, Filming in Africa, Jewel Scheme, The Third Party, The River Detectives, The Thieves, Julia Please, The Cuban Heels, The Royal Family, Comedy of Errors, Horse, Snapshots, Glasgow, Blind Allez, Wild River Apples, Shakin' Pyramids, China White, Rosie's Home, Farewell Parade, Amateur Hour, Kissing Bandits, Tonight at Noon, The McClusky Brothers, H2O, Chasar, Strangers and Brothers, Moni, The Dolphins, Happy the Man, the Crows, Hearts and Minds, The RBs, Menace, The Stingrytes, Runaway Train, Phobia, Heavy Pettin' . . . oh and the wee band I happened to manage, Drunken State.

Truth be told, Drunken State might appear at the bottom of my list but they're perched right at the top whenever I think of the Kelvingrove Festival.

That year, 1988 to be precise, everyone and their auntie and their auntie's wee Westie turned up on the Saturday to have a gander as the bands performed their sound-check. This happened in reverse running order, which meant my Drunken ones would be sound-checking last, at tea time, around 6 p.m., being first on the next day.

The day began so well. Glorious yellow rays bathed the park and the mood among the milling crowds reflected the summer sunshine. There was even an impromptu footie match between La Paz and Trident, who were headlining the gig. Actually, now that I remember, Trident had a rather big bee in their bonnet that day because the festival posters had all been printed with the soundcheck running-order back to front, meaning Drunken State were on top and the biggest stars of the bill at the bottom. To this day, on their official website, Trident still proclaim under an image of the poster: 'Honest, we headlined it'!

Now, bear in mind that in those days thrash music was just thinking about thrusting its petulant young way to the fore and a lot of mainstream music stations and their yes-men DJs hated this new and anarchic sound. I'd fought hard even to get Drunken State on the bill. I remember John McCalman coming up to me and saying he was taking a big chance on my boys because they were so young and because of the style of music they played. I assured him they were special and more than capable of doing the business.

And so here I am standing next to John Mac himself at the sound desk as my special, capable lads take to the stage for their soundcheck.

Let's not blame it on the boogie, let's not blame it on the sunshine, though I'm sure that inspired the initial thirst. Let's blame it on the crate of premium-strength lager that has been ladled into by everyone in Drunken State, bar lead vocalist Robert Traish, who never drank.

By this point in the night it's so freezing that rhythm guitarist Dougie Smith, who has bad circulation, finds his fingers frozen. Drummer Graeme Thomson, deaf in one ear, discovers the monitor is on his bad side. Guitarist Davie Leishman, meanwhile, is so drunk he can't find the hole to plug his guitar into the amp. To cap it all, bass player Michael Brash inexplicably falls off the stage.

To my right, the sound engineer, Johnny Ramsey, of EFX, is bent over in uncontrollable howls of laughter.

And then Mr McCalman turns round to me, his eyes like black stone and seethes through his teeth: 'You have two minutes to sort this lot out or I'm pulling you off the bill.'

Dear reader, you've never seen a grown man in leather run so fast since the day Jim Morrison woke up with a scorpion in his drawers.

Dougie's hands were stuck into his hot oxters, the drum monitor was heaved to the starboard, Davie's guitar was successfully docked with its amp and Michael underwent a Lazarus-like resurrection from beneath the stage. An incandescent rock manager, even one my size, can bring instant sobriety to his group and the remainder of the soundcheck passed off without event and we all staggered home to East Kilbride on the late bus.

Sunday, of course, went down like a storm. Drunken State, as I'd fully expected, stepped on to the stage and blew everyone away . Even John Mac came up to me afterwards and shook my hand.

'Excellent!' he said. 'Just excellent!'

Hey, Mr DJ!

All of the above shenanigans were ably compèred by the inimitable, gravel-toned voice of the music radio legend that is Tom Russell. It would be a grave error to underestimate what Tom has meant to the rock scene since his Friday Night Rock Shows first appeared on Clyde in the early Eighties – even if, back then, the radio bigwigs showed their disregard, if not downright contempt, for the burgeoning scene by offering a ghost-shift slot of midnight until two in the morning.

Tom was ever, if you can excuse the crude analogy, farting against thunder. Thank the louder gods of rock, then, for Jay Crawford and 96.3 Rock Radio for keeping the Russell roller-coaster going with Tom's new show.

Born near Kirkintilloch, Tom attended Lenzie Academy and from an early age he was intent on getting his hands on heavy metal: his very first job was as a metallurgist in Kirkintilloch iron foundry!

At the age of 18 he set off down south, not quite Dick Whittington style, for he was on a student apprenticeship with the Ministry of Defence, studying mechanical engineering at Durham College, don't you know? After working for a year as a stock car racer – I kid you not, when I tell you this man has had an eclectic working life – he then joined the Parachute Regiment, where he had a great time. In all, he leapt from a plane many thousands of feet in the air and strapped to a sheet, 17 times.

Next, he played guitar for a year in a band based in Newcastle, an outfit called Strange Brew. They recorded a single, 'Floating', which lived down to its name by sinking without a trace (somebody, somewhere must be able to find this gem).

The return of the native saw Tom open a record shop in Bishopbriggs, then another in Shettleston. A catalytic moment came at a record company party where he met Richard Park, then the big boss at Radio Clyde. Tom, as is often his wont, spent the entire night slagging Richard for not playing any rock on his station.

To his credit, Richard admitted to personally not liking the genre, but graciously phoned Tom a few weeks later and offered him a Friday Night Rock Show. The contract was for an initial six-week trial, but after the six weeks were up no one said anything so Tom just kept going in on a Friday and ended up serving for 25 years.

He recalls: 'I was really lucky throughout the Seventies, Eighties and Nineties to see almost every rock band around, including Van Halen, Guns N' Roses, Led Zeppelin, Bon Jovi, AC/DC, Deep Purple, Pink Floyd, Marillion, Thin Lizzy, Aerosmith, Genesis, Ozzy Osbourne, Yes, Def Leppard etc.

'And I was even luckier to get to interview most of them, as well as party with the best and worst of them. During this period I also worked as a journalist with Metal Hammer magazine and managed to expand my chain of record shops to four. However, the days of small record shops had come to an end and I closed them down at the end of the Nineties.'

In October of 2006 Jay Crawford called Tom and asked him in for a chat. Jay was programme director at Real Radio at the time and Tom suspected that he was going to be offered a weekly rock show.

You can imagine his surprise and delight when Jay announced that GMG were going to launch an entire rock station and he wanted Tom to present a show playing AC/DC, Led Zeppelin, Bon Jovi and the Rolling Stones five days a week.

Tom recalls: 'I hesitated for a millisecond, then mumbled: "Yes please" and walked out of his office convinced that I had dreamt the whole thing!'

It was no dream and Tom is now very much hands-on with 96.3 Rock Radio. As well as bringing us great music, he's involved in the promotional side of the business and it was a real pleasure to hear him compère the second Rock Radio birthday party in the Garage nightclub earlier this year.

When I add up all the years, which guys my age don't like to do very often, Tom has been in my life for more than 27 of them: firstly as my musical lifeline and educator on the radio and, finally, as a friend. He is singularly responsible for breaking many new bands throughout the years. One recent acknowledgement of his enduring influence, even for the freshest generation of up-and-coming rockers, came in a tribute from The Almighty, when they announced from the stage at their Glasgow gig in the Garage that, if it hadn't been for Tom, they would never have cracked it.

I can add a personal testimony to his unstinting devotion to the cause of rock. I remember when we organised a CD of unsigned bands on the Cathouse's Cat-scratch label. It was called, rather grandly, The Gathering of the Clans and Tom devoted a whole programme to playing the tracks and interviewing me. Never mind that not one of the bands was signed: it was all about the music.

Incidentally, not long after the show I got a phone call from Bobby Haines, from Clyde, enquiring about payment for the programme. I told him to f**k off and asked did I charge him for the two after-show parties in the Cathouse after the Kelvingrove gigs? The line went dead and I never heard from him again. Hey ho.

I have, however, heard often from Tom Russell: he is and always will be a true Glasgow rock legend in his own right but, more importantly, a great guy, a true friend.

Meet Ronnie And Henry

Another true star of the Glasgow rock scene in the Eighties and through every decade since is Ronnie Garrity and not just because the two months he spent ensconced in his studio, Heathman's Mastering in London, with his top engineer, Denis 'The Menace' Smith, remastering all of the tracks for the free listening post that goes with the book you now find in your hands.

Now, Ronnie, you see, was the bass player of the renowned Glasgow outfit, the Henry Gorman Band, whose line-up also included Henry himself on guitar and vocals, John Grant (keyboards) and Danny Gisbey (drums). Formed in the late Seventies from the raggle taggle remnants of Rivendel, one band to rule them all, who won the very first Melody Maker battle of the bands in Scotland, the HGB toured with some of the biggest names in the business throughout their illustrious career – among their stage pals were Frankie Miller, Wishbone Ash, Budgie and Girlschool.

Signing a major publishing deal with Jonathan Rowlands, who owned the Producers Workshop in London, they collaborated with producer Chris Adams and recorded the album that was to become The Official Bootleg Album.

The debut single was 'Chase the Night Away' (one of the tracks on the listening post, don't you know?) and the track was heavily promoted by none other than legendary Radio One DJ Tommy Vance on his Friday Night Rock Show and our very own Dougie Donnelly on Radio Clyde.

Gigging relentlessly nationwide, the band also flexed their musical muscle in Europe, playing gigs in Bulgaria and Poland during the Solidarity riots following the death of Brezhnev. These were groundbreaking times, indeed, so much so that – in true Spinal Tap tradition – the bootleg album was, erm, bootlegged and became the second-biggest selling album that year after the Rolling Stones!

The band relocated to London but broke up when Henry decided to move to the Big Apple in 1984. Such was his prodigious talent that he soon carved out a career in songwriting in New York and was signed to Geffen with his new band the Roo Ha Ha. As well as performing alongside such luminaries as the late, great godfather James Brown, Midge Ure and Robert Palmer, he has co-written with acclaimed writers such as Scott English (of Westlife and Barry Manilow), Kenny Young (The Drifters), Lisa Green (Britney Spears and Kylie) and Ray St John (Sade), to name but a few.

Henry was also a member of The Far Corporation, who made a successful cover of Led Zeppelin's classic 'Stairway to Heaven'.

Later he would go on to form the band Big Stupid Guitars, whose debut platter made it on to the credible New York Post's Album of the Month. Although now based in London, the HGB gets together in Gourock every now and then for charity work.

I first met Ronnie in the Nineties, when he had his own mastering studios, Waterfront, in Glasgow. Recently, he's been managing an all-girl band called The Roslins. Henry, meanwhile, has been helping out writing songs and performing his guitar magic and sound technician wizardry.

Apollo, We Have A Problem

In the middle of this decade, my old pals Uriah Heep would be involved in one of the Glasgow rock story's most poignant moments. After Abominog (1982) and Headfirst (1983) Mick Box, Lee Kerslake, Pete Goalby, John Sinclair and Trevor Bolder, who now replaced Bob Daisley, would cut the 1985 album Equator and become the last rock band to play the Apollo, on 16 May. It was a sad day for everyone.

Intent as I was on absorbing everything I could during the seminal moment, to this day I can remember everything, from the moment the family and I met up with the band for their photo call.

I'd taken the kids to Burger King beforehand and wee Cheryl still had her BK paper hat on in the pics, which brought smiles to the band amid what could only be described as an atmosphere almost of impending catastrophe.

Heep were not the only ones living that night under the cloud of knowing this would be the last supper of rock for the mighty Apollo. We met Mick Boyle, of Glasgow, outside and even he couldn't find his normal bounce that day. Pallas's Alan Reed, too, could hardly muster a smile.

I took a photo of my kids outside the great showhouse, at the main entrance next to a Heep poster that bore, in huge letters, the slogan: 'The Final Countdown'. I remember as I pressed the shutter on the camera, a huge orange bus passed right in front of me and my heart sank further.

I always liked the kids to experience the balcony at the Apollo but that night, unusually, we sat in one of the side-boxes. My eyes were as much fixed on the swaying crowd, drinking in the atmosphere of this ultimate night: although the overall atmosphere might have been more subdued than the walls were accustomed to, the fans themselves managed to be raucous enough so as not to insult the bands.

Heep's set that night included 'Sell Your Soul', 'Stealin'', 'The Other Side of Midnight', 'Too Scared to Run', 'Rockerama', 'Angel', 'The Wizard', 'July Morning', 'Bad Blood', 'PartyTime', 'Gypsy', 'Easy Livin'', 'That's the Way That It Is' and 'Look at Yourself'.

Looking back at ourselves that night, we were one huge swinging, stamping, singing family as the Apollo Choir said our final farewells.

Raging Bulls

Where did it all go wrong? What happened to so much potential? They had everything. They could be everything. They were special. They were regarded by many as the quintessential rock band. And they were ours, Glasgow city's. So how in heaven and on earth, did Heavy Pettin' manage to orchestrate their way out of assured and spectacular success?

Well, let's start with the basics. Now, I always was, still am, a huge fan. I own all the albums and the CD reissues and I saw Heavy Pettin' live many times. In fact, I was given the privilege of organising their farewell show in East Kilbride's Bruce Hotel in 1988. The line-up that night was Steven (Hamie) Hayman on lead vocals, Gary Moat (drums and vocals) and Gordon Bonnar (guitar and vocals). Punky Mendoza had left and been replaced by Alex Dickson (guitar). Brian Waugh, too, had gone, to be replaced by David Leslie, from Ransom, on bass.

Alex explains how he became involved thus: 'I got a call asking me to audition at the Venue in Glasgow. I was under the impression that it was Glasgow who were auditioning. I was taken into the room and, lo and behold, it was Bonnar, Moatsy and Hamie.

'They didn't have a bass player either, so I recommended David Leslie from Edinburgh band Ransom. I remember when they picked him up from Queen Street Station and were driving up the ramps of a multi-storey car park, David's first words to the band were: "Hey, guys, is this the Glasgow Tunnel?"'

So just what happened to Heavy Pettin'? You land a major record deal with Polydor (not to be sniffed at!). You're signed to ITB, one of the world's top booking agents. Brian May of Queen does your debut album. You tour the big wide world, supporting Kiss, Mötley Crüe, Ozzy, Ratt, Magnum and many more. There are women to your left, to your right and bang in the centre. And there, in my opinion, lies the key factor: no, not just the women – in the words of the Little Angels' song, it was all 'too much, too young'.

I think that, just like Hiding Place, a band I managed to get signed in the 2000s, Heavy Pettin' simply didn't realise just what it was that they had within their grasp. One minute they were scraping around, looking for the crumbs, the next top producers were clamouring for them and the lads were being offered the best of everything in the music business.

I liken Pettin's career to the maiden voyage of the Titanic. From the first day the plans were put on the table, wrong decisions were being made: about rivets, materials and just which way to go. What should have been a wonderful and spectacular creation was doomed from the very start, leaving it to be swallowed up and disappear without a trace.

Much like the problems that beset Little Angels and fellow Glasgow rockers The Almighty, who further down the line would be signed to Polydor, there was another massive anchor chained to Heavy Pettin's fiery meteor: their label didn't understand them. Quite simply, I don't think they could handle rock bands at all, because any label that enters their band into a 10-song play-off for Britain's entry into the 1987 Eurovision song contest – the event was hosted by Terry Wogan for goodness' sake! – isn't really on the same wavelength.

Pettin's Romeo entry came a miserable sixth. It had to win the play-offs to secure radio play and, er, didn't. So it wasn't played. In one fell swoop the career of, in my humble opinion, Glasgow's finest rock band was forever destroyed.

In 2008 Heavy Pettin' enjoyed a brief return to the fore with the re-release of their back catalogue: three albums (Lettin' Loose, Rock Ain't Dead and The Big Bang, all with bonus tracks) and the box set Prodigal Songs, all accompanied by liner notes from a good friend of mine for well over 20 years, Dave Ling of Classic Rock.

I therefore thank Dave for allowing me to blag his splendid Pettin' biog, which is appended below for your further delectation:

'The roots of Heavy Pettin' lie in Weeper, a regrettably named Glasgow pub band formed in 1975. Their ranks included guitarist Gordon Bonnar, bassist Brian Waugh and Drummer Gary Moat. When this trio met singer Steven (Hamie) Hayman and guitarist Punky Mendoza six years later, Heavy Pettin' were born. The quintet's timing was impeccable, as the summer of 1981 was a good time to be a hard rock or heavy metal band and Heavy Pettin' very quickly found themselves caught up in the tail end of 'The New Wave of British Heavy Metal'.

'That said, their American-orientated sound and image were a good deal more polished than that of Iron Maiden and their ilk. 'We listen to Saxon and Def Leppard, rather than Black Sabbath and Deep Purple,' Bonnar later told Sounds magazine. 'We've always been into heavy metal, starting off with Thin Lizzy.'

'Hamie was quick to own up to the band's US flavour in the same interview, acknowledging the influences of bands such as Aerosmith. 'They are more melodic and I like the way they look,' he told writer Dave Roberts, while Brain Waugh cut to the chase, declaring: 'We don't like the blatant and fast heavy metal that's coming out now, the thrash!'

'Young (their average age was just 20), gifted, ambitious and not exactly shy, Pettin' saw the opportunity and wasted little time grasping it. Within mere months of their formation, Kerrang!'s Geoff Barton was praising a demo comprising the tracks 'Love Xs Love', 'Speed Kills' and 'Hell is Beautiful', which the band had recorded in just 18 hours. It secured them a single deal with independent label Neat Records – home of Venom, the Tygers of Pang Tang and Fist.

'Roll the Dice' b/w 'Love Xs Love' won them acclaim from all over the world. However, with reams of positive press clippings in hand, the band were already thinking of bigger things, turning down all offers from Neat to record a full album. 'We haven't seen any [sales] figures because Neat would never tell us,' commented Hamie shortly afterwards. 'But the single must have done well to get to number six in the Sounds Heavy Metal chart.'

'Turning their attention towards the road, Pettin' plated their first gig at Glasgow's Virgin Megastore. Things didn't exactly go to plan. Upon arrival they discovered they were actually supporting the Cuban Heels. When they were informed they wouldn't be able to perform at all because the headliners needed time to soundcheck, the band responded with typical Glaswegian subtlety. 'It was either we played or the Cuban Heels couldn't,' recalled Gary Moat later. 'So, no problem. We went on anyway, then the Heels played after all or so we heard. Bunch of poofs!'

'Times were hard at the start and the band freely admit to being forced to steal food to survive. Revealed Bonnar: 'Me and Brian used to work in a butcher's shop. We'd work most of the week just to pay off most of our debts.'

'However, they eventually scraped together some communal dosh, invested in an old coach and set about gigging the length and breadth of the land. And when Tony Wilson, then producer of Radio One's Friday Rock Show (and now head of Total Rock Radio) invited them to cut a session, word soon spread like wildfire.

'Heavy Pettin' took to fame and its perks like schoolboys in the proverbial sweetshop. 'I've been a rock star since the day I was born,' Hamie told Mark Putterford during a Sounds piece, in which it was reported the group found themselves able to pull women at every available opportunity. Musically speaking, the self-belief of Heavy Pettin' was to be vindicated, first in the shape of a publishing deal with Warner Brothers, then a contract with Polydor Records. Better still, none other than Brian May and his co-producer Mack were being lined up to produce their debut album. Significantly, it was the first time that Queen's legendary guitarist had stepped outside the band to produce another act.

'Warner Brothers sent a tape to Brian in Los Angeles because they thought he would be the perfect producer,' explained Punky, with Gordon adding: 'Brian's been wanting to produce somebody for a long time. He told us he was just waiting for the right band.'

'I got really excited about their demos,' May later explained to Sounds writer Mark Putterford. 'The band are very much full of life and vitality. They know when to play and they know when to get drunk, go out and do silly things, but they can come up with the goods at the right time.'

'Recorded at the Townhouse in London with overdubs and mixing taking place at Union Studios in Munich, Lettin' Loose was released in October 1983, three months after a prize spot at the Reading Festival with Black Sabbath (the Ian Gillan-fronted variety) Marillion, Stevie Ray Vaughan & Double Trouble, Suzi Quatro, Anvil, Magnum, Mama's Boys and opening act Lee Aaron.

'Preceded by a 12" single of 'In and Out of Love' b/w 'Love on the Run' and a Friday Rock Show version of 'Roll the Dice', it was warmly received by Kerrang!, although writer Neil Jeffries did voice some mild reservations. He wrote: 'There's a very big buzz about this band at the moment. Polydor UK are convinced that the young Glaswegians are going to be huge. Lettin' Loose isn't a classic debut but Heavy Pettin' have hit upon a formula that sounds really good. They can write songs, electrifying riffs, super-crisp harmonies, lively solos and dynamic arrangements, a change of pace here, an acoustic guitar there. Nothing startlingly original but it works, Godammit!'

'On the downside, if you consider it as a negative, Jeffries suggested that May and Mack had made the band sound too much like Def Leppard, though he concluded that Lettin' Loose was a marvellous mixture of power and melody and offered the bold prediction that 'Heavy Pettin'' could well become the new stars of the 1980s.

'Mark Putterford, of Sounds, went a stage further still, proclaiming: 'I'd say Lettin' Loose is better than anything Def Leppard have produced so far and, amid the critical acclaim for Pyromania, that's quite a compliment.'

'With support slots on Kiss and Ozzy Osbourne's upcoming tours about to be confirmed, only a madman would have bet against Heavy Pettin' taking over the world, but unfortunately they'd figured without a strategically placed banana skin – namely the US market. Like so many groups before and since, Heavy Pettin' had been signed with an eye on America. Unfortunately, just like Tobruk, Lionheart, Airrace and the rest of their melodic hard rock rivals, it took ages to get within touching distance of Uncle Sam, if any of the others (all of whom were signed to majors) got there at all.

'And while Pettin' did set foot on US soil, numerous problems materialised. The video for 'In And Out Of Love' had received medium rotation on MTV – being played around three times each day – but ground had been lost due to Polygram's insistence upon an album re-mix and changes in both title and sleeve artwork (it was actually called Heavy Pettin' Stateside). Polygram's pet act at the time was Bon Jovi and Pettin' became something of a head-sore for the company. Explains Mendoza now: 'We'd toured with Mötley Crüe and made some noise but nowhere near the boom they expected. In some ways America was an eye-opener for us, in others it began our rapid decline from nothingness to less than nothingless.'

'The group put on a brave public face but during an interview with Mike Vergane, an American writer for the UK publication Metal Forces, their frustration was hard to hide. 'What's the push like from Polydor?' mused Hamie through gritted teeth. 'At the moment it's just so-so, but the promise from them is that it will get better and better.'

'Bigger careers than that of Heavy Pettin' have been founded from smaller acorns, but a gap of two years was to separate Lettin' Loose and the group's second album Rock Ain't Dead. Before the group returned to the studio they staged a free concert at the Astoria in London, filmed for video and later released as the Mike Mansfield-directed 'Heart Attack Live'. In July of 1984 Hamie, Gordon, Brian and Punky took part in a Band-Aid style benefit single for those who died in a riot at the European

Cup final between Liverpool and Juventus.

'Brian May's name wasn't in the new album's credits. When later asked if he had enjoyed producing their debut, he replied slightly more candidly:'50/50 at best. They were a fine band but the experience of dealing with managers and record companies was quite harrowing.' In response, Hamie criticised the sound of Lettin' Loose, commenting: 'We never even considered it could turn out as bad as it did – there was no bass and even bass drum missing on some songs. Can you believe that?'

'The band originally wanted to work instead with Mike Stone but he was busy with Asia. Ratts producer Beau Hill, whom they'd met in the US while touring with the Rockin' Rodents was another choice that fell flat. Lance Quinn of Bon Jovi/Lita Ford fame then entered the picture but the night before Pettin' were due to fly out to Philadelphia the record company decided to bring forward the start date for Jon and company's second album, 7800 Degrees Fahrenheit.

'Then Mike Stone fell out with Asia and re-expressed his interest only to hug and make up with John Wetton and company. The job finally went to Mark Dearnley, who had worked with both AC/DC and Krokus (and had overseen the US mix of Lettin' Loose). Mixing duties were by Jim Steinman's associate producer John Jansen.

'On top of all this Hamie had been experiencing vocal problems with the external problems of a paternity suit a possible cause. He later explained: 'My voice would simply cut out. It's a mental thing, similar to what Joe Elliot of Def Leppard experienced while recording Pyromania. Before you start the take you just know you're not gonna do it.'

'After one visit to a Harley Street specialist Hamie was given the all clear. Pettin' were back in business.

'If you love pure rock 'n' roll and if you love to see a band progress then you cannot help fall in love with Heavy Pettin', purred Kerrang! upon the album's eventual release in the summer of 1985. Its standout track was the first single 'Sole Survivor', but Kerrang! also poured specific praise on the song 'Rock Ain't Dead' ('a wave your knob about anthem'), 'Throw A Party', 'Dreamtime' and 'China Boy' (the band's most sophisticated song to date').

'Despite all the hassles, Heavy Pettin' still seemed confident to the point of cockiness. 'There was so much hype when we got signed that people expected too much too soon,' theorised Hamie. 'We are gonna be huge.

I'm convinced of it. This album is gonna sell well but the third one will really bust it open.'

'Polydor's lack of support suggested differently. In an utterly bizarre move, Heavy Pettin' entered their song 'Romeo' to the Eurovision Song Contest in 1987, even appearing on mainstream TV shows, such as Wogan, to perform it. When 'Romeo' lost out to Rikki's 'Only the Light' (which fared dismally in the final televised contest) the company axed plans for an already recorded third album.

'It was a hammer blow, especially given the third record's quality. The Big Bang surfaced through independent company FM Revolver in November 1989, with tracks like 'Born to Burn', 'This is America' and 'Don't Call It Love' surprising those who considered the band to be washed up.

'By that time Heavy Pettin' had already played a farewell gig in the Bruce Hotel in East Kilbride in 1988. I asked Punky a few months ago about Pettin's demise and quoted the above comment from Dave Ling about 'weans in the proverbial sweetie shop'. He laughed and said: 'More like raging bulls in the proverbial china shop!'

Looking Down The Barrel Of A Gun

As Heavy Pettin' made their merry way round the world, they proved to be an inspiration to the emerging new breed of rock band, one of whom was Cannes. I have to be honest and admit that Cannes were one of the few Glasgow bands I was never lucky enough to see, but I did get to know their guitarist, Ian Murray, when he played in Halloween and Five Past Midnight.

Cannes were an important branch in the whole family tree of Glasgow's rock scene, a limb leading to Blind Allez to Phobia to Gun and so their place in this tome is well deserved. I'll leave it to the late but great music journalist, Mark Putterford to tell their story when he wrote:

'Good rock bands don't tickle you under the chin. They punch you on the nose and I've been concussed since my first eye to eye contact with the jumpin', jivin', jock 'n' roll juveniles from Cannes.

As an amalgamation of fresh and fruity ideas forged from teenage frustration and itching ambition, Cannes sprang from the garage and bedroom bands in late '82, when flash-fingered guitarist Ian Murray and boisterous bassist Andi Burns fused with bright and brash singer/front-man Colin Peel.

'Nurturing the notions that cast a tunnel-visioned eye to the top, the trio acquired the tub-tapping talents of drummer Gordon Roberts in February '83 and quickly developed a thirst that could only be quenched by success.

'They burnt the boards on the Glasgow pub/club circuit, rearing a loyal and passionate support and their first demo, recorded in September '83, collared the attention of many more after receiving much Scottish airplay. Delving deeper into the dog-fight of hard rock hopefuls, the tartan terrors moved to the Big City in the summer of '84 and, under the managerial guidance of Bill Cayley, they have played numerous gigs around the London area, including the Marquee and Dingwalls, to much critical acclaim.

'Indeed, their live show is an entertaining and enterprising showcase of the band's tremendous wealth and depth of talent and potential. Cannes come with a potent pasticcio of various rock flavours, spiced with a youthful exuberance which excites and, armed with their useful arsenal of material plus the backing of Tony Platt [Gary Moore, Billy Squire and AC/DC] as their ultimate producer, they zipped into the recording studios again in October '84 to construct a thrilling three-track demo featuring 'Start It Now', 'Fightin'' and 'Castles in the Air'.

'Sharp and stylish, the demo signifies a further step in musical maturity for this young band (their average age is 21) and surely couldn't fail to have any A&R man with an ounce of suss knocking at their door.'

Despite this unswervingly confident prediction, Cannes did not, in fact, make it big and, when they called it a day, Ian Murray became involved with one of Glasgow's most influential bands, Blind Allez.

Blind Alley, as they were originally known, were formed in the early 1980s by a guitarist called Giuliano Joolz Gizzi. He hooked up with vocalist Peter Scallan and recruited bassist Cami Morlotti and the trio began writing and rehearsing acoustically in a bedroom flat just off Abercromby Street, Calton, Glasgow.

When they decided it was time to get serious, they started auditioning for new members. Friend and neighbour Chris Bowes was hired for guitar duties and all that was left to do was to find a drummer. After answering an advert in a local newspaper, Alan Thornton was auditioned for the job.

The lads rehearsed and gigged with this line-up for a short while before Chris left due to family commitments. The hunt was on for a replacement. Finally, the lads plumped for Ian Murray. With their line-up complete, they changed their name to Blind Allez, an Eighties thang and attempt to be that wee bit cooler.

After rehearsing in a dingy, damp studio under a railway arch in the west end of Glasgow, Allez embarked on a mission to play anywhere they could feasibly get a gig: the Venue in Glasgow, the Preservation Hall in Edinburgh, the Heathery Bar in Wishaw, the Pondarosa in Linwood, the Doon Castle in Glasgow, Fat Sam's in Dundee and, ultimately, in May 1985, a spot at the Radio Clyde Kelvingrove Rock Festival alongside Lyin Rampant, Abel Ganz, Zero Zero and Glasgow, where they stole the show.

Ironically, this successful gig was the last time Blind Allez would play together for another 21 years, with Ian leaving to form rock outfit Five Past Midnight and Peter joining another local band Chasar, before going on to work on a couple of projects with unshorn rockers Samson.

This was, however, not the end of the band. They chose to carry on, recruiting Mark Rankin and David Aitken and, after changing their name to Phobia, continued to write material and play live until 1986, when they secured a management contract.

The next year the lads won a recording contract with A&M Records, changed their name one more time to Gun and it was a line-up of Giuliano Gizzi (guitar), Cami Morlotti (bass), Mark Rankin (vocals), David Aitken (guitar) and Alan Thornton (drums) that I put on in the Bruce Hotel in 1987.

The band changed the line-up after Alan, Cami and David parted company and new recruits Dante Gizzi (Joolz's brother), Scott Shields and Baby Stafford joined. They released their debut album Taking on the World with Mark's cousin, Sharleen Spiteri, of fellow Scottish band, pop troubadours Texas and their own ex-drummer Alan contributing backing vocals to several songs. A single, 'Better Days', made the Top 40 in the UK and the lads toured the US and supported the Rolling Stones on their European Urban Jungle Tour of 1990.

At this point Alex Dickson replaced Baby Stafford, having gone along to the audition believing he was up for a role in a completely different band.

Alex explains: 'For the second time in as many years I was approached to audition for a band, only it was Slide this time. But when I arrived at Park Lane studios it was actually Gun.'

The second album was Gallus, from which the single 'Steal Your Fire' was a minor hit and Spiteri and Thornton again contributed backing vocals. For my money, this was the best line-up for Gun. Alex gave them a much rockier edge and the shows I saw, playing on the same bill as Def Leppard, displayed Gun at their peak. They rocked the house and, sadly, in my eyes, would never recapture that explosive edge again.

Both Alex and Scott left before the release of the album Swagger, with Joolz taking over all guitar duties and Mark Kerr, the brother of Simple Minds singer Jim Kerr, replacing Scott. Swagger was easily the lads' most successful album, propelled by the success of their out-and-out rock rendition of 'Word Up!', which was a Top 10 UK hit, charted well in many other territories and finally won an MTV award for best cover version.

The band took a break, only to return three years later with another new drummer, Stuart Kerr, formerly of Texas, keyboard player Irvin Duguid and yet another new monicker, G.U.N. The somewhat baffling reason for the full stops given at the time was to distance the name from the atrocious Dunblane shooting massacre and show sensitivity to those involved.

A new album, 0141 632 6326, produced by INXS keyboard player Andrew Farriss, was characterised by a much lighter, poppier sound than the more rock-driven sound of their earlier works. However, the album managed to simultaneously alienate existing fans of the band and fail to gain a new audience and sold poorly in comparison to Swagger.

The live showcase I saw in the Glasgow pub that used to be called Saints & Sinners was probably the worst I'd ever seen the band play – it was as if they were searching for a rock identity, all the while trying to be thoroughly modern and it simply didn't work.

The band finally split up in 1997. In 2005, Dante Gizzi resurfaced in the glam rock band El Presidente, with Alan Thornton collaborating on a debut album, playing nine of the drum tracks.

Scott Shields, meanwhile, was contributing music to the film soundtracks for Black Hawk Down and Bend It Like Beckham, as well as playing and touring with Joe Strummer and the Mescaleros until Strummer's death. Scott and other members of the band put the finishing touches to Strummer's last album.

Alex Dickson has played with Bruce Dickinson, Emma Bunton and the late James Brown since leaving Gun and is also a member of rock group Sack Trick.

Mark Rankin is currently working for Universal Records in London promoting up-and-coming bands.

Mark Kerr is currently living and working in Paris. He has been collaborating with many acts including Sly Silver Sly, Regency Buck, Scanners, Jackos One, Mellow, Bob's Symphonic Orchestra, Cathy Burton and DJ Daniele Tignino. He has also played drums on occasion for Simple Minds and for Les Rita Mitsouko.

Aside from a few one-off reunion gigs in 1998 and 1999, Gun (or G.U.N., if you prefer) themselves had not been active as a unit before a re-formation with Little Angel Toby Jepson as guest vocalist – the reason was a Rock Radio gig in aid of the Nordoff-Robbins Music Therapy charity in January 2008. Two new Gun CDs were also released (The Collection and The River Sessions, a double live CD) during their hiatus and all the previous individual members went on to other projects within the music industry.

The band announced on Rock Radio in April 2008 that would re-form and confirmed that Jepson would join the band on a permanent basis. In fact, Toby and I go back to 1988 when I gave Little Angels their first Scottish gig in the Bruce. In true Spinal Tap tradition, Alan Thornton was replaced on drums by ex-Graduation Day drummer Gordon McNeil.

Personally, I doubt whether the revised line-up can actually work very well, certainly not in the same powerful way as the original, but at least the diehard Gun fans should be happy.

The Man From Nazareth

Billy Rankin is a true Glasgow rock legend. He has everything going for him: he's a brilliant guitarist, he writes killer songs, he's worked with the best, toured the world and he is one handsome-looking chap. I know all of this because Billy told me.

He also has his own radio programme on 96.3 Rock Radio, so by now it's fair to say that he's used to talking the talk!

I had the pleasure of working with the man when we put on Nazareth in the Cathouse rock club in the early Nineties and it was always a pleasure to see him when he did his wee guitar spot in the Solid Rock Café.

He wasn't always a one-man music machine, however. His first band, Phase, were formed by Billy and a bunch of school pals – Allan Hendry (drums), Mick McAuley (bass) and John Burnett (guitar) – in 1972. Their first gig was at a high school dance, but by1975 they had been signed by Eddie Tobin to MAC, a top Glasgow agency. Eddie also worked with Nazareth, SAHB and as Billy Connolly's road manager.

The following year Phase signed to Black Gold records and accepted a Saturday night residency at the Burns Howff. Just five years after their school dance debut, they were supporting the likes of Marmalade, Slik, Dead End Kids and – high of career highs – played the Dougie Donnelly Roadshow!

Kenny Cobain replaced John Burnett on guitar but, in January 1978, Phase split amid rumours that our man Billy would be joining Thin Lizzy. Instead, Eddie Tobin took him to London to join the Zal (Cleminson) Band. They enjoyed brief tours of Sweden and the UK before Zal decided to jump ship from his own band to go to an outfit called Nazareth. The last gig, at the Marquee in London, featured Billy's first writing contribution, 'Jump Out the Window' but surely that wasn't what inspired Zal's exit?

Whatever the reason, Billy soon found himself put on a retainer with Mountain Records and spent three months rehearsing with Chris Glen and Ted McKenna of SAHB. The next shock came when all three were, as they say in the parlance of business, let go.

Billy then successfully auditioned for Euro rock pincers the Scorpions; language barriers made the band think again but, taking the sting out the tale, Billy formed The Mirrors with drummer Paul Simon, securing a deal with EMI.

The first single was to have been Preservation (it would later appear on Nazareth's 2XS album) but Billy opted, instead, for a solo offer from CBS, as the EMI deal was only for two singles. 'Love Leads to Madness' was also premiered at a showcase gig for EMI.

In 1979 Billy signed to April Music (now CBS Songs) and Delta/CBS Records, forming a writing partnership with Peter Shelley (of Alvin

Stardust fame, ladies and gentlemen) and, with the help of Chris Glen and Tommy Eyre of SAHB and Pete Phips of the Glitter Band, he recorded two singles: 'I Wanna Spend My Life With You' and 'Can't Stop Now' – both of which were backed by 'Jump Out the Window'.

Using April Music's in-house writing rooms, more than 40 songs were written in the space of just four months, including 'Dream On'.

A year later a CBS and Delta falling-out saw Billy dropped, but Delta's Colin Robertson agreed to keep him on a retainer of £60 a week if he returned to Scotland. In November, Eddie asked him to call Pete Agnew, as Zal had quit Nazareth. It would be the shortest ever audition that saw Billy accepted into the Nazareth fold.

Pete: 'What type of guitar do you play?'

Billy: 'A Gibson 335.'

Pete: 'You're in, son.'

In December the STV In Concert at the Gateway in Edinburgh and a solo Buddy Holly tribute on the Hear Hear show meant Nazareth enjoyed exposure through two TV appearances on consecutive nights. US tours followed from January to May, promoting the Fool Circle LP. Gigs were recorded with the Record Plant mobile, resulting in the 'SNaz album and Billy's first Nazareth studio recordings – 'Crazy' for The Heavy Metal Soundtrack then 'Morning Dew/Morgentau/Juicy Lucy' for the 'SNaz bonus single.

In 1982 2XS was recorded at the AIR Studios, Montserrat, after which the band toured in Europe. At this point, impressed by Billy's writing skills, A&M records financed solo demos at Ca Va studios in Glasgow. Four tracks were delivered and a solo deal offered. It was then, too, that John Locke left Nazareth, just before a series of Euro dates with Rush.

The lads chose the AIR - owned by legendary Beatles producer George Martin - to create Fool Circle and 2XS. They arrived shortly after the departure of Glaswegian chanteuse Sheena Easton and her band and it wasn't long before one member of the resort's staff felt forced to declare: 'You guys spilled more drink than Sheena's entire entourage drank during their stay.'

In fact, history has it that the final bill for the band's alcohol intake was so outrageously gargantuan it was queried by their manager – George Martin duly wrote to each Nazarene personally asking them to own up!

In January 1983 Nazareth recorded demos in Pencaitland, while the next two months saw them record the Sound Elixir album at Little Mountain studios in Vancouver. While it may not be regarded by the diehards as one of the best Naz albums ever created, its birth was certainly eventful enough.

During the recording, Billy struck up a friendship with Canadian rocker Bryan Adams, who had also signed a solo deal with A&M and would be responsible for getting Billy shit-faced as his daughter, Anna, was being born back in Scotland. Darrell broke the news to Billy next morning by replacing the milk with Scotch in the cornflakes at breakfast. Neither of them made it to the studio until late that evening, when a crate of champagne arrived, courtesy of A&M.

Billy also became firm friends with Brian 'too loud' McCloud from Headpins, who unwittingly gave Billy's second solo album its title. After a jam on stage, Brian said he'd finally met his match in the volume stakes, adding to the half-deafened crowd: 'Too loud McCloud? This is Crankin' Rankin!'

Noise was, of course, an integral part of the songwriting process. All Nite Radio's intro is actually the pinball machine at the Little Mountain studios – Billy and Pete recorded the ping, clang, beep racket then went back to their rented condo and wrote an entire song around it.

When not creating music, the lads would be creating merry hell. Billy and guitar tech Davie Horner had to flee a downtown bar after buying onyx totem poles from an Eskimo who proceeded to fondle Billy's leg under the table. The following week the local paper listed the bar as Vancouver's number one gay venue. Suddenly, it all made sense!

This wee gem, however, is topped by the day that the Vancouver Police Pipe Band, arrived next door to Nazareth's studio to record their new album. Armed only with four crates of Johnny Walker Red Label, they took Nazareth to their 'club' and, for once, trounced the entire Naz entourage in a contest of macho drinking prowess. Billy and Pete got so wasted they left and attempted, in a one-step-forward, two-steps-back trance, the short walk home.

Suddenly, sirens surrounded the lost boys and an officer hollered through a megaphone: 'Nice try, boys, but we're takin' you in, cos we ain't done with you yet!'

The bewildered rockers were taken straight back to the party and placed under arrest until sufficient drinking had taken place. All of the above perhaps goes some way towards explaining the patchiness of the finished album!

There were no such shenanigans for the next recording, however, which took place at Jacobs Studios in Farnham, a thoroughly British location, don't you know, old bean, which had been suggested by none other than Alan McGee of A&M UK – which was rather ironic when you think that they eventually withdrew release of Growin' Up Too Fast in the UK because it was 'too American'.

Rather than rock 'n' roll mayhem, the album was a respectable affair that involved Billy's growing family – Billy Junior appears on the back sleeve of the album and baby Anna on the promo postcards for 'Baby Come Back'.

The project's producer was one John Ryan, chosen by Billy after a series of auditions that had been held at Le Park in Hollywood earlier in the year, during which Billy grilled a dozen potential head honchos, including Mack (of Queen and Rolling Stones repute), Ken Scott (Bowie and Supertramp) and other noted millionaire music moguls, some of whom, when asked why they wanted the Naz job, looked at Billy disbelievingly and blustered: 'For the money, asshole!'

In the end, Mack was just deemed to be too 'out there' and first choice Ken phoned Billy the next day to say he was unable to fit the job in (actually, this problem recurred on Crankin' remixes, which were undertaken eventually by Steve Nye).

John Ryan was the only candidate who didn't want to change the band's demos, 'just record 'em better' and his work with Santana and the Doobie Brothers had more than impressed Billy.

One noteworthy incident, involving neither totem poles nor bagpipe-playing cops, involves the arrival of Zal Cleminson in the studio. John couldn't understand why Billy wanted another guitarist for a few solos when, after all, he could have done them himself.

'You'll see,' replied Billy.

Zal unpacked his gear and listened to the backing track for 'Rip It Up' as Billy pointed out the chords. He then sat on a stool looking for all the world like a bored librarian. John, meanwhile, reclined on the couch, fat cigar in mouth and, more than bemused, suggested a dry run. Billy told the engineer Ken to record this one and John shook his head in disgust, his face still saying: 'What's he doing here?'

When the solo slot arrived, without warning, Zal leapt from his stool and adopted the spread-legged stance of a rock god, his whole body shaking, his face contorted and he yelled and he growled and he threw his guitar up and down.

John Ryan bit his cigar in half, choked and cried out: 'Holy shit!'

His solo stint finished, Zal sat back down on the stool and scratched his nose. It had taken just 15 seconds. One take. Job done. Alistair Zal Cleminson is a true one-off, no contest!

Well, 'Baby Come Back' was a US Top 40 hit and Billy got to be an MTV celebrity for a month. TV shows followed and the first solo tour was booked. Asked on Thick of the Night show to reveal his most and least favourite places to play, Billy revealed Detroit as the most. Least should've been Singapore or something equally non-US but he stupidly said Buffalo, NY. Three weeks later he headlined an outdoor festival in Buffalo, NY. The promoter praised his guts for getting through one song, then helped him get out of the building alive.

Other memorable gigs included (surprise, surprise!) Detroit's phenomenal three-night sell-outs at Harpo's, the LA Palladium with the inimitable Stevie Ray Vaughan and upstaging Molly Hatchet and Pat Travers by going on stage during a hurricane, thanks to a radio mic, non-conductive footwear and a fortitude made from girders.

Then there were the two nights as a support to 38 Special, after which the headliners were honest enough to inform Rolling Stone magazine that 'Rankin's too awesome!' as their excuse for removing him from their Michigan dates.

Billy recalls: 'I think they were being genuine enough. Closing my half-hour set by leading 18,000 voices through a rendition of "Baby Come Back" was maybe too much of a "Follow that, ya bastards!" for Donnie & Co to deem acceptable!'

A&M were so pleased with the success of Growin' Up Too Fast, they requested a second solo album to capitalise on Billy's new-found popularity. In a wholehearted tribute to his roots, he turned down four top US studios in favour of using Glasgow's own Ca Va studios, a decision he still stands by. He is also rightly proud to be noted as Ca Va's first major label project and even prouder that they've gone on to become a 'Hit Factory' for so many top acts worldwide.

All would not be so well with A&M, however. After the LA Palladium gig, a big party was thrown in Billy's honour at Le Dome. Everything was going swimmingly until our man was tipped off about a minor disturbance in the car park. Outside he found his manager, had A&M executive Charlie Minor pinned over the bonnet of his Rolls Royce. It took six people to drag him off.

As the crowd finally shuffled back inside, Charlie was heard to yell: 'Rankin, you're finished on this label.' And he was.

Things dragged on for a year or so. There were remixes, re-covers and re-titles before, ultimately if all too inevitably, Billy's calls began to be ignored. His final call was with Jordan Harris (A&R, mentor, now at Virgin) who couldn't have been more brutally honest and to the point: he wasn't to speak to Billy anymore, on company orders.

The rest of the Eighties were spent signed up to a succession of production deals. John Ryan, Doug Banker (Ted Nugent's manager) and even Uncle Pete Agnew all tried and failed to get Billy out of whatever mess he had created, whether simply by association or happenstance. At one stage, Doug even made it into Jordan's Virgin office before he dropped Billy's name and was forcibly removed by security guards.

Then came a phone call straight out of the blue from Pete: 'Manny's oot. We want you back!'

After a phone call to Manny, who confirmed he was indeed 'oot', before adding 'Best of luck, Bill, you'll f*ckin' need it!', Billy rejoined the band as sole guitarist for the first time. They toured the States with Ten Years After and Blackfoot, then Europe with Kansas, Saga, Uriah Heep, Wishbone Ash and all the old guard.

Suddenly, the word 'revival' was being bandied about and it seemed that if anyone could engineer a Lazarus-type raising of the dead for the band it was the man from Nazareth.

Before rejoining Naz, Billy had written 'Cover Your Heart', 'Every Time It Rains' and 'Right Between the Eyes' while playing with La Paz, demos that were featured on Radio Clyde's Rock Show. A fourth track, 'Johnny Don't Dance', was also intended for a new album, No Jive, but Dan felt it didn't do full justice to the band, despite his liking for the song. Demo

The Poets Poster

Jimmy Miller & Willie Henderson (Rangers FC) with me, The Olympia, 1963

Studio Six

Family holiday, Butlins, 1965

Dave Wilson (Rangers FC) & Me! The Olympia, 1963

NSU, Turn on or turn me down

The Stoics & Frankie Miller

Apple Records WHITE TRASH 3 Savile Row, London W1

White Trash

The Beatstalkers

Beggars Opera

the only
AUTHENTIC
BEATLE WIG

WOW! the BEATLES ARE HERE!

Authentic
Beatle Wig

Captain Marryat

Findo Gask

Jude

The Flying Squad

JSD Band

Tear Gas

Zal Cleminson *Guitar*   Ted McKenna *Drums*   Chris Glen *Bass*   David Batchelor *Vocals*

Tear Gas

Jimmy Barnes

THE SENSATIONAL ALEX HARVEY BAND CHRISTMAS SHOW

The Sensational Alex Harvey Band

CHRISTMAS SHOW 1975

Official Programme

The Sensational
Alex Harvey Band,
Christmas Show poster

Me

APOLLO CENTRE

P.A.S.S

date 18th November 1973

First Apollo Pass, 1973

North Wind

Uriah Heep's Mick Box & Big Lee Kerslake with my son Wee Lee (Apollo '73)

Uriah Heep's Gary Thain and Wee Lee (Apollo '74)

Uriah Heep's Dave Byron and Wee Lee (Apollo '75)

Big Lee with my daughter Cheryl and son Lee (Apollo '85)

Heavy Pettin'

String Driven Thing

Henry Gorman Band

Alex Dickson

The Apollo, Glasgow, 1985

Abelganz

Blind Allez

Billy Rankin

Glasgow

Baby's got a Gun

Big George, Greg & Shifty

Dolphins

First Priority

Trident

Midnight Blue

Ransom

Ozzy Osbourne, Big Lee, Wee
Lee & Cheryl, The Apollo, 1980

Underhand Jones

Drunken State

The Crows

Monkey See

Crisis

Pink Kross

Marcha Fresca

Gun

Robbie Williams Birthday
party, Strawberry Fields, 1999

Rock God! Cathouse, 1993

Buddah Grass Harbour

Tom Russell, Rock Radio

Calvin Macro, Christian Watson and
Me (AC/DC) 2009

The Hedrons & Johnny Rotten

time in a Coatbridge studio was taken and rough versions of 'Every Time It Rains' and 'Right Between the Eyes' recorded. However, the versions done on Billy's own humble four-track at home were deemed far superior and the project moved to Dunfermline. At this point 'Cry Wolf' was also demo-ed.

No Jive was written and arranged at Shorties Rehearsal Studios, Elgin Street, in Dunfermline just prior to the band's departure to St Ingbert-Schuren, Germany, to create the album proper. The four-track was used after agreeing keys, harmonies and structure and so a regular tape recorder was also set up which recorded the entire time spent thrashing out each song.

Pete's 'Tell Me That You Love Me' evolution is particularly interesting. The idea was to have everything demo-ed to save time in Germany, including transferring drum machine patterns to samplers. The band members met at nearby Jinty's Bar and Billy would eventually depart to Shorties, either to lay down drums and guitars for Dan and Pete to play to or with either of them, if required.

A shortlist of songs – 'definite, possible, naff'– was compiled, which featured future Boogaloo tracks 'Open Up Woman', 'Lights Go Down', 'The Robber & The Roadie', 'The South' and 'Kremlin Party'. With the exception of 'Cover Your Heart', the track listing was set and approved by all, with the addendum that 'Open Up Woman' would only be included if they could knock it into shape in St Ingbert.

Ian Remmer's credit as engineer on No Jive was possibly unexpected by the man himself. 'Most lucky to be alive' was his true and agreed position within the first week's recording. From then on he would set up the required mics and patches for the day's schedule (vocals/overdubs etc.) and leave. In return, the band spared his life.

Billy controlled the desk and Pete took on the role of co-producer for Dan, Billy or Darrell's dubs. Billy and Pete took two days solid, alone and the bass guitar tracks were completed.

After a hard day (pints of champagne and orange juice all round!) everyone wanted a playback. Normally, the engineer would have to realign the desk, change reels and generally cater for the wants of the client, but fear of Nazareth and fear of wiping the tape prevented both sides from risking it. Instead a DAT machine was linked up from where rough mixes could be blasted safely through the monitors. A second pair of 100-watt speakers and DATs were installed upstairs in the TV room – just in case anyone couldn't make it off the couch!

The response to No Jive proved a major boost to the band. In particular, it took care of the 'Where's Manny?' nay-saying section among the band's fan base and promoters and Billy no longer felt as though he were playing in his predecessor's shadow. Indeed, in a much appreciated seal of approval, Manny himself was complimentary.

For the first time in years, Nazareth were getting airplay and MTV coverage as a band with something new to offer. Billy threw himself into the next batch of writing and Move Me was ready to record a few months later. All they needed now was a deal.

David Krebs (of Aerosmith's Lieber & Krebs) flew to Scotland and, following much backslapping, gave the go-ahead to record Move Me. He never asked to hear any of the songs, stating simply: 'Billy wrote 'em? That's good enough for me!'

Once in Germany, Krebs backed down, however and the band found themselves stuck in a studio they couldn't pay for, recording an album that had no deal. In stepped old friends from Polygram GMB, Karin and Astrid, who'd been impressed with the reaction to No Jive in Germany. A deal was done and the album saved, to be released on a real label again.

The year 1994 also saw Billy, Pete and Dan undertake two short, unplugged UK tours where songs such as 'Simple Solution' and 'Shapes of Things' were given the acoustic treatment. These shows are particularly memorable for their intimate nature and humour content.

At this time, Billy was also a member of two 'fun' bands, as he termed them, playing many weekend gigs in pubs and clubs around Glasgow. The Broons, featuring Pete Agnew on bass and his wee bairn, Lee (now part of the new Nazareth line-up), on drums and The Party Boys with Zal, Ted McKenna and bassist Nick Clark.

The initial response to Move Me was positive and a major European tour, which was backed by Polygram, was scheduled for February and March of 1995, a move that sent the band into their rehearsals in optimistic mood.

Then it all hit the fan.

Billy recalls: 'I have no intention of bad-mouthing any of my former bandmates or stirring things up. My expulsion from Nazareth (I was fired) occurred due to circumstances identical to Manny's dismissal in 1990 and, like Manny, I wish them all the best.

'We last got together for Darrell's funeral and shared many happy memories together, I'm never likely to forget. Hopefully we'll do it again some time in less tragic circumstances.'

After his unexpected expulsion, Billy began writing and demo-ing songs for his old pal Karin at Polydor, who was keen on a third solo album. However, despite her own confidence in the material, the genre simply was not being heard, played or signed anymore.

Billy remembers: 'Eventually I decided to give it one year of concentrated effort, using every contact I could and exploring alternative possibilities: gigs with The Spiders From Mars, which led to a single, a deal for All the Madmen being offered and knocked back and even an audition for The Wildhearts, which I was particularly crushed to lose out on (I was told I was too old).

'Eventually, I took an HGV driving test and got a "real" job!'

Finally, by dint of the new technology, which means we can all make recordings in the back room without the need for record company involvement or financial support, Billy came up with another fantastic solo offering, Shake.

At the time, Billy commented to the press: 'It's great to finally see all the hard work come to such a perfect album. I'm well chuffed!'

And quite right, too. He deserves every success.

I'd like to end our wee tale of the man from Nazareth here, but the story continues apace. Billy's musical journey carried on with another few gigs with Nazareth on vocals, in the shape of a Spiders From Mars tribute band, with Joey Elliot of Def Leppard and now, most recently, with a brand new career on 96.3 Rock Radio.

It's been a chequered musical life for Billy Rankin, if I may say so and it's certainly not over yet. How do I know this? Because Billy told me so, of course!

Robert The Bruce

By 1986 Uriah Heep had replaced Pete Goalby with Steff Fontain and Phil Lanzon was on keyboards. Fontain himself was soon replaced by Bernie

Shaw, who had been with Lanzon in Trapeze, as had Goalby. In 1988 the lads recorded Live in Moscow and became the first Western rock band to play there, a pioneering move swiftly followed up with Raging Silence in 1989. This bunch would prove to be the longest surviving Heep line-up, lasting till 2008.

The year 1986 was also seminal for Yours Truly, for it was the year I first became much more personally involved in the music industry.

My son Lee was by this time in the Scouts and looking forward to going on a trip to Kandersteg in Switzerland. The Ging Gang Goolie committee called for all us parents to attend a night where they asked us to get involved in helping to raise the £2,000 needed to cover the trip. As I've always been a huge Beatles fan, a love affair that withstood my traumatic wig-melting moment, I came up with the notion of trying to put together a Beatles and Sixties music night.

The masterplan was not only to raise the necessary £2,000 for the trip in four big nights but also a further £35,000 for charity through events over the next three years.

I was still working for Craig Nicol so I knew I could shift a few tickets in there – as it happened I sold more than 200 – and I left the other parents to get rid of the remaining 200 between them.

The ticket price was £3 and I'm proud to say that this princely sum also bought the bearer a raffle ticket, a snack at the interval and their bus rides there and back. In the end, the numbers were so great that three buses had to be laid on.

I was in seventh heaven. Everyone had such a whale of a time: yes, even the Celtic workmate of mine who found he'd won a signed Rangers football, presented by a young whippersnapper by the name of Ally McCoist. Don't worry, he wasn't too bothered, as he swapped balls, as it were, with a Rangers supporter who'd been handed a rotund raffle prize by Danny McGrain.

In the wake of my first night as a promoter of Sixties music, sausage roll canapés and signed Old Firm footballs, I was called into a life-changing meeting by the Bruce Hotel's dynamic duo management team of Lenny Wilson and Graham Boyle.

It was suggested by Lenny and Graham that I might have a very small yet burgeoning talent for organising events. Would I consider doing a live band night at their East Kilbride hotel?

Well, fast as the proverbial rat up the drainpipe that's followed us through this book and haunted my entire career, I said I'd come back to them quick pronto with a business plan. Just two weeks later we had agreed on the Wednesday Night Rock Club, which would for the next ten years be the major player in the history of live music in East Kilbride and Glasgow-wide, showcasing not only the freshest local talent, but attracting top touring bands from all over the world.

I guess we were picking up the gauntlet that had been laid down continually by the Olympia in the Sixties until its demise in the early Eighties, when it finally went the way of the Howff and eventually the Apollo.

To get the ball rolling, I got on the phone to my old mucker Tom Russell, who at the time was in Radio Clyde and, fine man that he is, he gave me contact numbers for all the bands he rated. I also got in touch with young Gordon Bury at the East Kilbride News to place an advert asking all local bands to send their demos into the paper, from where they'd be passed on to me.

The response was magnificent and so a series of nights was put together: Wednesday, 18 February, would feature Zero Zero, Wednesday the 25th a band called Trident, Wednesday, 4 March was the turn of Ransom (all the way from Edinburgh, boys and girls) and La Paz, who were slotted in for the 11th.

I invited the featured bands to a sell-out opening night, where I announced to all the local band members that they'd get a regular gig but only if they supported the place. I'm happy to say that down through the years they and their contemporaries from all over Scotland did indeed support our rock night.

My DJ for the opener was my Sixties music night man and mate, Gillie Martin -- truth be told, the real reason for this was I had an amazing rock collection and didn't want it all scratched, so I made up tapes which Gillie played.

It became obvious, however, that a bona fide vinyl-spinning DJ was needed, so I took on first Brian Peebles, then Peter Mclean and finally Tom Russell himself.

The only momentary pause when I thought it might not be working quite as anticipated came just after the first two years, as there seemed to be a dwindling in numbers.

I remember one very important night in the nearby Key Youth Club when I had a copy of local band Drunken State's soon-to-be-released debut album Kilt By Death. We were doing an advance playback for all the local kids when I was approached by a very young and confident Cammy Young, of local band Dirty Dollar. They were a fine rockabilly-influenced outfit but Cammy complained to me that indie rock bands in general couldn't get a gig in the rock club as it was a purely rock-only venue.

Not without some reservations, I agreed to put his band on and, in doing so, changed the musical goalposts to include a much more varied selection of music and bands. And from that moment on, our humble wee club in the heart of a Glasgow spill-over town took off quite spectacularly.

Bruce The Almighty

Anyway, back to that amazing opening bill at the Bruce Hotel, a first foray into the biz for me and one small step that would eventually change my life forever. The band that night were Zero Zero, formed in 1983 and their line-up was Stevie Doherty on guitar and lead vocals, who was formerly of Underhand Jones and China White Andy McAfferty (bass), Joe James (drums, formerly of Red Ellis), Duncan Macrae (lead guitar, formerly of Sidewinder) and Dave Ramsey (keyboards, also ex-Sidewinder).

The Zeros quickly established themselves as one of the most popular bands on the Scottish rock music scene. Due to the same old musical differences, Duncan and Dave left, while a chap by the name of John McMillan stepped in on lead guitar.

In 1985 they won a competition run by the Glasgow Evening Times newspaper to find a new band whom the judges felt could go on to bigger and better things. From hundreds of songs submitted, 'Runaway' was chosen and Zero Zero won a day of recording in Glasgow's Ca Va studios.

Somewhat strangely for a Glasgow band, things really took off when the band started playing gigs in Edinburgh. One of the first nights saw them team up with PA company EFX and a reunion with an old friend, Digger Cockburn, who would go on to mastermind their live sound.

Now EFX was run by Johnny Ramsey, who also happened to be the sound engineer for Simple Minds and Johnny himself would sometimes be found behind the desk for the Zeros. Within a short time the band was playing to capacity crowds in venues such as the Jailhouse and the Preservation Hall in Edinburgh and Shadows in Glasgow. In fact, at the height of the Edinburgh Festival, the Zeros took over the Jailhouse completely, playing every night for a week with a different local support band each time.

From Zeros, to heroes, the band went from strength to strength, gaining a following within the record companies and championed by none other than Kerrang!'s Derek Oliver. Sold-out showcase gigs at Shadows, attended by coach loads of fans from Edinburgh, led to a number of companies being interested in signing the band and a couple of gigs at the renowned Marquee Club in London.

Forever, it seemed, on the verge of something big, Zero Zero, like their contemporaries La Paz, never quite took the step onto the next rung of the ladder – despite the fact that they had everything going for them: the image, the playing and, most importantly, the songs, any one of which would and could have graced a Journey, Bon Jovi or Bryan Adams album with ease.

At the time of the Zeros I was just making my way in the business at the Bruce, of course and had very few contacts of my own, so the situation was very much out of my hands. When, inevitably, the band split, John formed The Whole Earth, Stevie joined Midnight Blue, Joe disappeared from the music scene altogether and Andy formed The Almighty, one of the greatest Glasgow bands.

Before I forget to mention, I would persuade the lads to re-form in the Nineties, this time with the greatest drummer on earth, Paul McManus, beating the skins: thus were Monkey See Monkey Do was born, but more of them in the next chapter.

From Zero Zero and straight to my next band at the Bruce opener, this time Trident (this is how quickly those early nights seems to fly in, too). These lads got together in Kirkintilloch and, like Anaconda, Centurion and their ilk of the day, you knew exactly what you were going to get at a Trident gig: a no-frills, 100% rock 'n' roll frenzy.

One of my favourite memories from that first gig was when vocalist Martin McGuire burst out through the fire doors, all the while serenading, via his radio mic, the punters still queuing to get in. Brilliant theatre. Until he tried to get back in himself and was refused entry by the bouncers.

With the band? Nice try. No, really, I'm the singer. Not tonight, son, not unless you put your hand in your pocket.

All the while, thanks to his mic, we could hear him squealing and the entire crowd were ending themselves in laughter.

Poor Martin finalised a line-up that had been formed back in 1983 by drummer Graham Hendry and guitar player Campbell Burns, with Tommy Wilson added on bass.

The band were soon well known for their energetic and fast-paced performances that took them all over Scotland as one of the hardest working bands of their day: Shadows, the Venue, the Doune, Radio Clyde's Kelvingrove Festival, were just a few of the classic venues that Trident would spear then shake to their foundations with a full-on, let's-be-havin'-a-party sound influenced by AC/DC, Quo and Waysted.

While Glasgow at the time was in the frenzy of glam and sleaze rock, with a de rigueur uniform of lipstick, Spandex and candy-flossed hair, Trident were having none of it and were one of the few bands who stuck to their roots: they were, all said and done, the basic rock animal.

They headlined the 1988 Kelvingrove Festival when they were at their peak, then when a few internal differences saw the original line-up split after five years of constant and gruelling gigging, the band bravely fought on in various formats.

It wasn't until 1994 that the four original members got back together for the odd gig, until the year 1997 saw a period when Martin was not available and the three remaining amigos drafted in ex-Centurian frontman Jim Jamieson on vocals. This was quite a line-up and the band recorded a CD called The Answer, which has some of the finest songs the boys have ever written. Truth be told, this line-up was more about the recording than playing live, though they did perform a handful of gigs in Glasgow, including one at Strawberry Fields.

In 1999 the classic original line-up got back together for some local concerts, which are remembered with some nostalgia, if not irony, as some of their most fun gigs ever. Alas, Graham moved to the wilds of Aberdeenshire in 2003, then Tommy went to Canada to start a new life in 2006.

It was time for the band to call it a day and bow out gracefully after 23 years of amazing rock 'n' roll.

The third of my Bruce's babes for the opening night were Ransom, formed in Edinburgh and with this east-coast pedigree - apart from Uriah Heep - the only non-Glasgow band in this book. They earn their place here, however, because they were, quite simply, a great band and an integral part of a west-coast institution's historical opening bill. In fact, they would go on to play the club many times over the course of the opening few months.

Ransom were vocalist Bryan Taite, Iain Gordon (lead guitar), Alan Melrose (guitar), David Leslie (bass) and John Clelland (drums). A glam sleaze rock band, they owned some great songs, one of which, 'Shipwrecked', to this very day still dances around my frizzy napper.

They were only together a few years and when they split up Iain and David would join Donald MacLeod's Crows, while David Leslie teamed up with Heavy Pettin' for their farewell show in the Bruce.

Page Three Stunners

To be blessed in any generation or decade with a special band is exciting, but to be blessed with two is downright indulgent – yet, cutting their own path alongside the trail being blazed by Zero Zero, locally and nationally, La Paz were one of the greatest unsigned bands I've ever had the pleasure of seeing live.

Like the Zeros, they were never signed to a major label and worldwide recognition proved all too elusive. But this is, after all, one of the main reasons this book had to be written: to pay tribute to the unsung heroes of rock.

La Paz boasted killer songs, but they were playing melodic rock when, in the late Eighties, that particular wave was being overtaken by the terrifying tsunami of Thrash Metal.

Chic McSherry (formerly of Red Ellis), Doogie White (Tryxter) and Alex Carmichael formed the original La Paz line-up. Their musical influences lay in Purple, Rainbow, Journey and Gary Moore. Their first decision, however, was to find a sound that would take them one step beyond the all-guitar bands who dominated the circuit in the early part of the decade. This meant introducing keyboards and several players were auditioned before the lads chose Andy Mason.

It wasn't a match that initially looked great on paper. Andy was a public schoolboy and, by their own admission, La Paz 'were just a bunch of schemies from Motherwell, Wishaw and Viewpark'.

The band recall: 'Andy was still at school when he joined and looking at him in the photos, which were taken at our first demo recording, it's hard to imagine that he was allowed out on his own, never mind with us lot.

'He likes to think that he brought an air of civilised sophistication to us but we have some photographic evidence that proves we corrupted him totally. In reality, we saved his life because a career in the Civil Service clearly beckoned before he met us.'

Now all they needed was a drummer, though this proved slightly more problematic. In all, the band would try five drummers at different stages in their career: Dougie 'the Brickie' Hannah, Paul McManus, Stuart 'Bunty' Brown, Spanky Harris and Colin 'To' Morrow. Paul is now back playing with La Paz, having been given the accolade of being 'unquestionably the loudest and the most accomplished'.

With the line-up established it was time to find a name. It wasn't a love of South American geography that inspired their moniker, but rather a Page 3 model in the Sun, Caz Carrington. She was spotted by Chic bearing her all under the headline: 'Ever been to La Paz, Caz Has'. To this day Chic claims it was the rhyme of the words, rather than the raunch of the bird that proved so inspirational.

Whatever the reason for its conception, the name La Paz soon became well known across Scotland, as the band embarked on a gruelling, relentless schedule of gigs, often playing twice a week.

They recall: 'Although we never played outside the UK, we felt that we had played in the USA by proxy as we were regulars at various US military bases in the UK and we had a huge fanbase amongst the enlisted men stationed here.

'These gigs were marathons – sometimes we played up to three one-hour sets per night – but they were the only ones on the circuit that paid good money and it was from those earnings that we funded all of our recordings.'

Feted by music journalists, most notably by Kerrang!'s Derek Oliver, it seemed that stardom could only be a signature away. In fact, terms were finally agreed for a three-album deal before, suddenly and inexplicably, they were shelved.

It was a major blow for the lads, after six years of blood, sweat and tears and the end for this incarnation of La Paz came on 15 October 1988 with a farewell gig in Falkirk. Doogie moved down to the Big Smoke to join an outfit called Midnight Blue with Alex Dickson, before moving on to Ritchie Blackmore's Rainbow.

There was a reunion gig a year later – by then I had my own Glasgow club, Strawberry Fields – where the lads and I celebrated Chic's fortieth birthday.

But it was our old pal Tom Russell who would trigger a La Paz renaissance in January 2008. By that time DJ-ing at 96.3 Rock Radio, he called Doogie and asked if he would be interested in singing some songs at the Garage for the station's birthday party. Doogie agreed and asked Chic to play. Armed only with one flamenco guitar, they took to the stage in front of 1,000 screaming rock fans.

Chic recalls: 'We had such a blast and it woke up so many great memories in both of us that we decided to give it a go with the full band for my fiftieth birthday in November.'

Chic, Alex and Paul got together to rehearse a set of covers and, after just one rehearsal, it was clear to the three amigos that they hadn't lost the phenomenal La Paz vibe. Three dates were booked to work with Doogie's touring schedule and early in 2009 Doogie flew in from London the night before the first show to rehearse.

They went down a storm and, truthfully, I wouldn't have expected anything less.

'The point of doing these gigs is simple: to have fun,' says Chic. 'We're not out to prove anything or to recapture our youth or to answer any critics or even to look for a new audience. It just feels great to be doing something again that was so important to us all and was such a big part of our lives.

'We won't be writing any new material or rushing into the studio to record – those days are long gone. But we know from the reaction so far that lots of people want to hear us play again and that is just fantastic.'

Fantastic indeed!

Well, with such a fine calibre of bands already appearing at the Bruce, I was intent on also trying to bring through the younger unknowns and set out on a mission to attend rehearsals and gather demo tapes.

One of the first tapes I received was from a young band called Samoyed. It was well recorded (in a bathroom) and featured the guitar histrionics of a 16-year-old by the name of Alex Dickson. I recalled having seen Alex with my son Lee, who was at school with him and, even at that young age, he already looked like a star: imagine a miniature version of Jake E. Lee, one of his heroes. At the time I thought, if he can play as well as he looks, he's destined for great things. Boy, could he play guitar.

The Samoyed line-up was Alex, Mark Christie (vocals), Alex's big brother Hugh (bass), David Christie (guitar) and Rory (drums).

Having been won over by their tape. I went along to a rehearsal at the Key Youth Centre one sunny summer's night. They were so nervous, it was criminal and Alex kept bursting his strings. It was the first time in my life I remember seeing someone recycle the wires and put them back on. I left the room at one point and came back with five cokes and Mars Bars and, from there, everything went fine. They made their debut at the Bruce weeks later, joining the ranks of other local acts: Drunken State, The Entwined, Pteranadon, Crisis, Trumpet Worm, Twin Town, Sadistic Death, Easy, Psycho Flowers and so many more.

Samoyed changed their name to Jinx and also their drummer Rory for James Jazzar Rae (of Halloween), with Big Alan Sands (may he rest in peace) replacing Hugh on bass.

They were the first band I ever managed and will always have a special place in my heart. They then went on to win the first annual Impulse Records Battle of the Bands competition in the Bruce and made their debut (two nights in a row) in the much renowned Shadows bar in Glasgow.

They split up in true rock band style while at their peak. Alex went on to a glittering career as a guitar hero extraordinaire. His first good move was answering a phone call from one of the guys from the band Glasgow, asking him to audition for them at the old Venue in Sauchiehall Street. He packed his axe and headed into town only to be confronted by Hamie, Gordon Bonnar and Gary Moat of Heavy Pettin', whose members Punky and Brian had just left.

In fact, Heavy Pettin' had been checking out Alex's playing weeks before, when Jinx were supporting Glasgow in the Bruce. Alex nailed the audition and recommended David Leslie of Ransom for the vacant bass job.

So was born the Heavy Pettin' line-up that would play the farewell gig years later in the Bruce. It really was that kind of place: where many dreams were born, some were lived and others laid to rest.

The Venue

It was during one of these club nights in the Bruce that Tom Russell informed me the Venue was looking for an experienced rock DJ on the Saturday night. I hadn't even thought about DJ-ing in the Bruce back then, but Tom let me dabble for a few weeks and he believed I possessed a knowledge, understanding and, most importantly, a passion for rock music, so he put my name forward.

There was no one more shocked than me when I landed the job and no one less surprised when I was sacked halfway through my first night!

I was armed with my treasured album collection, recently topped up to the tune of £300-worth of discs from 23rd Precinct in Glasgow's Bath Street. And yet no one was dancing. I stood petrified in front of 300 staring punters and an empty dance floor.

The then manager, Big Tam, came over and announced I was 'shite' and this would be my first and last night!

My first, admittedly rather feeble, line of defence was to argue that it was, in fact, his punters who were shite, but I'd have every one of them up jigging once the amber nectar kicked in.

It was all to no avail: I was to be Joe the Toff at the end of the night.

Imagine my delight, then, when moments later there was a sudden shuffling of humanity on to the dance floor and the night kicked off.

Tam immediately reinstated me.

After the gig he told me he'd been flummoxed by the fact he'd received no fewer than fifty complaints about yours truly . . . all after only three songs! The reason why, it transpired, was down to a Machiavellian attempt by a rival to scupper my first night. Apparently, a certain wannabe and his girlfriend, who shall remain faceless beneath veils of undeserved charity, had stationed themselves in the toilets, where they set up a campaign to persuade everyone to report the DJ as mince and boycott the dance floor.

Tam's girlfriend Jean was in the girls toilet when she heard the poisoned dwarf telling her tale and Tam went into the Gents, where he heard the same line in propaganda.

At once the big man stormed round the hall, telling anyone who would listen, but especially those who wouldn't, that Robert Fields was here to stay and, if they didn't want to dance, they could f*ck off.

Hey presto! A merry time was had by all. So merry that not long afterwards I landed the Friday night slot as well, a gig that lasted into the Nineties, when the Cathouse came courting.

So, let's find out a little more about my new place of work of a weekend. Well, the Venue opened in 1981 and the rock night was kicked off by Tom Russell, who could only DJ there from 10–11.45pm due to his commitments with his Friday Rock Show with Clyde on 261 (at that time the station was in the Anderson Centre in Glasgow and not Clydebank). The rest of the night was handled by Gary Lovett, who would go on to be Tom's engineer at Clyde and was on the audio crew for the mobile recording shows at the Apollo and an all-day live broadcast from Donnington's Monster of Rock Festival piped into the Venue in 1984.

Now that I think of it, I can recall it was Gary's sister, Sheena, who caused such a stir in her thigh-length boots and long blonde hair way back then and can, therefore, lay the claim to be one of the first bona fide Venue rock chicks.

My good friend Stuart Eadie helped Gary for a while and together they guided the Venue to its first anniversary in October 1982. Their success meant a Saturday night slot was added and a whole weekend of rock was in place.

The Venue's promoter, Alan Mawn and owner Ross Bowie, decided that Tom's spot should be changed from the Friday to the Saturday, allowing him more time on the decks and Kenny Buchanan from Listen Records took over the Friday night. As he only played a selection of 7"singles, there was now time for live bands to appear.

For an 18-month period the Venue closed its doors, amid much in-house political turmoil, but reopened in February 1987 with Peter and Kenny taking control on Fridays, then Kenny and a young up-and-comer,

George Bowie, on Saturdays. I was also approached, in the wake of success at the Bruce Hotel, to add some rock to the proceedings on a Friday night.

It worked well for the best part of four very special years and we enjoyed many a great night and live gigs in the place, simply by merit of playing the right music at the right time – and by playing requests. Anyone who frequented the Venue in those heady days will remember the pen and paper I left for all the dedications and requests and the paper fights I used to have with the paying punters.

We had our fair share of celebs in through the doors over the next few years. I remember Tom putting Roger Daltrey on the guest list, as he was interviewing him on Clyde. Between records, I went over and introduced myself. He was lovely to talk to, polite and attentive and all he asked was that I didn't mention he was there or, worse, play The Who. Aye right! No sooner back in the DJ box I was announcing the presence of a rock legend at the front of the stage and slipped on 'The Kids Are All Right'.

Roger's cute wee face transmogrified into that of Mad McVicar. He gave me the finger and left.

Lemmy, of Motörhead and Ace of Spades fame, was in one night too, again as the guest of Tom. My band Drunken State had their album Kilt By Death out at the time, with the sleeve depicting Death as a manic Celtic warrior, complete with kilt and sabre – the original was painted by 2000 AD's Slaine artist, Simon Bisley.

Like a proud father, I showed the artwork to Lemmy and all he could find to say was that we'd stolen the title from one of his songs, 'Killed By Death'. Well, quoth I, didn't he steal that himself from the Goons, Messrs Milligan, Sellers and Secombe?

'F*ck off, smartass!' says Lemmy, to which rejoinder I pointed at the mole on his face and asked: 'Can I squeeze that by the way, big man?' (I know, a real witty riposte - not)

The look in his eyes was enough for me to beat a sharp retreat but when I played 'Killed By Death' a couple of minutes later he, too, gave me the finger. What is it with rock legends and giving the bird?

The music from that year, 1987, onwards was special, with hip hop crossing over into rap, metal, thrash, glam, funk, melodic rock, heavy rock, Gothic rock. Everything and anything went, was dissected and experimented upon, cloned or spliced and in the Venue those were the best of nights - the charged atmosphere, the music beating in your head, heart and chest, with the mirrors steamed up, the floor soaking wet, the rooms filled with the smell of fresh sweat fanned by toss of long, saturated hair and that was just the women!

I doubt there will ever be another club good enough replace the Venue in the history of the Glasgow rock scene.

Midnight At The Mayfair

After cementing my foundations within the Venue, I also landed the job of DJ and compère at all the top gigs upstairs in a club called the Mayfair. Faith No More's first gig, with Mike Patton replacing Chuck Mosley, was one such event and I've never witnessed a band on stage or off who hated each other as much as that lot.

Watching the soundcheck from stage left, Mike was gracious enough to sign my copy of The Real Thing LP. I asked if he might get the rest of the guys to sign, too, when the booming voice of Faith's guitarist, Big Jim Martin hollered: 'Where's that bastard?'

Mike turned to me and said: 'Ask them yourself. I f*ckin' hate them.'

Worse was to come. At one point Patton bent down to check the set list and Big Jim booted him up the arse so hard that poor Mike fell off the stage.

Another Mayfair lowlight were those Swedish doom merchants, Candlemass. Their singer, Messiah Marolin, who wasn't an ounce under 20 stone, told me that when I saw him dive into the crowd that would be their last song and I should stick on a certain favourite tune of during his mid-air flight. The problem was that when the kids saw their Messiah hurtling towards them, a laudable sense of self-defence kicked in and they parted like the Red Sea.

The force of the vibrations from Marolin hitting the floor caused the turntable arms to skite all the way up Sauchiehall Street, leaving me with nothing queued up. In the deathly silence Marolin lay sprawled on the floor, with all the kids and band members and crew staring at his gargantuan prone body. Finally, with a twitch from the Messiah's legs and a deep groan, the silence was shattered by the roar of 400 kids and one DJ pissing ourselves silly.

It wasn't all laughter. One of my nastiest moments at a gig happened in the Mayfair. Just to put you in the picture, this was a manner of venue that regularly played host to the Irish band The Wolfetones, an outfit with decidedly Irish Republican persuasions, whose politics went down very well with most of the in-house bouncing staff.

Now, the band playing this certain night were American Nuclear Assault and, like a lot of overseas acts, they'd never fully taken on board the fractured and fraught religious climate in Glasgow. I was at the front door with their tour manager, where we had just peeked outside to look at the sell-out crowd queuing all the way up the street. He wanted to greet the first few fans with some promo gifts.

Finally, the doors burst open and, slam!, the first punter is punched out and unceremoniously set upon by the bouncer, in a one-man nuclear assault of muscles and tattoos.

All hell is breaking loose until the wee guy fights his way up and screams: 'Warraf*ckwizzthatfur?'

The knuckle-scraper grabs the guy by his chest and replies: 'It's your offensive T-shirt.'

Lo and behold, but isn't the wee rascal wearing American Nuclear Assault's official T-shirt, the one advertising their new single, 'Hang the Pope', depicting the Holy Father himself strung up in his frock on a gallows?

Having witnessed this felony upon a stalwart fan, Assault's tour manager, somewhat understandably, flies into a holy rage and threatens to cancel the sell-out show.

Encamped in the dressing room with the band and entourage I try to explain the intricacies and implications of wearing such a vestment in the heart of Glasgow. Like strolling into Harlem wearing a Ku Klux Klan tour T-shirt, I venture.

Word comes from Big Tam, the head bouncer, that all miscreants currently assembled outside can get in, but only if they take their tops off.

Band says no.

Finally, after an hour, I broker a deal that sees Assault's fans troop in wearing their bullish heraldry turned inside out. The gig is saved.

If only the bigotry that so many of Glasgow's sons and daughters wear in their hearts could be turned inside out as easily. Final thought, though, for American Nuclear Assault, the poor sods: their next gig was in Belfast.

And On This Rock

It should be no surprise to any fan of rock in Glasgow that our last, but not least, Eighties mention should go to the city's Solid Rock Café. No pub past or present will ever have the same impact as Robert Alexander's place in Hope Street, which is 22 years young this year, still kicking serious butt and seeing off all competition. In fact, its enduring, battling spirit typifies the city's entire rock movement.

My first encounter with the building was in 1970, when it was my regularly indulged habit to go inside to watch live bands. Back then the place was called La Gondola and it was well named, for I remember often having to propel myself precariously through a maze of amps, mic stands and surprised rock stars to the toilets, located directly behind the band's stage area.

A decade later I used to frequent the Pig And Whistle on Buchanan Street, where I'd have wee chats with its owner, Robert Alexander. Now, he wasn't deliriously happy with its passing trade and, at some seminal point, decided to buy the old Gondola building, by then Black Jacks bar and turn it into a rock pub, which became the Solid Rock Café.

The move didn't surprise me. Robert and I are cut from the same cloth, though granted these days his may be a tad more expensive than mine, for we are both first and foremost Big Bad Rock Fans. Both of us experienced our Road to Damascus moment early in our youth on hearing Uriah Heep's 'Gypsy' for the first time, before buying Black Sabbath and Deep Purple albums. I bought mine in Paterson's in Buchanan Street, opposite the same Pig and Whistle, while Robert, being a shy wee boy who wasn't allowed into the big bad toon, bought them in Gloria's in the more residential Hampden area.

I could have written an entire book on the Solid Rock Café itself. It has and always will have, a special place in my heart. It's not just a pub, it's a way of life. Down through the years Robert has made a point of getting to know all his regulars and often puts on special nights for them.

A great wealth of talent has played the place: worldwide stars such as

Status Quo, Billy Rankin, Nazareth, No Sweat and Wet Wet Wet.

Robert has also been kind enough to help me with my own bands, organising showcases downstairs: Quarantine for BMG and Adam 8*1*2, who landed their Kelvingrove slot playing in the Solid.

When times got tough in 2000 Robert was one of a handful of mates who stood by me and I'll never forget him for that. Let's have a special toast to the Solid, a true Glasgow rock legend.

And as the decade comes to an end, let's raise a glass, too, to the exciting times that lie ahead. For these will be the years when the gods of rock deign to smile on me and I get to set up a wee four-gig scene for local bands, work with the top international acts and, finally, have my own nightclub. We're moving on to fresh Fields, boys and girls.

THE NINETIES

Omission Impossible

AS we've seen, Eighties Glasgow rightly laid claim to some of the world's most groundbreaking and influential rock groups. The Nineties, however, would welcome a brand new breed of international band, beamed into our lives via music television and a new medium, the mighty, ubiquitous World Wide Web: Pearl Jam, Metallica, Rage Against the Machine, Soundgarden, Smashing Pumpkins, Tool, Green Day, Offspring, Weezer, Radiohead, Alice In Chains, Dream Theater, Machine Head, White Zombie, Blind Melon, Coal Chamber, Korn, Cypress Hill, System of a Down, Marilyn Manson and, of course, Nirvana, the band who brought us Nevermind, an album that inspired another million bands and launched the entire Grunge movement.

Locally, something very exciting was happening, too: a sudden blossoming of bona fide rock venues. The Venue, which had been Glasgow's premier rock club without contest for years, suddenly had a rival in new kid on the block, the Cathouse, an establishment that went from strength to strength, attracting big bands and increasingly bigger crowds. While the Venue's Brown Street building was briefly taken over by the Rat Trap, also on the scene was the Power Station and, on a Thursday, you could rock all night at the Warehouse with Peter McLean. Sauchiehall Street's Nice 'n' Sleazy was also established in this decade, while at the tail end of the ten years I'd be midwife at the birth of the Strawberry Fields club.

Glasgow's bands were quick to tap into this newfound love of rock.

Their fervour soon became a stage frenzy, as new groups sought to unleash their music in every packed venue throughout Scotland's Central Belt: Drunken State, Crisis, Dr Pop, The Flys, Freeview, Gobstopper, Real, Churn, Ramp, The Ocean, Fireball, Hellfire, Subway, Mudshark, Baby's Got a Gun, Bleeding Hearts, Buddha Grass Harbour, Indian Bone, Nerve, Pink Kross, Just Another Dream . . . there seemed to be almost as many rock bands as there were rock fans.

When not satiating their hunger for live performance, these same fans could also, as the decade aged, log on to their computers for a hit, as the Internet was beginning to play a big part in music in the shape of downloads and file-sharing sites. What began in 1999 as an idea in the heads of teenager Shawn Fanning and his uncle Sean Parker in Boston redefined cyberspace, the music industry and the way we all think about intellectual property. Napster is now back in business as a legal, pay-per-song music-download site, having started with P2P 'peer to peer' files before upgrading to the more popular MP3s. File-sharing is now commonplace in the music industry, of course, with Limewire and Spotify the most popular sites.

As we greeted new bands, new technology and new publications – in the shape of Classic Rock Magazine – we also said goodbye to fallen heroes and cherished friends:

Mark Putterford, Steve Clark, Rory Gallagher, Frank Zappa Andrew Wood, Johnny Thunders, Stevie Marriot, Chas Chandler, Brian Connolly, Tom Fogerty, Gerry Garcia, Stevie Ray Vaughan, Rob Tyner, Ronnie Lane, Jerry Nolan, Michael Hutchence, Ray Gillen, Mick Ronson, Cozy Powell, Freddie Mercury, Tommy Tee and the bleach-haired lost boy, Kurt Cobain.

The Art Of Promotion

And so, ladies and gents, boys and girls, we come to the Nineties, the decade I would begin to try out my own promotional skills in and around Greater Glasgow. What was being achieved with a relatively small budget in the Bruce Hotel in East Kilbride hadn't gone unnoticed. Many nationally known rock bands had trodden the boards there, after all. In fact, we'd provided the debut Scottish shows for bands such as Little Angels, whose bass player and rabid Leeds United fan Mark Plunkett remains a trusted friend to this day, Wolfsbane, Chariot, Acid Reign and Onslaught. On top of these were gigs by Heavy Pettin', The Almighty, Big George and the Business and every local band worth their salt.

Of course, as a result, I'd get on all the major promo lists and one contact in particular gave me some cracking rock recordings and myriad knick knacks: RCA's Dave Shack. Now, a few little words in passing about Shacky, if I may. The man is a legendary scribe, who kick-started his career writing for the Yorkshire Post before becoming a regular contributor to Kerrang! – all while he was still a book-brained brat at university.

Now recognised as one of the UK's top rock specialists, he was asked to produce at Radio One, with Tommy Vance and Alan 'Fluff' Freeman as his charges and co-presented on Steve Wright in the Afternoon and occasionally the Friday Rock Show.

In 1991 he was employed by BMG as a rock consultant and has worked his way through the ranks to the title of vice-president of Sony/BMG. He is, however, still the same down-to-earth mate as ever he was - despite the fact he must be sick of me reminding him that his beloved Leeds United were slain, both home and away in Europe, in 1993, by the Glasgow Rangers triumvirate of Durrant, Hateley and McCoist.

Anyway, while I was growing more busy by the day in the world of rock, my mates in Uriah Heep would play Glasgow only once in this decade, on 12 May 1991, in the Mayfair, this time in support of their Different Worlds album. They would also release Sea of Light ('95) and Sonic Origami ('98), their last album for ten years until the quite magnificent Wake the Sleeper.

Although it must have seemed that Britain had cooled on them, Heep were kept busy gigging worldwide.

Okay, I confess, there was one other UK gig they were booked for but didn't play and, yes, that, too, was in the Mayfair in 1990. And, okay, I now admit I may have been instrumental in the no-show. Well, sometimes the art of promotion, for bands and self, is as much about what doesn't happen as what does.

That night the Heep gig's organiser was, well, let's just call him Bart. Now Bart had booked the event after putting on a few wee shows in the Saints & Sinners club, most notably Little Angels on their Don't Prey For Me tour. Like all wannabe promoters, he was found wanting, however, when it came to upscaling his production. Truth be told, this is where most wannabes fall down. You have to get all of your costs bang on, right down to the last detail and, most importantly, read the contract – all of it!

Well, I got a phone call on the morning of the Saturday show from the bold young Bart, who knew of course that I was in regular contact with Heep. Could he just run a few things by me? Shoot, young fellamelad.

Well, first, was it okay for the support, his own band Metro, to use Heep's kit and backline? I think I snorted into the phone.

Erm, secondly, then, as he hadn't hired any lights or stage extensions for the show, would the in-house stage and disco lights be up to the job?

Silence. Finally, I asked if he was winding me up? No? Well, did he know that he was dealing with a worldwide major touring act here and not Joe Bloggs and the Feckin' Nose Pickers from doon the toon? In fact, says I to the strange, strangled sounds on the end of the line, did he know that he would be in breach of his contract because the lights and the stage were totally inadequate for Heep – the stage alone wouldn't hold Lee's drums and Phil Hammond's keyboards all at the same time, never mind the rest of the backline.

Well, in the end, Heep didn't get to play that night and the bold Bart was never seen on the scene again. I suspect a wee fortune may have been lost in the process, but at least the plates of munchies that had been laid on backstage were saved. In fact, they tasted braw and, with my tummy lined, it was off to the Solid Rock Café for a few bevvies, then on to Central Station Hotel for a few more with the lads from Heep.

Well, I knew they weren't doing anything else that night. Cheers!

One For All

A few of our highest hopes had hit the skids in the Eighties and chucked music altogether, so it was goodbye to Zero Zero, La Paz, Heavy Pettin' and Jinx. From the ashes of that little lot, however, came the quite magnificent phoenix that was Midnight Blue.

Zero Zero's former frontman Steven Doherty was down in the Big Smoke, where he was introduced to Jem Davis (ex-Tobruk, on keys), Eddie Fincher (drums) and Niall Canning (bass). These three were looking for a frontman for their newly formed AOR group Midnight

Blue. They also lacked the lynchpin of a rock outfit, the guitarist: it's fair to say that, although Stevie could strum along to make an approximation of an axe during rehearsals, he wasn't what you'd call a lead player.

Midnight Blue had made several moves for a young guitarist who was strutting his stuff with Jagged Edge (who'd made their Scottish debut in the Videodrome that year) but Myke Gray was intent, instead, on setting up a new band called Skin.

Finally, after auditioning all of the London hopefuls, Stevie decided enough was enough and recommended Alex Dickson. The young laddie was sent for posthaste. Of course, he blew everyone away.

At that point, Midnight Blue had recorded some songs without the vocals. Although I did have a rough copy of a demo from Alex called Party, featuring Stevie on vocals and guitar. The same demo song was played by that great patron of the genre, Tom Russell on Clyde 261 and for Midnight Blue the future looked bright.

The problems began when Stevie was asked to actually front the band and quite literally drop his guitar. He recalls: 'What they were after was some guy in Spandex with a candy floss hair-do, strutting his stuff on stage and it wasn't me – I had to have my guitar!'

One weekend, hopping on to a train to visit his sister, Stevie decided that he wouldn't be coming back. It was then that I received a call from Alex to say Stevie had just quit the band and he was looking for the number of former La Paz singer Doogie White.

Doogie did, in fact, join Midnight Blue and turned them into one of the best melodic rock bands I've ever seen. I was lucky enough to do a couple of great gigs with them, one a Friday night in the Venue and then as part of a killer seven-band all-nighter in the Mayfair, which also included Drunken State, Engine (from Liverpool), Marcha Fresca, The Crows, Baby's Got a Gun and Big George . . . oh and a comedian-cum-compère called Stu Who?

Midnight Blue would eventually secure a publishing deal with Chrysalis and record one album Take the Money and Run. What next? Well, as a famous Goon once said: 'And then, suddenly, nothing happened.'

Just like so many other melodic rock bands of that era Midnight Blue imploded, folding before realising their potential. Indeed, the album was released, in Japan, long after their demise.

The three musketeers – Stevie Doherty, Doogie White and Alex Dickson – would, however, go on to find many major successes throughout their careers and here are their own stories. The first is told by the great man himself, so sit back, boys and girls and pray silence for Mr Stevie Doherty . . .

'It all started one night at the Glasgow Apollo. One of my friends had given me a ticket to go see a band I had vaguely heard of and I thought: 'Why not . . . can't do any harm.'

'Up until then I wasn't really into music and had wanted to be a journalist, as my uncle was the sports editor for the Sunday Mail and I thought that looked like a great job, hanging out with all the Celtic players!

'Anyway, all the studying and passing of exams were about to mean absolutely nothing as I sat in the stalls and watched a band called Status Quo and in particular some guy called Rick Parfitt, make the best noise I'd ever heard. The next day I asked for a guitar. I didn't get it until Christmas and that was it. I think that was 1973 or '74 and after that nothing else mattered! I tried to knuckle down at school but it was a losing battle.

'I formed a duo with my mate Gordon 'Jeff' Jeffrey playing Quo songs and that then became the band Shade, which became Orion. In 1978/79 I left that band to join Underhand Jones, one of the biggest Glasgow bands at that time. After a year or so I left to join Hijax, a band based in Balfron.

'It was around about that time that I auditioned for AC/DC, shortly after Bon Scott died and pre-Brian Johnson. I sang half a dozen songs with them, which was an absolute dream come true.

'When Hijax split, myself and guitarist Ian Stewart put another band together, which would eventually become China White. We had our own studio in Yoker, where some of the big Glasgow bands like Scheme would record and rehearse. We went through a few drummers and eventually got Davie Edgar from the Dolphins: this line-up would eventually become Strangeways.

'We signed to Canadian record company Bonaire. I left the band (musical differences!) in '83/84 and met up with Andy McCafferty, Joe James, Duncan McRae and Dave Ramsey to form Zero Zero. In '85 Duncan and Dave left and John MacMillan came in on lead guitar. We had a great few years, almost (but not quite!) signing to Atlantic Records in New York. During that time I was offered the job with a Yugoslavian band, Wild Strawberries and also auditioned for and got the job with Uriah Heep, but decided to stay with Zero Zero.

'After Zero Zero split I formed a band called Liaison with some guys from Edinburgh and also played with Glasgow's Peter Goes To Partick. I then reunited with John and Andy from Zero Zero, along with drummer Paul McManus, to form Monkey See.

'We did a few gigs, including supporting Izzy Stradlin at the Barrowlands and a showcase at the old Marquee, then we recorded down in Sawmills studio in Cornwall, but it was shortlived.

'Around that time I had been one of the guest singers with The Party Boys, who were basically the Sensational Alex Harvey Band without Alex and involved various singers like Dan McCafferty (of Nazareth), Fish and myself coming along and belting out a few covers.

'When the band decided to re-form as SAHB I got the job as singer and spent a great couple of years touring with them and recorded the Live in Glasgow album. I moved to Suffolk in '94 and joined Bury St Edmunds-based band Dream Thief, who had supported SAHB at the Railway Bike festival in Ipswich a year before.

In 2009 I released my new solo album Desolate Horizon; I play in the Pink Floyd tribute band A Saucerful of Floyd . . . and life is grand!'

After Midnight Blue's demise, the second of our musketeers, vocalist Doogie, embarked on a trip to Japan in 1991, singing with Praying Mantis, which was followed by the band's revival tour. Doogie was also busy laying down tracks with Cozy Powell and Neil Murray for a solo Powell project.

A few years earlier, a demo tape had been forwarded to Ritchie Blackmore's management, only for it to languish forgotten in a box. That is, until Candice Night discovered it and presented it to Ritchie, who was at the time looking for singers to audition for Rainbow. As a result of Candice's find, Doogie joined the band in 1994.

After the end of Rainbow in 1996, Doogie worked with Alex with the intention of securing a solo deal. Sessions on several tribute releases, including the Whitesnake tribute Snakebites and tracks on 666 – Number of the Beast, a two-volume tribute to Iron Maiden out on Deadline.

A contribution to Royal Hunt bassist Steen Morgensen's solo project

Arrival, under the moniker Cornerstone, was released in late 2000. Doogie also guested on Nikolo Kotzev's conceptual Nostradamus, which was released in 2001.

Doogie also joined Yngwie Malmsteen's band, touring South America in late 2001. Attack, released in late 2002, was Doogie's first studio effort with the Swede.

Once Upon Our Yesterdays was the next Cornerstone album and a set of dates for the band across Europe marked their live debut.

In 2005, Doogie fronted another Malmsteen offering, Unleash the Fury. In this year, too, he recorded an album with guitarist Bill Liesegang and formed a part-time band, White Noise, made up of Mostly Autumn personnel. A DVD from their support stint in the UK with Uriah Heep features a live airing of 'Tarot Woman', as well as other Rainbow tracks.

The year 2007 saw the release of a fourth Cornerstone album, Two Tales of One Tomorrow. Later the same year, Doogie replaced Tony Martin as the frontman of the German band Empire, who released a fourth album, Chasing Shadows, in November, with Doogie on vocals.

On 26 February, 2008, Doogie announced that he'd no longer be a member of Yngwie Malmsteen's Rising Force, but some months later was singing for a band called Tank, a heavy armoured outfit who had found success as part of the New Wave of British Heavy Metal genre.

Never one to be work-shy, Doogie is currently performing with La Paz again, as well as Tank and is recording vocals for an English version of the latest album of Argentinian rockers Rata Blanca.

When the names of Glasgow's top guitarists are spoken, often in hushed and reverential tones, Alex Dickson, the third of our Midnight Blue triumvirate, might not glide off the tip of the tongue as quickly and easily as the likes of legends Leslie Harvey, Zal Cleminson, Jimmy McCulloch or Brian Robertson. Those in the know, however, will be only too glad to tell you that Alex is the guitarist of his generation. Just ask Rab Andrew what impact Alex had on Gun. If you saw Midnight Blue at their AOR peak, or Gun supporting Def Leppard, or Bruce Dickinson's Skunkworks, you will know what I'm talking about.

Add to this little lot major stadium tours with the likes of pop prankster Robbie Williams (on whose I've Been Expecting You album Alex played), Godfather of Soul James Brown, Ronan Keating, Emma Bunton, Matt

Willis and, most recently, Calvin Harris and it's easier to appreciate just how far the boy from East Kilbride has come; indeed, he's now one of the industry's most sought-after gunslingers.

It's all a lifetime away from his first outfit, Samoyed/Jinx, when he was a Duncanrig School pupil with my son Lee. Even way back then, we knew he was going to be a star and he didn't disappoint. Add to the mix his collaborations with the genius Sack Trick and his own solo band Fling, who did an In the City gig in 1987 in Strawberry Fields (the following year, Alex would return the favour by bringing the entire Robbie Williams entourage into the same venue for a private party and gig).

I've already spoken much of Alex in this book, but of all the local bands and musicians I've worked with, his story makes me most proud. He is the most gifted individual I've ever had the pleasure to manage and work with and is a true Glasgow rock legend.

Kross Purpose

It wasn't all testosterone and tight trousers in the Nineties. One of the bands I did manage to get into T Break, the scouting contest for the T in the Park festival were a wonderful three-girl punk band from Glasgow called Pink Kross.

Sisters Jude and Vic Boyd and Geraldine Kane had never played a note together when Bill Bartell met them in 1992 when they were in the audience at the Phoenix Festival, Arizona, USA. Bill is the man who broke cult group Shonen Knife, but at this point he was with Courtney Love and Hole's entourage. The Californian was so impressed by the girls' enthusiasm, that he told Sonic Youth's Thurston Moore about them. Come Sonic Youth's set, Moore booms out from the stage: 'This one's for Pink Kross from Scotland. They're here to rock!'

What better way for a punk band to be born?

The girls chose new stage names and Pink Kross became Vic Blue (drums and vocals), Jane Strain (bass and vocals) and Jude Fuzz (guitar and vocals). What had begun as a bit of a laugh grew from musical malarkey to serious gigging, with the trio playing extensively in Glasgow, Edinburgh and London throughout the early Nineties.

Having discovered they actually enjoyed their messy mishmash of Black

Flag, Ramones and Redd Kross-inspired noise, they eventually released a debut single, the Punk or Die EP, on their own Bouvier label. It was named Single of the Week on BBC Radio One's Evening Session and a Peel Session quickly followed. The Abomination EP marked the last release with the original line-up, as Geraldine left in April 1996 to concentrate on her full-time mum duties.

Jane Chalmers took up the bass mantle and the adventures continued, including the release of the Active Dalmatian EP, a UK tour with Urusei Yatsura and Number One Cup and a number of contributions to various sampler compilation CDs. Tours of the east and west coast of the US, the release of the Chopper Chix From VP Hell album and the Scumbag EP were all highpoints in the girls' career, as were playing with lifelong heroes the Lunachicks, the Muffs, Gas Huffer and Man Or Astroman?

Though not quite the Active Dalmatians they used to be, Pink Kross can still belt out the punky fuzz trash cacophony of their craft. Geraldine tragically died in December 2008. There would have been no Pink Kross without her.

Is There A Doctor Iin The House?

In the early Nineties, for the first and last time, I made the mistake of trying to manage two bands simultaneously. In most cases this shouldn't cause problems, but it did, as one band was an all-female funk rock band Adam 8*1*2, who hailed from Dundee and the other was Dr Pop from East Kilbride and Glasgow. The problem was that both bands' promotional packages were given to the same people at the same time but the girls got all that was going: two television slots, a Kelvingrove Festival gig and eventually a deal with Polystar in Japan, which the singer took for a solo deal.

Although both bands did get to feature on the Cathouse's Gathering of the Clans CD and played the tour to promote it, the pressure of having to justify myself to the boys every time the girls got something and they didn't was too much and finally we parted company. Thankfully, the lads remain my great friends.

They formed in 1990, an outfit that consisted of Stevie Greer on guitar, Dave Hillis (bass), Affy Ahmad (drums) and Jim Hillis (vocals). The first meeting was in the rehearsal rooms at the original Soma Records building above the Sub Club in Glasgow, where Stevie was playing with blues rockers Loose But Tight and on the lookout for a bass player. Jim, who was also rehearsing at Soma with his band the Lost Boys, suggested his 17-year-old brother Dave and brought along a bedroom demo tape the next week. Stevie recalls: 'When I heard Dave's incredible playing, I knew he wasn't right for the band, but I realised neither was I really and I knew we could start something better together.'

Meanwhile, Affy's band Screaming Tear was dissolving, so the idea was pitched to him that he join a new funk rock project with Stevie and Dave. It took a few phone calls and some persuasion – Affy was a brilliant, in-demand drummer – but he eventually agreed to a jam at Berkeley Rehearsal Rooms. The three musicians gelled instantly and set about looking for a singer. After several months of weird and wonderful try-outs, they were still rehearsing and writing ideas when Dave happened to mention that his brother's band was splitting up.

'Jim was the perfect fit,' recalls Affy. 'We knew he was a good frontman from seeing the Lost Boys, but he wanted to do something different, funkier, with a bit of rapping and a sense of humour.'

Stevie adds: 'We really wanted a proper heavy funk sound, so that means real brass. A lot of other bands were using samplers and stuff, but we wanted that big sound.'

Stevie's brother Dave and his mate Pete Drummy were recruited on tenor and alto saxes to put the missing pieces in place. The horn section would vary enormously over the coming years, with up to five players on board at times, but it was this consistently strong mix of big brass, a punchy funk rock rhythm section and snappy, satire-laced lyrics that established the definitive Dr Pop sound.

The first gig was at a rock night I ran in the Gemini Disco in East Kilbride. The band was well received by a large and diverse crowd and I offered to manage them.

Dave remembers: 'I don't remember any formal contract. It wasn't really needed with Robert. You knew he'd just get on with doing his best for you without meddling with the music.'

Well, I set about getting the show on the road, setting up gigs in key venues in Glasgow and Edinburgh, where the lads did me proud by putting on stormers.

The Hillis brothers' appreciation of the ridiculous was something that became an integral part of the music, especially at live shows. Stevie recalls: 'Dave and Jim have a very, erm, unorthodox sense of humour. I think they're actually both slightly mental. But the whole band embraced that and their ideas.'

At a time when most bands were either into the dressed-down grungy look, or hanging onto the sleaze glam rock thing, Dr Pop would variously be seen dressed in pink dungarees, extraordinary hats, three-piece French-flared suits straight from the Seventies, sequinned Ali Baba suits, Thai boxing shorts . . . anything unfashionable or entirely inappropriate was the order of the day.

This irreverence also extended to the rest of the show, with outrageous axe solos, cover versions of telly theme tunes or maybe even something by the Osmonds.

Typical of the band, when asked to contribute to a Spinal Tap night at the Apollo Club in Glasgow, where bands were asked to play a short set of their own music and one Tap cover, they entirely ditched their own songs, dug out the Spandex, leotards and foil-wrapped cucumbers and performed an entire Tap set.

By 1994 it became obvious things would have to get a little more serious if the band were to progress, but it became difficult to put the genie back in the bottle. Over the course of some showcase gigs in London, a few of the founding members began to lose heart and so the band, still fronted by Jim, moved on to the MkII version.

This consisted of Jim on vocals, Steven Raeside (guitar), Thomas Big T Moonan (bass), Mick Pryde (drums), Alan 'Muff' Moffat and Terry McEwan (keyboards). The band marched on for about ten more years, playing regular gigs in London, including the Marquee, the Orange and Camden Underworld. En route home to Glasgow after this last gig, Jim leaned against the bus door, got his chain trapped in the handle, springing open the door and was left dangling from the bus as it stormed down the motorway.

Luckily no harm came to the bus and it lived to face another day. Jim, too, was still in one piece for a sell-out night in Glasgow in King Tut's Wah Wah Hut.

The band's sound developed from funk rock to a more rap metal sound and, despite changes in the line-up, mostly guitarists, their gigs always attracted a loyal fan base. Perhaps this popularity was as much to do with the band's sense of humour. Indeed, many reviews referred to Dr Pop's members as having comedy personas stand-up comedians would kill for.

The final punchline came in 2007 when, because of the road crew's other work commitments and Jim's family responsibilities, Dr Pop retired from the world of music and mayhem. This may not be the end, however . . . the word 'reunion' is being bandied about, so who knows? Best look out the Spandex breeks from the bottom drawer and grab a fresh cucumber just in case.

What A State To Get In

The next band I managed was East Kilbride's 'other top band', Drunken State and what a hoot we had: I think the whole of Duncanrig, St Bride's, Claremount and Hunter High schools were in the band at one point, such was their popularity among musicians and ardent metal fans.

Colin Lowlands, who went on to form the fantastic Dream Disciple, was the original singer, alongside guitarists such as Steven Flanagan and Darren Callaghan, with wee Alistair 'Limpet' Sneddon on drums. The classic Drunken State line-up, however, was Robert Traish (vocals), Dougie Smith (guitar), David Leishman (lead guitar), Michael Brash (bass) and Graham 'Psycho' Thomson (drums). It was this line-up of lads who released the Bags Not Carry the Coffin EP and the Kilt by Death album on Heavy Metal Records America.

At they were settling into this line-up, thrash metal was just peaking and, unsurprisingly, the State's influences were cited as Metallica, Iron Maiden and Thin Lizzy. This was no mere tribute band, however. Drunken State were a dedicated bunch of musicians who, in the wake of Holocaust from Edinburgh, were rightly considered to be Scotland's top original thrash band.

You could point to many attributes that made Drunken State stand head and shoulders above the crowd – even when they weren't sober! For me, however, the wholly unique quality could be found in frontman supreme Robert Traish: the voice, the madcap antics, the genius, meant or otherwise, of his vocal and physical gymnastics.

I've read elsewhere that Robert had said we didn't allow him to move about freely on stage. This, of course, is a load of mince, because Robert was so entirely unpredictable on stage all we could ever do was try to give him safety guidelines about where he could and could not go, then stand back and hope for the best. More often than not the best was a miraculous escape from life-threatening injury.

It didn't help our cause that Robert was inspired to increasingly dangerous flights by every new act he saw. One night we were watching Acid Reign, whom I'd brought to Scotland for their north-of-the-border debut. At the start of the Eighties, they were at the forefront of the UK hardcore scene and had drawn eager crowds to Billy Potts' Rooftops venue.

Now their rather energetic frontman, known simply as 'H', began, mid-song, to climb the viewing boxes at the side of the stage. Bearing in mind we were playing the same venue the very next week with Holocaust, Drunken State to a man turned to a smiling Robert and cried: 'Don't even think about it!'

He was thinking about it, of course. This was confirmed by the fact that the following week our man Icarus lost his grip on the edge of a box and fell head-first into a rack of guitars. That death evaded him is a miracle of chance rather than design.

Not long afterwards, at a gig in the Edinburgh Venue, supporting Onslaught, I endured a long night at the bar keeping a young mosher and his girlfriend sweet after Robert Edmund Hillary Traish had decided to climb along a beam the length of the hall during the instrumental number 'Eric'. When, inevitably, he came plummeting back down to earth, his fall was broken by the moshing couple, causing both some serious GBH and a pair of aching, long-locked nappers.

Luckily, the amber nectar at the bar was going down faster even than our flying frontman and by the time I and the bar had finished with our unfortunate human runways, not only had they forgotten their injuries and completely shrugged off their shock, they also had plum forgotten they were in the Edinburgh Venue. In fact, they were so pickled they missed the bands.

The head of A&R at London Records, on the other hand, didn't miss a thing. He'd travelled up to watch his band Onslaught and, like most folk who came along to the gigs, he immediately recognised a support band by the name of Drunken State was blowing away the main act.

It should have come as no surprise then, when that same night I was approached outside by Onslaught's manager asking for permission to speak to our young singer and wannabe trapeze artist about leaving Drunken State to join his own outfit.

I replied by reminding him it was a nightmare to get back inside the Venue on a busy night and, oh, did he remember all those terribly steep steps on the way in?

The poor man looked confused and said, quite, yes he did, but why?

'Because you'll be sent down them headfirst, if you go anywhere near our singer!' I hollered into his shocked face.

No more was ever said on the matter (sorry, young Robert!).

Anyway, as we discovered earlier in this record of rock ribaldry, Robert was the only one of the Drunken State kirk who didn't drink. The rest of the lads more than made up for that, of course and it came to the point where I decided the mantle of responsibility should rest squarely on their manager's shoulders. This drinking would have to stop, I argued in the morning's wake of one particularly tempestuous night.

Guitarist Douglas K. Smith entered into the spirit of the debate with gusto, deflating my argument with an admirable display of impeccable dialectic logic.

Did the band not play better when bevvied? They did.

Had they ever played a bad gig or so much as hit a bum note while under the influence of said bevy? Errr, no.

Did the ambience of all-round bevviness add a certain frisson to the evening's entertainment, both for entertainers and entertained? Indubitably.

We celebrated Dougie's insight into the chemical composition of thrash metal with several pints of the bar's best elixir. The truth is, it really was all in the name: Drunken State, however they might look to the casual onlooker before the start of a gig, were consummate professionals when they took to the stage, a world where for the players and the listeners, it suddenly all made sense.

Well, it did to most of us. That night in the Edinburgh Venue, it had all made sense to Onslaught's manager. Apparently, it had not been as easy to fathom for the head of A&R at London Records.

After the gig I approached him and asked what he thought.

He looked at me for a few seconds then said: 'At one point during that gig I almost considered signing them . . . till I noticed how pissed they were.'

Apparently, the icing in the cake that became a huge custard pie in Drunken State's face, was when the seemingly drunk, unpredictable and dangerously erratic singer had clambered along a beam and 'nearly f*ckin' killed two of the punters!'.

Not even my attempt at Dougie's Philosophy of the Transportive Qualities of the Drunken State would work.

'If you shut your eyes, didn't they sound super?' I asked. 'With your eyes closed to everything, did you hear a bum note or any mistakes? Were they not one of the tightest bands, with the best songs, that you will ever clap your ears if not your eyes on?'

'Yes,' said the man from London Records, very politely. 'No,' quoth the man from London Records, with a smile. 'Yes,' replied the man from London Records, wiping his brow with the sleeve of his suit jacket.

'Well, then, what's your problem?' I asked, exasperated.

'I didn't close my eyes at any point during that gig!' screamed the man from London Records. 'That's my f*cking problem!'

We never did get a call from London Records.

We did enjoy some great shows at the Marquee in London, however. And at the Kelvingrove Festival in Glasgow, with supports to Heavy Pettin', Acid Reign, Onslaught, Holocaust . . . we even did a guy's twenty-first birthday party somewhere in the darkest memories of my mind. I think it was a function suite above a pub in Wishaw, or maybe Airdrie. The notion of thrash among the sossie rolls and party hats sits somewhat uncomfortably alongside memories of searingly good reviews for Kilt By Death in Kerrang! and Metal Hammer and countless music papers across Europe: indeed, the lads still get lots of fan mail from Greece, Germany and Spain.

Well if the twenty-first birthday party did not seem quite the acme of thrash metallurgy, it must have sparked some strange desire in our restless young Robert, who decided he'd had enough of Drunken State – he was already earning top pennies singing cabaret and telegrams and was keen to join a comedy band who dressed up in cowboy gear and covered themselves in talcum powder.

So we wished him good luck – it did after all, offer the perfect platform for his comedy fits – and replaced him with another quality singer by the name of Robert, this time Irvine. Robert MkII joined us on a tour, including a showcase for a mooted second album at the Marquee in London for Heavy Metal Records America.

Another two songs were written, appearing on the Gathering of the Clans CD and then Drunken State split up.

We had taken the rock story as far as we could. Grunge was on its way and the old school, all of a sudden, was out for summer. We'd shared many great nights, even more great laughs and as a promoter and manager, I'd learned a lot working with the lads: not least, wear a safety helmet when working with Robert Traish.

They really were that good a band and then it was all over. If only they had taken it a wee bit more seriously . . . aye, right!

Kicking In, Bowing Out

By this point in the Nineties the Bruce Hotel Rock Club was kicking in fast and furious and so were the local bands, the next two of whom boasted two musicians I could not help but immediately admire and respect: Knightrider with Tam Toye and Lyin Rampant with Eddie Trainer.

A Kerrang! scribe once wrote of Knightrider that they were 'an unstoppable rock juggernaut that just keeps rockin' and rollin'. Even if it makes me want to say '10–4 for a copy, Rubber Duck!' rather than don a David Hasselhoff chest wig and say into my watch: 'Get in here, Kit, I need you!', the analogy goes some way to describing the incredible raw force of Knightrider.

Joining Tam (bass and lead vocals) were Jim Cosgrove (drums), Dave Grocott (guitar) and Craig Ross (guitar); in fact, it was this very same line-up I put on at the Cathouse in 2008 and I was blown away not only by how good the lads still were but, more importantly, how relevant to the current music scene.

Formed by Tam in the Eighties, I always remember the adverts in all the music press for the band's seven-inch single, Knightrider. They were one of the first outfits to play the Bruce in those heady days of 1987 and I remember that their line-up then, apart from Tam but including a very young Paul Polosi on guitar, were all left-handed and so I introduced them as The Corriefisters.

They were anything but hamfisted, however, when it came to playing rock, being voted Scotland's 'best local band' of 1983 in a Radio Clyde poll organised by Tom Russell. Their prize was a gig in Tom's Paris Disco in 1984 and, to this day, they have gigged relentlessly ever since – making them the longest-running rock band in Glasgow's long rock history. In an industry where most bands split up faster than you can say 'musical differences', their durability alone earns Tam Toye's Knightrider a place in our book and in our hearts.

Cut from the same cloth as Tam – denim mostly, with a hint of leather – was guitarist Eddie Trainer, who made his name in the local pub band scene with a young and embryonic band called Weeper. From these beginnings he was asked by Stewartie Adams to join his fledgling Lyin Rampant, a bold-as-brass-balls outfit who fitted well into the cock-o'-the-rock scene of the late Eighties and early Nineties.

Glasgow-born guitarist and vocalist Stewartie had only recently returned from the Big Smoke, following the demise of his first band, London-based rockers Tytan, whose record label Kamaflage had gone out of business, pushing already delicate band relationships to the breaking point. (Luckily for Tytan's fans, most of the band's unreleased songs were cobbled together by Metal Masters and released in 1985 under the title Rough Justice.)

Joining Eddie and Stewartie in Lyin Rampant were Tam Creamer (drums), Georgie Pringle (bass) and finally Paul Stephens (keyboards).

The band's album, hilariously titled in an inspired Carry On moment as Up And Cumin', was described in one memorable critique in the Record Magazine as 'a light-metal amalgam of Rush, Journey and REO Speedwagon, indistinguishable from much of the music of its genre'. Ouch! There was some comfort to be taken perhaps in the addendum: 'However let us not forget Stewartie Adams, self-styled walking distillery and one of the best new rock singers I've heard in ages. His vocals make this album worth a listen, at the very least.'

For me, they were so much better than indistinguishable wannabes. I gave them a gig in the Bruce Hotel, where they excelled in playing great and original songs. Of course, excellent performances and originality often count for naught in this dirty business and, just like so many others before them, Lyin Rampant couldn't make that big leap from being great to being amazing. With the untimely passing of Prism records, Lyin Rampant also furled their flag in 1991.

After the split our man Eddie remained undeterred, however, putting together another class act called Danger and I would give the lads a few cracking shows through the Nineties. The highlight of them all was a support slot with No Sweat, a melodic rock band from Ireland, in front of a sell-out crowd in the Videodrome.

Out Of The Frying Pan...

Ah, the Videodrome . . . I got the phone call early one Monday, the morning after I'd just done a seven-band gig in the Mayfair club in Glasgow. Truth be told, I was feeling a little fragile from a hangover and perhaps not at my most enthusiastic picking up the phone. My mood brightened to hear the voice of a good friend, Johnny 'Fury' Cameron. Back then Fury was lead vocalist and guitarist of East Kilbride band The Force, with his brother Duncan (bass), Barry Hilton (keys, vocals and guitar) and Rab McQuillan (drums). They had blagged a major deal with Atlantic Records in New York but were still known locally as the singing taxi drivers as they were all, yes you guessed it, taxi drivers.

But Fury wasn't calling because there was a cab outside my house. He was calling on behalf of Colin Robertson, owner of the Videodrome, who would like to meet to discuss my taking over the Sunday Tennents Live slot in his venue.

I arranged to meet Colin the next day but, I must admit, I had a few reservations. The Tennents Live circuit at the time was, not to put too fine a point on it, crap. It featured a stable of the usual suspects: Hearts and Minds, the Wild River Apples, the Pearl Fishers, then later Win, Thrum, Whiteout . . . the list goes on and on, with the same bands playing the same venues, week in, week out. Even their TLN magazine was crap, despite an annual budget of over £60,000, but more about that later.

My biggest issue, however, was the trepidation of working with a guy who had very quickly become one of the most respected figures in the Glasgow music scene. Colin had been a major force in the Unicorn Leisure team, who not only managed some of the biggest worldwide bands and artists to come out of Glasgow, but who single-handedly restored an ageing Green's Playhouse to the legend that would become the Apollo.

Despite my nervousness, the meeting went well. I had my hair tied back in a ponytail in those days and the first words Colin uttered were: 'Jackie Pallo, how you doin'?' I'd never before been addressed as the famous Sixties wrestler, but that certainly broke the ice – in fact, Colin still calls me Jackie even to this day.

The partnership with Colin was just what I needed. Until then I'd received financial backing from the Bruce Hotel to the tune of £30 a show, later raised when I began DJ-ing too.

Colin taught me so much in our few months together. The budget was £150 a week and I spent £20 of that on monthly billboard posters and fliers and £100 on the PA to ensure that any band playing the Bruce or the Videodrome would have a killer sound. The PA company I used, Storm, belonged my old mate Wilson Reid.

I recently read a bizarre criticism on a web forum from a punter bemoaning the fact that the Nineties' Tennents Live sound was monopolised by Storm or EFX from Edinburgh: 'Everywhere you went it was either one of those two companies but, don't get me wrong, it was a good sound!' So, what are you complaining for? What other issue is there than guaranteeing a good sound?

In fact, my faith in Wilson's talents led me in later years to bring him into Napoleons and the Cathouse. When bands worked with Wilson they got a guy who had worked with the best: Pearl Jam, Dream Theater, the Buzzcocks and hundreds of other world-renowned names.

So, with most of my Videodrome budget spent in advance, I still had to pay for the DJ, catering and security. Success would depend on enough people coming through the doors to cover everything. Well, as they say, I built it and they came.

After the first couple of weeks, when we reluctantly inherited bands left over from the original club, we kicked in big style. I brought in, at considerable expense, Circus of Power from the States, Pat Travers from Canada and Magnum. This last band couldn't get the Barrowlands, so they played my wee club in front of 300 punters rather than miss out on playing for their fans in Glasgow.

We also had Jagged Edge, Heartland, Jezebel and one of the best nights, already mentioned, when Irish rockers No Sweat were more than ably supported by our man Eddie and his Danger crew.

I'd like to think that the lure of live rock was the Videodrome's primary attraction, but I'm sure our midnight licence, which offered a full hour more than most pubs in Glasgow at that time, was a bonus for many patrons. The excuse for the extra-late drinking was the kitchen – so long as I could stick sandwiches and chips and stuff on the tables during the evening, we were laughing.

Well, most of time we were. One night I got a tip-off from a friend up in St Vincent Street that the licensing police were on their way to check the food situation. Unfortunately, the punters had just scoffed the lot and the tables had been cleared, with no evidence left of the picnic. In real danger of losing our extra hour, we panicked, turned on all fryers and bunged in a barrel-load of chips and burgers.

The band on stage at the time must have thought I'd gone to the trouble of buying in dry ice; the truth is the kitchen had become a crematorium for frozen food.

Just as my son Lee came over to say the polis were at the door, I arrived armed with a mountainous plate of fried food and offered the guardians of all that's good a sample of my greasy wares. They politely declined, instead sticking their nappers in to witness the frenzied feeding of the 2,000, looked at me as if to say 'We'll get you next time, Shields.' And departed.

That wasn't the end, though. Early next Monday morning I was woken by an incandescent Colin Robertson screaming down the phone demanding to know where the f*ck were all his chips and burgers for the crowd he'd invited on a VIP golf outing. All I had to offer was humble pie.

Thankfully, most of the time at the Videodrome help was soon on hand for such potential emergencies. Two great pals from my days at the Venue stepped up to the plate: Trisha and Lorna, aka Wax On and Wax Off. Let's just say they earned their nicknames from a reputation for being able to take care of themselves.

All was going well, then, with our culinary reputation until No Sweat came up and the girls found themselves distracted by the lads' Irish charm. We went from staple fare to à la carte dining: every two minutes it would be 'We need more money because the band want this and that'. It was so bad that when, finally, a full-bellied No Sweat left the building and I totted up the catering budget, I hadn't a button left to pay the karate kids their wages.

It took a heartfelt promise of double next week's and glares and a lengthy staff meeting at the bar before normal service was resumed. We never pandered to a band's gastronomic preferences again.

Oh, by the way, Danger played a blinder that night supporting No Sweat. It would become a common refrain, with our local acts often outplaying the big guns.

It was a formidable venue and a great time to be in the rock business in Glasgow. I think Colin realised quite quickly that working with me was going to be a roller-coaster of ups and downs, but with never a dull moment. His Videodrome manager at the time was big Gordon Brown (no not that one!) and we got on wonderfully. The front-of-house bar manager was Old Firm and Scotland footie hero Alfie Conn and completing our top team was the front-of-house DJ, Ian Donaldson, former front boy of boy band H2O.

I must admit I had reservations about a former pop star as a rock DJ and after a wee chat with Gordon we agreed the pub would pay Ian while I gave him a crash course in rock music. I decided the easiest way forward would be to leave a box of albums, with three options for songs on the cardboard sleeves and a few singles – foolproof, you would think.

So it proved for a while, with lots of folk coming in from the bar when the Videodrome's gig doors opened. It all backfired spectacularly, however, when Mike Patton and Faith No More entered the building by invitation after their Barrowlands show in April 1990.

I'd been at the Barrowlands earlier on in the day and met Mike at the soundcheck. He remembered me from the band's Mayfair slot and I joked had he recovered from being booted off the stage by his colleague in rock?

He smiled and accepted my offer of food and free bar and so we had two bands on that night. The headliners were UP, who were formed originally by Bobby Hodgens Bluebell, Stuart Bearhop and Kenny Hislop in 1988, then joined a year later by David Aitken when he left Gun. When Kenny left, the band would bring in Stevie Barker on drums and Raymie Docherty, formerly of Big Dish, on bass.

Managed by Graham Wilson, of Subclub and Night Crawlers fame, they played and recorded prolifically, even shooting a video for a track called 'What's That Song', but broke up shortly afterwards, in 1991.

That night at the Videodrome I told UP I would hold them back for when Faith No More came in. And I told Ian Donaldson that when I gave him the thumbs up he should make a special announcement and announce the arrival of our special guests and play a song. My son Lee was on the door with his mate Stuart Beale when Mike and co. walked up. He waved them all in, gestured excitedly to me and I gave Ian the thumbs up. He made an amazing speech, wholeheartedly welcoming the band, then played 'We Care A Lot', a track sung, of course, not by Mike but by former singer Chuck Mosley.

Heaven preserve us. The band thought I'd orchestrated the entire thing to take the piss and it took a river of free beer to placate them. Dealing with such unforeseen events was never in the job description but, hell, it was part of the fun.

The Free World

The fun was often hard work, too and things were only getting busier. I also took on a Tennents Live slot at Napoleons in Merrylee Road and so I was now doing rock nights at Napoleons on a Wednesday night, the Bruce Hotel on a Thursday, the Venue on a Friday and Saturday and the Videodrome on a Sunday.

With so much rock and so little time, something in my personal life had to go and, after much deliberation, lasting say a sneeze, it was my full-time job.

This was fine because, after a final warning about my timekeeping (the gaffer hated me because I was earning a crust outside work), the offer of voluntary redundancy came up and I left with £4,000 in my pocket. 'Tis a pity the gaffer, in his haste to get shot of me once and for all, chose me to go instead of an engineer just in the door, whose exit would have cost the company nothing. More pity that, had he waited another fortnight, he could have binned me for free anyway because I was taking time out to hit the road with Drunken State on a UK-wide tour. Ah, but only fools rush in.

Freed at last from the day job, it was during this tour that I could focus much more on my management duties, formulating what would become the blueprint for my London showcases. The catalyst for this was Drunken State's disastrous debut in the Big Smoke, set up for Metal Hammer and Kerrang!. The album was just out and doing well and I'd allowed bass player Michael Brash to book the gig in the Royal Standard in Walthamstow, which is in London as much as Aberdeen is in Glasgow.

Humped, the aptly named local band who were headlining, didn't show up, nor did the promoter but around 100 kids did, clutching their albums and EPs to be signed. After a great soundcheck, the Drunken ones were asked to play a full set and encores and, at this point, I heard Humped's manager telephoning the AWOL promoter: 'Get your f*ckin' arse down here, there's a great Scottish thrash band about to take the stage.'

The promoter didn't show and we didn't get paid. We did get great reviews in Kerrang! and Metal Hammer but after the gig the tour van was broken into and a guitar went walkies, as did a jacket with all the band's bank cards in it. We were skint and had been relying on the gig money to get home.

In the end we had to drive the van to a vacant car park and sleep in it until next morning, when the guitarist Dougie Smith could sign out cash from a bank and bail us out.

Badly stung, I swore I'd never get caught like that again.

Thankfully, there were some fine bands finally getting their sound together and being able to experience their live act offered more than enough rewards for me to put up with the trials and tribulations of working in the business.

One such band, if only too briefly, was The Whole Earth.

After the demise of Zero Zero, John McMillan got together with Niv Dyer and a great wee pal of mine, the talented Elaine Downie on backing vocals. In fact, the Downie family seem blessed with more than a fair share of talented singers: Jim Downie is a formidable chanter and my hero Robert Downie fronted his own outfit Cortez, a band I worked with in East Kilbride before taking them down to London.

By this time John was working as a community musician for the Glasgow City Council, organising Open Days and music workshops and drew on the pool of talent before him and thus The Whole Earth were born. The full line-up was John on guitar, keys and vocals, Niv (lead vocals), Tony Regan (guitar and keys), Phil Zambonini (bass), Ian Murray (drums), with Elaine and Pat Stuart (backing vocals).

Their music had a strong funk-rock feel to it – think along the lines of Prince and the Dan Reed Network – while the backing vocals gave a much fuller, more melodic sound.

They were a big seven-piece but always a treat to work with and I remember them fondly as a great melodic rock band who, in the end, simply had the knack of finding themselves in the wrong place at the wrong time musically.

Also cooking in the early Nineties were The Almighty, fronted by former New Model Army and Rough Charm guitarist Ricky Warwick. Joining him were Andy Tantrum McAfferty on bass, Floyd London (lead guitar) and Stumpy Monroe (drums). Andy and Floyd had swapped instruments at a practice and so their rough and ready sound was born.

Ricky was very focused on what he wanted from the band, having spotted a niche in the market, between Motörhead and Zodiac Windwarp. I was introduced to him by his then manager Rhona Walters (Rhona and I go back to the late Eighties, when she was managing La Paz and Hold the Frame). It was at a show I was putting on in the Village Theatre in East Kilbride, featuring Wolfsbane, Drunken State and Centurion, that the bold Ricky turned up in his newly painted biker's jacket, emblazoned with the full Almighty logo.

Ricky and the lads were signed by Polydor in March 1989 and the next year released their first album, Blood, Fire and Love, which had been recorded at gigs in Edinburgh and Nottingham. In the same year they were voted into third place on the Kerrang! readers' poll for Best New Act.

In 1990 they toured the UK before setting off on a short American tour in an attempt to break into that market. A more extensive follow-up tour did not go ahead, although they did embark on a European club tour. Recording began of a second studio album, Soul Destruction, in December 1990 and it was released in March 1991, along with the lead single, 'Free 'n' Easy'.

In February and March they toured the UK, supporting Motörhead and Megadeth, then, in June 1991, embarked on a headline UK tour. The concert at the Town and Country club in London was filmed and released later that year on video as 'Soul Destruction – Live'. Later in the year they supported Alice Cooper on a European tour.

In March 1992 band differences came to a head and the fall-out saw guitarist Tantrum throw one and leave the band. He was replaced by Canadian Pete Friesen, who had played for Alice Cooper and met The Almighty when they had supported the US rocker.

In the spring the band were invited to tour Australia in support of the Screaming Jets, who had just released their Living In England EP and wanted a British band as their support. That summer the band were the opening act at the Donnington Monsters of Rock Festival.

A third album, Powertrippin', was released in 1993, followed by a European tour supporting Iron Maiden, their longest tour to date. This was followed with a support slot at that year's Milton Keynes Bowl festival. In Autumn '93 they finally toured America, but failed to make the hoped-for impact.

On their return they started a headline European tour, but were forced to abandon it after just two London dates due to poor health. In November they parted from their long-time manager Tommy Tee and moved to Sanctuary Records. At the same time they left Polydor and signed with Chrysalis.

Their fourth album, Crank, was released on Chrysalis in late 1994 and they were guests on Top of the Pops to promote the first single, 'Wrench'. More touring followed, then in May 1995 they recorded four tracks for a proposed EP. However, the band decided the tracks were good enough to form the basis for a fifth album and arranged two more recording sessions, recording four tracks each time, so that they would have enough for an album release in 1996. Just Add Life was released in 1996, but later that year they disbanded.

Re-forming in 2000, they released the self-titled album Almighty, replacing guitarist Pete Friesen with Nick Parsons and adding new bass player Damon Williams, formerly of Horse London. A second album, Psycho-Narco, followed in 2001, with Gav Gray replacing bassist Floyd. The band disbanded again, with vocalist Ricky Warwick pursuing a solo career.

In 2002 a compilation album, Wild and Wonderful was released, which included material from the band's three Polydor albums, along with covers.

The Ricky, Stump, Floyd and Pete line-up reformed for benefit shows in January 2006 and then appeared at the 2006 Bulldog Bash. A five-show tour followed at the end of December 2006. In 2007 a second compilation album, Anth F***in'Ology: the Gospel According to The Almighty, was released and this covered their entire career and included a DVD of all their promo videos to date. A lengthier UK tour took place in January 2008 to mark the band's twentieth anniversary.

In November 2008, Floyd announced on the band's forum and MySpace pages that he had decided to leave the band. In December of the same year Tommy Tee passed away and the Glasgow rock scene lost a true legend and a genuinely nice guy.

The heartfelt tribute from the band themselves, in honour of a great guy, says it all:

'Tommy managed The Almighty from 1988 to 1993 and, even after we parted ways, he remained a firm friend throughout. Ricky first got to know Tommy when he joined New Model Army as a live guitar player for their world tour back in 1987. Tommy was their tour manager at that time and would later go on to become their manager. The rest of us were lucky enough to meet him shortly after, as he was one of the main catalysts that started what was to become The Almighty.

'Tommy was one of those people who, when you first met, you liked straight away. He had a huge zest for life, a fantastic work ethic and, above all, a huge sense of fun.

'Tommy was manager of The Almighty from day one, when the band first formed. It is fair to say that he was as much an integral part of the band as any of the rest of us. No idea was too big and he instilled a confidence in us that made us all believe that anything was possible.

'He helped guide the band, from playing to 12 people at our first gig to playing in front of 80,000 people at Castle Donnington and having hit singles and albums.

'We always, to this day, consider him to be part of the band. He always remained a loyal and true friend to all of us, a great family man and, above all, a true gentlemen. He will be terribly missed.

'Tommy, we love ya!'

Ricky, Floyd, Pete & Stump, The Almighty

Songlines

In my quest to bring to you a few of Glasgow's unsung heroes, I had to track down a fair number of people and it was a great joy to find two of the greatest Glasgow vocalists of the Nineties, more so for the fact they are still belting out the songs.

In the late Eighties the foundations of what was to become The Hardline were laid by 20-year-old singer-songwriter Jimi Anderson, who had teamed up with his school friend, drummer Keith Crozier. Under the name Sahara they gigged together with various band members until they placed an advert in the Evening Times for like-minded musicians and recruited guitarist Iain McPhie and bass player Peter Dorman.

Jimi, Iain and Peter hit it off immediately and their combined talent for writing killer songs shone through in 'I'm A Believer', 'Hold On' and 'Out of My Life'. Glasgow's Ca Va recording studios were booked to produce the fruit of their hard work. Peter's younger brother Stag was working at the time as a roadie for Wet Wet Wet and he gave a copy of the lads' demo to Wets manager Elliot Davis. Impressed by the strength of the writing, he gave the band the use of his Pet Sounds studios in Maryhill.

It was both a constructive and instructive period, with the band learning a lot about songwriting and stagecraft from Elliot and production guru Jim Mitchell. The band was off and running.

It soon became obvious, however, that drummer Keith was being left behind and he became the first in a series of line-up changes that was to hamper the band throughout their short-lived career. Todd Macleod was brought in as a replacement, the level of playing and songwriting went from strength to strength and a showcase gig in the Renfrew Ferry was arranged, with a favourable review in the Evening Times by Russell Blackstock added to the CV.

It was at this point the band changed their name to The Hardline, a moniker inspired by an album Elliot had lying on his desk by Terence Trent D'Arby, Introducing the Hardline.

Just as things seemed to be going really well, Jimi broke his leg and was out of action for more than six months. On his return, however, The Hardline were offered a management/publishing deal by Elliot's Precious organisation who thought, quite rightly, that the band's time had come.

Unfortunately, the lads were having serious problems with their gifted guitarist Iain and he was asked to leave the band. Jimi recalls: 'This was to be the biggest mistake we made, because Iain had such a unique style of guitar playing and he was possibly the reason that The Hardline were different sounding to all the other rock bands at the time.

'We could never really replace him or the sound he brought to the table and, in hindsight, we should have brought in a second guitar to beef the sound up a bit more'.

A replacement guitarist was found, however, in Jamie Margey, whose improvisational skills and blues style proved inspirational – his input on songs such as 'Oh Why' and 'Reach Out' kept the band on track. The downside was Jamie didn't keep too well and the pressure being put on him from being in a successful band in full flight took its toll, finally forcing him to bow out.

The next guitarist would be Alan Murray, who was working in Park Lane Studios. Another great player, his was a completely different style from both the band's previous axe men and once again The Hardline's sound would be pulled in a different direction. That said, his playing on 'Same Old Song' and 'Hold On' was particularly inspired.

Once again the band believed they were back on track. The next major setback – yes, it does get rather Spinal Tap at this point – was when Todd left to get married, citing his reasons as a lack of financial support, or to put it another way, being skint and having to be able to earn cash to pay his mortgage.

Todd was replaced by Billy Morrison, formerly of Bronz, whose out-and-out rock style once more changed the band's direction.

Undeterred, the lads went on to play sell-out gigs - including two for me - one in the Bruce and one in the Videodrome. There followed a tour of Scotland, after which Alan decided to leave. This would prove to be the final nail in the coffin. Although the band soldiered on with Steve Vai-styled guitarist Mickey McCluskey, the sound just didn't sit right and they were no longer gelling as band.

By this time Elliot had lost interest and dropped The Hardline altogether. There was one last gig at the Borderline in London but, with no deal and no money for The Hardline, as for so many of the melodic bands of the Nineties trying to make it big in the face of the rising Grunge movement, their 'tea was oot'.

Jimi now lives in York, where he is still singing his heart out and God bless him for that, for he is an amazing rock singer. Don't take my word for it, however. Check out The Hardline track on this book's online listening post.

The second singer I managed to track down only after much hunting high and low was John Higgins, who was frontman for a band called Frontier.

Born in Maryhill, John grew up in Stewarton in the heart of Ayrshire and had put Frontier together in the late Eighties. The core of the band included guitarist Brian Cunningham and bassist Alan Greenwood, with session players Rupert Black (keyboards) and Dave Watson (drums).

The lads sent a home-recorded demo to a handful of record labels and three months later got a call from Polygram Records in London who loved their sound. Several record-company-paid-for Indian curries later and Frontier scored a seven-album deal on Polygram's Vertigo label alongside Texas, Robert Plant and Dire Straits.

They spent over a year recording an album with producers, engineers and session players onboard, luminaries such as Gary Katz (of Steely Dan); Ian Kewley (Paul Young); Dave Bascombe (Tears for Fears); Kenny McDonald (Texas); Steve Jackson (Bryan Adams); Adam Mosely (Rush); Tony Philips (Seal); Wix (Paul McCartney); Tony Beard (Jeff Beck; Hall and Oates; Crosby, Stills and Nash); and Graham Broad (Go West).

With such a stellar cast working with them, it seemed fated that Frontier would push the boundaries and become stars themselves, yet, quite inexplicably, they were dropped weeks later. In the end, only two singles were released: 'Lonely Heart', produced by Gary Katz and a cover version of the Graham Parker song 'The Sun Is Gonna Shine Again', produced by Glaswegian Kenny McDonald.

Frontier should have been huge. With the incredible voice of John Higgins, a great live band and well written, superbly recorded songs, the formula for success was mixed to perfection. And 'Lonely Heart' wasn't even in record stores when Frontier were playing sell-out gigs supporting Wet Wet Wet in 1992.

All the talent in the world doesn't mean jack when fans can't buy your CD, however.

John took off on a new trajectory altogether, rehearsing and recording at the Brill Building for a couple of years with a new band, John Harley and the Pack, which included members of another Glasgow band, Wanted: Donny Little (now guitarist for Paisley popster Paulo Nutini) and bassist Chris Thomas. Drummer George Lundy was later added to the mix.

Producing the new songs, however, was a long and drawn-out process and the results, to be overly kind, were eclectic to say the least.

At this point, John decided to begin working solo alongside producer Sandy Jones, who now owns Foundry Music Lab in Motherwell with Wet Wet Wet's guitarist Graham Duffin.

These new songs had a strong direction yet sounded spontaneous. Sandy seemed able to capture John's great soulful rock vocals with ease. However, his manager, The Wets' Elliot Davis, wasn't convinced. After many shows in and around Glasgow, John decided the track he was on had reached a dead end.

Having met his future wife around this time (an Ozzie lass based in Glasgow as PA to well-known hair-dooist Rita Rusk), John made a momentous decision: he got as far away from the entire experience as he could by moving to Australia in search of a new audience and even adopting a new name, John Harley Weston.

Since then, in a fabulous riposte to those who let him and Frontier down so badly, his career as an independent musician has gone from strength to strength. He won the Australian National Songwriting Contest in 2005, has received accolades from Billboard and Unisong, written for Aussie Rules football team the Brisbane Lions (much like being asked to write for Rangers or Celtic) and has held the number one spot for six months solid on the Australian Indie Radio Charts.

The boy from Maryhill has even been voted one of the top five best vocalists in the independent music world by a heavyweight US publisher.

Although John is in Australia, Frontier are not dead. After placing high in the MySpace band charts, their fans recently demanded new material and with the magic of modern technology, crossing oceans and continents, John and guitarist Brian Cunningham recently wrote and released a new song, 'Be Careful What You Wish For' – unless, of course, you're wishing for a full-on Hardline revival.

The Blues Is His Business

My favourite gig at the Videodrome was when Pat Travers, the blues legend from Canada, came a-calling but this was more for the gutsy performance of the support act. In fact, it had been no-brainer when it came to choosing his warm-up (I always insisted to agents that I wasn't interested in paying £50 support fees to a band no one had heard of who couldn't pull the skin off their own porridge, never mind a crowd) and so the call was made to Shifty and Big George, aka Big George and the Business.

Pat's gig had sold out in advance so I offered George a choice of the support fee plus beer, or beer and a free, limited guest list – the Business had attracted a huge following of bikers and I had no intention of letting them all in for nothing.

George went with door number one, the fee and the beer, with the kicker: 'F*ck that lot, they should have paid for their tickets.'

And so with my son Lee minding the door and no guest list, George and I hid through the back guzzling the beer. Sure enough, it wasn't long before Lee came hunting for me. There was a large contingent of ladies and gentlemen at the door seeking free entry.

Reluctantly, I approached the assembled mass and right away sensed an air of hostility emanating from the herd of black leather. When I informed them of George's decision regarding guests, their self-proclaimed leader took me aside, with a huge bare arm around my shoulders and very quietly and politely informed me that it wouldn't be good for my health to refuse hospitality to his gang of scallywags.

At this point he opened his coat to reveal a rather large sword, one that would have made Excalibur look like a toothpick. At once, I shouted: 'All in! Women, children, cats and dugs first, then anyone else who fancies it!'

It wasn't worth getting a my head cut off. And, anyway, we wouldn't be losing cash as the gig had already sold out.

What a gig. Pat Travers would be brilliant, but Big George and the Business had all but blown him away. I watched Pat standing at the side of the stage, looking somewhat sheepishly on in admiration at the big man who is George Ross Watt living his blues, slamming his guitar like the impossible love child of Jimi H and Stevie Ray Vaughan, singing in smoky tones that could make Joe Cocker sound like a pre-pube choir boy.

And yet George had been born under a less than auspicious star. He came screaming into this world in Glasgow in 1958 and was brought up in the slum housing that in those days was home to the Clyde's shipyard and engineering workers. It was a hard school beginning that gave him a reactionary and insatiable lust for life. It also made him uncompromising when it came to the blues rock he loved and composed – and, as the years have rolled on, that he has shown to have been blessed with a God-given talent to write and play.

After playing in the local rock band circuit for many years, he was hired by one of his all-time heroes, James Dewar, he of Stone the Crows and the Robin Trower Band. Unfortunately, after four years, James's ill health forced the break-up of the partnership. With James retired, Big George knew the time was ripe to form his own band.

At first he tried a number of different formats, using his immediate network of local musicians, until he finally contented himself with a three-piece band. Greg Orr played drums and Tam 'Shifty' McLucas played bass. Shifty also took over managerial duties and his innate organisational skills propelled the band on to the next level.

Theirs was a raw, gutsy, uncompromising style of blues and it was only a short time before they had found critical acclaim for their live shows, first in Glasgow and before long across the UK. A debut recording, The Alleged Album, enhanced a growing reputation for a rocking style of blues that, try as they might, no other British band could quite match.

The next logical step was for Big George and The Business to hit the road and they toured extensively throughout the UK and Europe. When time permitted, the band eventually managed to return home long enough to write and record a second album, All Fools' Day. By this time their reputation had spread across the Atlantic and, in 1992, they were invited to appear at the Montreal Jazz festival, following this with a series of gigs in Canada.

Since those days the band has made frequent returns to Canada and America, sharing many a stage with the likes of Buddy Guy, Larry Davis, John Campbell, Bo Diddley, Mick Taylor, to drop only a few names.

It was during one of their many sojourns in Canada in the late Nineties that the band stayed long enough in Montreal to record half of their next album, Home of the Wolf. The title track was inspired by Big George being made an honorary member of the Mohawk nation in the wake of a rapturous gig at the Kahnawake reservation.

While the first album was gutsy and raw and the second saw the band expanding with piano and other instruments, Home of the Wolf explodes with the fulfilment of the potential shown in the first two.

In recent years, between touring and penning music for television shows, George has become closely involved with the Glasgow community, teaching kids the magic of music, in particular the art of playing guitar. He has also produced and recorded a large number of young up-and-coming bands from all over Scotland in his custom-built home studio.

I can honestly say it's been a privilege to have worked with such a talented and blessed musician; indeed, he was one of my main inspirations for this book.

At the time of writing, George is recovering from a mild stroke and I wish, along with you dear reader and the hundreds of thousands of people all over the world who have witnessed his genius, that he has a speedy recovery. The Blues just don't feel the same without Big George and the Business.

At Least No One Got Shot

The end of the Videodrome came very swiftly. After seven glorious months, Mitsubishi bank bought Robertson Street, Brown Street and York Street to form part of a huge redevelopment plan and that was that. It wasn't long afterwards that Napoleons went bust, too and so that was me back to putting on shows at the Bruce Hotel and the Venue.

As if I'd nothing better to do, at the same time I approached Stuart and Tam with regards to a Sunday rock club. Thus was born the shortest-lived rock club in the history of Glasgow. The idea was to host an afternoon gig to bring in shoppers and day walkers then stay open all day till midnight. Everyone thought this was a mighty fine idea and, in the wake of a few weeks' advertising, I'd booked the first month's bands. We were set to open the Time Warp Rock Club on a Sunday in early January 1991, with local lads Indian Angel.

The gods of rock 'n' roll mayhem had other ideas. Didn't the River Clyde burst its banks the same day? The club was below river level and the Clyde came pouring in. In the Monday edition of the Evening Times, my old mate Russell Blackstock reported: 'After the loss of the Videodrome and now the Time Warp, Robert Fields has set up a stall in the Barras selling lucky white heather.' Ha, bloody ha, Russell.

Despite our near biblical wash-out, we were able to relocate over the bridge to the Hacienda, where we had a few great months, despite making do with a wooden dance floor that swelled up to near bursting point whenever it rained.

Thankfully, Glasgow's rock scene seemed to have more to offer.

It was at a Birdland gig in the Mayfair on 24 February 1991 that I was made an offer I couldn't, but did, refuse. The blond mop tops were one of my favourite indie bands at the time and so I went along to the gig in the Venue's big sister armed with my album and a 12" single ready to be signed. Always the groupie!

And here didn't I meet a man by the name of Stuart Clumpas at the bar? Now, Stuart and I went way back. As well as the damp dance floors, I'd been managing a great band from Dundee called Adam 8*1*2 and Stuart and I crossed paths frequently in Dundee's premier night bolt, Fat Sam's and whenever he braved a trip down into Glasgow to do his university union gigs.

Well, Stuart said he wanted to talk to me about a wee business proposition. Nae probs, says I, but could he get my stuff signed?

He was too busy, I'd best seek out his better half, Judith. This I did and I finally found her in the cloakroom and handed over my vinyl. Had I spoken to Stuart? Yes, well I'd best get my bahookie to the office in King Tut's Wah Wah Hut in St Vincent Street on the morning of Monday.

Being the inquisitive wee beggar I am, I squeezed it out of her.

'Stuart and I want you to put your rock bands on in our pub. How do you fancy the chance to manage the big gig as well?'

The gig was big. Although it hadn't quite grown into the huge commercial monster it is today, Tut's, or the Pub as I like to call it, was a big deal. I repaired to the bar to mull it over.

Ah, but the curse of being a rocker at heart. Try as I might, it wouldn't and just couldn't add up. Tut's was never a venue where rock punters hung out. It isn't to this day. Yes, these days they will turn up in droves to frequent the place when the bill suits, but at that time, in the Nineties, everyone with rock in their heart hung out in the Solid. More importantly, the Venue was still cooking big style, so it all felt wrong. Come on, even their juke box was mince. It still is.

At the end of the night I met Judith and enquired about my Birdland stuff.

'You can pick it up on Monday at the meeting.'

I never did see it again. I phoned on the Monday, made my apologies and thanked them both for thinking of me, but explained I didn't feel Tut's was the right place for rock bands and punters.

Thankfully, to keep my mind off what I'd lost out on – I really liked that Birdlands12" – at this time I received a call from Donald of the Clan MacLeod. Donald, who had gone to school in East Kilbride and was the driving force behind First Priority, had teamed up with a young glass collector from the Howff in the mid Seventies by the name of Michael Pagliocca.

Together they had opened a rock club in Bathgate and now were of the opinion that the Venue needed a wee kick up the butt. In direct competition they stuck in £50 each and hired the Hollywood Studios in Brown Street and relaunched it as the Cathouse.

Why was I called? As the DJ and promoter of the Venue, they wanted me not only to DJ their new gaff but plug it as well in my current capacity. You couldn't fault their business acumen.

But I couldn't do it, as the Bruce was the same night. So I papped off the dark-haired one who was helping me in the venue to do it with all my records sent on in a taxi every Thursday for a few months until he got his own collection.

Glasgow's rock punters welcomed the Cathouse with open arms – this is quite easy when you consider most of them wore sleeveless jerkins. In fact, so successful were the first three months, Donald and Michael decided to buy the lease for the place and take on the Venue head-to-banging-head by opening up Thursday through to Sunday.

Now here comes the best bit. Donald had become involved with a band called The Crows and he was champing at the bit to put on live bands. The problem was and it wasn't just a wee hiccup, that back in the Nineties, unlike today, bands' agents were very loyal to their regular venues. It didn't help that the man responsible for putting on rock acts in Glasgow and who had been the oil in the machine for the past few years, was yours truly, still engaged to the Venue.

Thus it came to pass that the first band to play the Cathouse were Donald's Crows, playing under the pseudonym Wild Spirit.

Donald's Crows were fledglings who took flight from the abandoned nest of First Priority. Ross Allison was vocalist and he was complemented by Donald (guitar), Ross Thom (guitar), Billy Bowie (bass) and Keith Falconer (drums). Falconer? Should he have been allowed near crows? I digress. Again.

Anyway, their very first demo attracted major airplay on the wireless, with Radio Clyde, Forth and BBC Scotland very kindly strengthening the bands' reputation. Their debut single, 'The Sun Went In', released on their own Raven records, was played on Radio One by Janice Long and extensive local and national airplay followed.

A major deal with EMI followed, as did tours with big acts such as The Damned. The lads released another couple of singles and would later contribute a couple of tracks to my Gathering of the Clans CD, by which time they had been joined by the former Ransom duo, drummer John Clelland and guitarist Iain Gordon.

After the Crows played their debut Cathouse gig, I was asked to meet Donald again. They wanted me to put on bands. What the hell? I decided that it wouldn't do any harm. This was a Sunday gig and so it wouldn't affect the Venue anyway.

The first major band I booked into the Catty was the aptly named Tigertailz, a bunch of Welsh glamsters. It was a great night and the place was well suited to be a rock venue: the right acoustics, the right atmosphere and a crowd who appreciated the music. It was just round the corner from the Solid Rock Café, so we had a market on our doorstep.

Things were going well and, asked for a third time to join the Cathouse full-time, I finally said yes. The Venue lay down and rolled over like a wee puppy and wouldn't fight back for me.

The Cathouse turned out to be one big roller-coaster of a ride; it was all very exciting but the pressure that was put on me to organise the bands was almost overwhelming.

My main mission was to book all the bands and help the DJs fill the three floors with punters. The basement floor, meanwhile, was handled by Mr Harry Margolis, who had captured a niche market through the decades with his big band sound. He was a very much respected figure in the Glasgow music scene and a perfect gentleman to boot.

Every weekend he compèred a club that catered specifically for singles and divorcees and it was all I could to stop the rock kids wandering downstairs to have a sneaky peek at the clientele, not to mention scupper all manoeuvres from the oldies, who liked to climb the stairs.

Ach, it was fine and dandy; sometimes it worked, sometimes it didn't, but everyone was having fun.

The only time trouble came calling was one Sunday night. One of Glasgow's most, shall we say, celebrated businessmen came to the Cathouse door and immediately set off the metal detectors as he was carrying a gun. The gentleman in question was sent packing and his first reaction was to begin threatening to shoot anyone who stopped him gaining entry.

To their credit, if everyone else's astonishment, the Honey Monster and Wee John on the door stood their ground. There was a tense stand-off until, much to everyone's surprise, mine especially, our would-be guest asked for me by name. I'd later learn that he remembered we had once met at a party in a Glasgow club, appropriately named Bonkers. And so Michael flung me down the stairs to the front door and promptly locked himself inside his office.

I tried to compose myself, first by visiting the loo. At the door I was greeted with a smile, a firm handshake and the reassurance that hell would freeze over before he came inside a club unarmed. Valiantly trying to ignore the climactic grumbling of my own bowels, I suggested we moved round the corner for a wee chat, where I reassured my new best friend that we could sort this out. On a spur, I asked if I could see his piece.

Now, I know nothing about guns, but it was one of those black ones that has a magazine for the bullets that slides out. I put it to our VIP, in a way that suggested he'd thought of it first that if I kept the magazine out of harm's way in the club's safe, then as far as anyone else was concerned the gun was still loaded.

He smiled, shook my hand and handed me the magazine. I slipped it inside my pocket – boy did that thing feel heavy in my breeks – and we strolled back round the corner.

I flashed the Honey Monster a quick glimpse of the bullets behind our VIP's back and told him that our guest would be enjoying the dancing this evening so could we please turn off the metal detectors. Our man entered the Catty. On the guest list, of course.

I put the cartridge, inside a brown paper bag with a raffle ticket

Selloptaped to it, in the safe. It was faithfully collected at the end of the night when our man took me aside and complimented me on the way I had handled it. He'd just wanted to see what I was made of, he told me, with a bellowing laugh. Right then, I was thinking, I was potentially made of a big trooser-full of jobby.

I met our man again recently and we had a laugh about that night. He told me he still has the raffle ticket. Apparently, it makes him laugh. It still makes me want to go the toilet.

Catty That Got The Cream

We had a great team at the Cathouse, but nothing works so well as the personal touch – or so I had to keep telling myself – and it was yours truly who replicated the 60′40 billboard poster campaigns from Napoleons and the Videodrome, who delivered the posters and fliers by hand and on foot (never had a car), in person contacted all press and media contacts. But there was, still is at the Cathouse, a huge professional team, including Storm PA and my old mate Wilson.

I honestly believe no other rock club, before or since, could host such an incredible range and variety of rock talent so early on: Pearl Jam, Dream Theater, Paradise Lost, Fudge-Tunnel, Terrorvision (with the Henry Rollins-managed all-girl band Die Cheerleader in support), Badlands with Jake E. Lee and Ray Gillan, Rubicon (who were actually The Fields of the Nephilim), the Buzzcocks . . . yes, the Buzzcocks . . . and not forgetting all the local bands worth much more than their centurion's pouch of salt.

Local talent. Boy, did we have Glasgow's finest Nineties rock bands playing the Cathouse in the Nineties!

Let's start with Balaam and the Angel. This outfit had formed in the Eighties around the core of the three Morris minors: Jim, Mark and Des. They began their career playing working men's clubs – where else? They were brought up in Motherwell.

A children's cabaret act, they were South Lanarkshire's answer to the Jackson's, encouraged by a father who made sure Top of the Pops was mandatory viewing. Relocated to Cannock in Staffordshire, an early gig saw the bare-footed trio playing cover versions of Sixties love paeans. Nice. But not rock.

Shoes or not, having founded their own Chapter 22 Records with manager Craig Jennings, they made a debut album, World of Light, which appeared in 1984, inspiring a support slot on tour with The Cult.

Virgin Records saw the potential and The Greatest Story Ever Told came out in 1986, followed by support slots with Kiss and Iggy Pop in the US of A. Another album in 1988 was followed by the addition of a new guitarist, Ian McKean, who was enlisted to perform additional guitar parts on Live Free or Die.

Ah, but the garrulous Goon rears his head again for then, suddenly, nothing happened. They were dropped by Virgin and their first tour for over four years took place in 1990. Press speculation that Mark would join The Cult as a replacement for bassist Jamie Stewart came to nought when Cult singer Ian Astbury publically decided the boy from Motherwell was 'too much of a frontman'.

In the Nineties, when they were playing the Cathouse, the lads truncated their name to Balaam, marking the switch with the release of a mini-album, No More Innocence. Today, they're still playing away on the club scene and releasing fine albums.

Young Guns

Baby's Got A Gun were an East Kilbride-born band from a time when everyone you knew was in a band. They were born into a New Town, which had everything you needed and nothing you wanted. No rehearsal rooms, no guitar shops, nothing. Anything you wanted you had to find, make for yourself or leave town.

Garry Borland was vocalist and he was joined by Richie Simpson on guitar, Murray Dalgliesh (formerly of The Jesus and Mary Chain) on drums and Jackie Crane on bass.

Their first gig was at the Heathery Bar in Wishaw and soon they were playing all over Lanarkshire and east to Edinburgh. At the time Garry and Jackie were living in Edinburgh and found it easier to promote gigs in the capital, particularly at the Jailhouse and La Sorbonne, regularly playing around the city and out into Fife.

At this time Jock McDonald of the Bollock Brothers took a shine to them and quickly hired some recording time at Pier House Studios, where the band recorded a 12" single called 'Suicide Girl', produced by Donald McLeod.

Sales were good but were increased substantially by a poster produced by the band themselves promoting the single and live gigs. It was plastered all over Glasgow and, unfortunately, all over the newly laid mosaic stone side of the Bruce Hotel in East Kilbride. As if this wasn't bad enough, at the bottom of the poster was a further information number and the line: 'Ask for Liz.' Nothing unusual in that until you telephoned and were put through to the Queen's personal secretary.

The boys from New Scotland Yard were not impressed and scurried up to East Kilbride and nicked poor Murray.

It may not seem like much now but when the local and national papers got hold of the story the band gained huge notoriety and gigs became crazy, dangerously over-wrought affairs. Finally, Jock McDonald got the band out of the country by inviting them to play at a gig to help the families of the victims of the Herald of Free Enterprise disaster off the port of Zeebrugge.

The group was riding high at the time but things were not well within the band. Inside weeks of each other both Murray and Jackie left, leaving Garry and Richie looking for new members to keep up the momentum. Enter Billy Duncanson, a Glaswegian drummer who had recently been playing with local band the Special Guests and long-time friend from East Kilbride Bill Cochran, bassist with another local band, The Ceremony.

The new members revitalised the band and were soon writing and recording new material with a harder, tighter sound than was evident before. Baby's Got A Gun were gigging constantly at this point, trying new songs out in smaller clubs before showcasing them at large support gigs with David Bowie, Thunder and touring with The Almighty.

Pretty soon the lads came to the attention of Dave Ramsden, the man behind Oh Dear Management and plans were laid out for a foray into Palladium studios with Keith Fearnley to co-produce an album and a single to be released on the No Mercy label.

And so it came to pass that the start of the Nineties saw the new Baby's Got A Gun fully fledged. The band announced the release of their studio album Up, a ten-track album of tough yet melodic rock songs that brought out the best parts of their live performances.

Excellent reviews, months of touring and full-spread features in the music press led to radio sessions for Tommy Vance and more gigs, notably at the Marquee with Zodiac Mindwarp, Glasgow's own Barrowlands with both The Damned and The Almighty and Edinburgh's Usher Hall, opening for Little Angels.

The lads also took time out to produce a promotional video for the single 'Take the Ride' with TV producer and husband of Scots journalist Muriel Gray, Hamish Barbour, which received significant broadcast time and airplay. Unfortunately, the group found their relationship with their manager becoming increasingly precarious. They fired him and signed, instead, for London-based Management Group International, who had at various times Paul Kossoff and Jim Capaldi on their books.

Rejuvenated by their new deal, the lads performed a scorching showcase gig at Nomis Studios in West London for the Warner Chappell Publishing Company. Within days they were once again heading south to sign a publishing deal with the prospect of some major financial backing.

Hoping to capitalise on their deal, Baby's Got a Gun renamed themselves the Bleeding Hearts, hoping to distance themselves from their previous manager and to polarise their musical direction. Again they entered the studio with money from their publishing deal to record a four-track EP called God Save Us, released on an independent Dutch label in 1994.

The EP, however, took its toll on the band. It took a full year to record and with management wrangles and diminishing public appearances, the lads dropped off the radar altogether.

Bill left the band in 1995 and has since recorded an album and gigged with members of Jane County and the UK Subs, in hard-edged Glasgow punkers Them Or Us.

Garry, Richie and Billy, meanwhile, have recorded under the names Smiler and, more recently, the Heavy Drapes, supporting the New York Dolls and playing gigs in the underbelly of Scotland's Central Belt.

Many more Glasgow bands would come through the doors of the Cathouse. One night I got a phone call from Derek Forbes. He had just left Simple Minds and had formed a new band called The Flys and wanted to play the Cat.

His new band comprised Derek, Ray McVeigh, the guitar player from

The Professionals, a London band who had Paul Cook and Steve Jones of the Sex Pistols in their ranks. On vocals and guitar was Roy White, erstwhile singer of pop duo White Torch and on drums was Brian McGee, who, like Derek, was a former member of Simple Minds and Propaganda.

Of course, I was more than happy to get the lads on for a gig, but was flummoxed by the name. Derek explained: 'The name we chose, The Flys, was originally Dangerous Flys, a hastily written note posted on the fridge in Charlie Burchill's kitchen, left by his father, with the proclamation: "Be careful Charles . . . dangerous flys hovering". I knew at that moment where Charlie got his eccentricities from and it wasn't Scottish Power.'

The wee beasties, dangerous or not, recorded Signs of Madness at the studio of Scot's singer Fish in Haddington. In all, they would playing only a handful of gigs, but the greatest – yes, you knew I would say this – was at the Cathouse.

Another great, yet shortlived, band at the Cat were Goth heroes the Dream Disciples, who were formed in 1990 by singer Col Lowing, Sid Bratley (guitar and keyboard), Gordon Young (guitar and keyboards) and later Karl North (formerly of Rosetta Stone, bass).

Their musical style, which combined elements of Goth, industrial rock and electronic, saw them sell around 16,000 albums. Their real thing, however, was working onstage and they toured extensively around Europe, culminating in a swansong at the Whitby Gothic Weekend in April 2004.

With so many bands clamouring to get on stage at the Cathouse, I was having to work 90-hour weeks and the pressure was mounting. I realised it was time to enlist some help, so I brought in Lesley Glenn Bryden to help me with the running of the PR side of things.

If you look at the Cathouse nowadays they have around five or six people doing my job, but back in the Nineties we were all self-taught, learning the business as we went along: there were no college or university courses then, so it was just a case of rolling up the sleeves and hoping that, if any mistakes were made, eventually it would all even itself out.

Having eked out a little spare time, I turned to my next adventure in rock, persuading Donald and Michael to form a record label. My idea was to put out a compilation CD of all the best unsigned Scottish talent playing the Cathouse once or twice a year.

The debut for Catscratch Records was the Gathering of the Clans CD and a special tour was put together to showcase the songs. Eight bands were represented, each providing two songs: The Crows, Adam 8*1*2, Drunken State, Crisis, Real, Gobstopper, Dr Pop and Dunderfunk. The CD was well received in the press nationally and we were commended for at least trying to stir the stovies in the face of what was becoming an alarmingly apathetic and downright glib Glasgow music scene.

Thankfully, not all of us old rockers were giving up the ghost and there were plenty of talented young musicians coming through who were willing and able to take up the torch.

Marcha Fresca were fronted by the energetic, if unfortunately named, Michael Jackson on vocals and backed up magnificently by Blair Sutherland (drums), Gary Taylor (guitar), Carl Bridgeman (bass) and James Savage (keyboards).

They were a musical chimera, a creature whose DNA evolved from a musical stew that incorporated funk, rock, pop and dance. Listening to Marcha Fresca for the first time was, as you might expect, a rather confusing experience. But once you got it, theirs was a truly unique sound: they were and still are one of my favourite bands from this era.

I put them on an all-nighter bill in the Mayfair and Marcha Fresca just blew everyone away. Consummate musicians, they were also charismatic on stage, bare of chest and soul. If I'd been their man, I'd have bussed the lot of them straight down to London for a major showcase, but their management waited another full year before trying that and by then any momentum, certainly the freshness of their sound, had been lost. They were just one more band whose tea was oot.

Of them all, only Carl is still playing away with a nascent band, Destino. He is also a music tutor and does masterclass bass sessions with the Glasgow Music Academy.

Lest we forget the magic of Marcha, let's take a look at what List scribe Fiona Shepherd wrote when they were at their peak.

'If there has been nothing new and original in rock music since the mid '50s to '70s, or wherever you choose to draw the line, then no one has told Marcha Fresca. After months of self-incarnation in a Paisley rehearsal studio they're itching to untether their all-new hybrid of dance and rock. But before you point them on the road to Manchester note that the rock is with a capital H and M. 'Music has been going in so many different ways,' states Michael Jackson, lead vocalist. 'So much music's been factionalised: that's why we're not one certain thing anymore – we're trying to bring it back together.'

'To the point that they've taken it upon themselves to conduct their own descriptive term for this unholy marriage. Thus the science of Frescology is born, beckoning bare-torsoed from the gaggle of posters that currently mantle the hoardings of Glasgow.'

Michael enthuses: 'We take the best bits of every style of music. I used to go to dance clubs but I like raw guitars, so the perfect logic was to put them together but leave out the dodgy elements of heavy metal – like the cucumbers and the sexism.'

He makes their genesis sound so simple, but for the band Frescology was as much a learning process as a natural evolution. Drummer Blair explains: 'We used to think that if we mixed rock with a dance element we had to have four bars of rock, then four of funk then back into rock. We were trying to force the busy bass lines on rocky songs when all we needed was a straight one.' On paper this sounds incredibly diffuse but in performance it makes sense, as an audience at the Paisley studio recently discovered.

There was this girl dancing the way they do in the clubs and there was a guy next to her head-banging and that really summed it up for me. Perhaps there is nothing new in music, but there is nothing sacred either. Marcha Fresca are free to do what they want any old time.

Another Cathouse favourite in the Nineties was an outfit called The Ocean, who were made up of the cream of a number of disparate local bands: Gun, Up and The Right Stuff. David Aitken was on guitar, Brendan Moon on bass, Jackson Wilson drums and Stevie 'Hammond' Doyle on keyboards. The head honcho, however, was their frontman Ger Craig.

I can still vividly recall a stunning show at the Cathouse when they supported Aussie rockers, the Screaming Jets. When Drunken State split up before the Gathering of the Clans tour, The Ocean took their place, putting on a great show in the Marquee.

The lads were riding high on the wave of debut album Silver and so I helped set up a showcase in the Swan in Fulham for Dante Bonutto of Atlantic.

'It should have been a big shoo-in. Silver was earning rave reviews at the time. Consider this tribute from Steve Athwal of RAW magazine, ignoring, if you can, the ridiculous portrayal of our nation as some God-forsaken Arctic tundra:

'Hailing from the frozen wastes of Scotland, where they've already cut a considerable swathe, Glasgow's self-proclaimed 'visionary rockers' The Ocean have released an album chock-full of killer songs. Silver is a power-hungry, Hammond organ-imbued sleazy slab of Stones-like grooverama, all wrapped up in silver trousers. The Stones' influence is more apparent in Ger Craig's vocals, which recall Jagger at his early Seventies best, but there is enough originality here to cast aside accusations of plagiarism.

'Midnight Heaven and Stay Crazy are infectious proclamations, while Take Me Back to the Ocean really shows off the band's ability to pen a memorable song. Here the guitar of ex-Gun slinger David Aitken develops into an aural tornado, ably backed by the rhythm assault of Brendan J. Moon (bass) and Jackson Wilson (drums), while Stevie Doyle liberally douses everything with his living, breathing Hammond.

'The peeling screaming intro of Silver Into Gold (cut me up and eat me) gives way to a precisely executed guitar solo but it's the Jaggerisms of 'TV Heads' that really grab the attention. The Ocean are really brimming over with an almost zealous self-confidence and Silver does nothing but confirm that their belief is well justified.'

I get the impression our man Athwal quite liked the album. The cover was painted just like the Gathering of the Clans sleeve by artist supreme Brian Waugh who, of course, was the bass player with Heavy Pettin'. I remember, on seeing his portfolio of science-fiction paperback covers, for which he later became renowned, I asked him why Polydor never allowed him to contribute to Pettin's sleeves. Apparently, at that time they had an army of in-house artists and used them. Brian added: 'They told me I was a bass player and just to concentrate on that.' Brian is now one of the world's most sought-after artists, with exhibitions on both sides of the Pond. Most recently he's been producing one-off stained-glass masterpieces.

Needless to say, nothing came from the gig and the band split up after giving it their all. Stevie still runs his studio in Glasgow, David Aitken is playing in Ireland, while Brendan Moon went into band management.

Ger, the last time I saw him, was having health problems and Jackie

Wilson has disappeared off everyone's radar.

One of the last bands I put on before leaving the Cathouse for the first time, were one of Glasgow's best-kept rock secrets, the McCotter brothers' Mudshark. I'd worked with them in the past, through all their incarnations, such as Phoenix and High On Water, but they'd really brought it all together this time and secured the interest of Rab Andrew. Rab had been a van driver for Beggars Opera in the Seventies but now he was one of Britain's top managers. Along with his sidekick Gerry McElhone, he ran the much-respected G&R Management company, who handled Gun, Texas, Slide and Primal Scream.

Signing Mudshark in Germany, where, it seems, for reasons perhaps best known to Freudian analysts, there will always be a healthy metal scene, proved a masterstroke as Britain at the time was busy wallowing in that slough of despond called Grunge. The band released their debut album and single in 1995 and toured both Britain and Europe, supporting bands such as Dog Eat Dog, Sugar Ray, Prong, The Melvins and Iron Maiden.

Jason Newsted of Metallica voted Mudshark's the best album of 1995, while earlier the same year Jerry Ewing wrote in Metal Hammer:

'Chances are that Mudshark are the heaviest thing to emanate from Scotland (Drumchapel) since the heady days when the N.W.O.B.H.M. offered up the near legendary Holocaust (from Edinburgh). But don't let that put you off. They sound nothing like each other. Mudshark·are very much a family unit . . . the brothers Ian (guitar and vocals), Sammy (guitar), Derek (bass), joined by cousin Peter Haggarty on drums, have just completed a stunning set at this year's T in the Park festival and by the time you read this will have played at In the City in Manchester.

'Things are beginning to happen for Mudshark and their debut album will be released on Pony Music this month. A strong set of solid metal wavering between (if one has to make a choice) Metallica's uncompromising power and Soundgarden's ear for melody. But throughout, Mudshark stamp their own youthful identity, especially on tracks such as 'Showtime', coming across like a young British rock band full of hope.

'Like many young bands today, Mudshark don't comply with any musical movement in the way that the late Eighties saw myriad lousy AOR bands trying to emulate Bon Jovi, but are instead forging their own metallic path with enough suss and originality to suggest their future could be a rosy one.'

Alas, just like so many bands in this book, even though they'd got off on the right foot in Germany, for Mudshark it turned out to be a case of 'wrong time, wrong place'. So it came as very welcome surprise to hear that the lads have re-formed and a new album is being recorded. I, for one, though I'm sure I'm not alone, cannot wait to hear it.

Moving On

The Cathouse and the Bruce Hotel were going from strength to strength. The Catty, in particular, was hitting all the right notes, especially when it acquired a new addition to the family. Jackie Lamb, erstwhile of the Venue, was the very first female rock DJ in Glasgow. She was also the best.

Sadly, while we were ecstatic to gain her services, my inspired move killed the Venue stone dead. Oops!

With new signings and such a huge buzz emanating from our live gig scene, a lot of people were beginning to sit up and take notice of the Cathouse. After I'd put on Grunge gurus Pearl Jam, I was approached by Mark Gillan of Tennents Live. At the time they had a monthly mag called TLN. It had taken them until now to admit defeat and declare the ridiculous rag a failure; instead, they would use the money to sponsor an outdoor festival and I was approached with a view to putting on what was, in essence, the very first T in the Park.

Now this was a big deal, too big for us at the time. It was 1992 and we were doing well at club level and our first Barrowlands show was coming up. In the distant future big festivals and gigs could be organised, but this seemed premature.

My feeling was it was far better not to be known as the first people to make an arse of T in the Park. Much to Donald's annoyance, I knocked back Mark's offer.

We all had a lot of learning and growing up to do and the reality of our situation bit deep soon afterwards, with two horror Cathouse gigs that culminated in both Les and myself leaving.

Fish, former frontman for Marillion and at that time held in regard by many as something of a Scottish legend, wanted two nights in the Catty for a certain fee. I was told in no uncertain terms that no way were we going to get caught up in proffering that kind of money for a 'has been'. A heated argument ensued.

I went back to the big man Fish and offered him a different deal for less cash but whereby, if he sold the two nights out (piece of cake), we would double his money by giving him, less expenses, all the money from the door. He thanked me and we shook on the deal. On stage and at the door he did the business for all of us. But it was the first time that my judgment had been called into question and, on the night itself, what was already a tense situation was further inflamed when at the end of the two shows both bars had record takings.

I was called a Mickey Mouse promoter in front of the bar staff by one of the powers that be: why hadn't we given Fish the fee he'd asked for in the first place? The Cathouse could have split the rest.

You just can't win sometimes.

It all came to a head a few weeks later with the Average White Band, who turned up at 4.45 p.m., having forgotten to mention in their contract that all their gear was American and therefore needed a couple of AC/DC transformers.

Les and I raced around the corner to a plant-hire firm to grab the necessary gear before it closed at 5.00 p.m.; in fact, the salesman, God bless him, gave us the essential free and gratis, because Average were his favourite band. I put him on the guest list, along with his wife and son, later taking him upstairs to meet the band.

All was well, the night was saved? Nope, I got destroyed because, unbeknown to me, I had arranged to let in a former manager and worse, on the guest list.

The big bad cauldron well and truly boiled over the next day in the mother of all arguments. I decided to make a sharp exit, as is my normal defence mechanism in such situations.

Once it had all calmed down, we kissed and made up, but for me, it was all over. Things were too fraught and, anyway, how could I top the few special years that I had put together in there? Les felt the same way.

My last act would be putting on the Buzzcocks. But it was now time to move on and take my next step in life. I had by my side my trusted and, by now, knowledgeable brother in arms Lesley Glenn Bryden. Like me, he was relishing a fresh challenge without the threat of anyone 'going f*ckin' bananas'.

New Faces

The first thing when setting out a new business plan is to identify your market and, as I've always worked with rock bands, our new company would use live rock music as its lifeblood. The name we came up with was Face Two Face Promotion and Management and, as Les didn't want the logo to look like that God-awful vase that was kicking about at the time, the one where the two faces are in silhouette and could be taken for a vase if looked at a certain way, we asked Brain Waugh to design a logo. It came out like the Top Gun emblem. Smashing!

By leaving the Cathouse, I would have to relinquish my connections with all the agencies for our Glasgow shows. The Bruce, however, was still dealing with major touring bands so I still kept in touch and got a couple of juicy wee shows. The first gig we did was Babylon Zoo's Sony showcase in Sauchiehall Street's Nice 'n' Sleazy prior to their number one single 'Spaceman'. That went well, aside from the anti-beer human shield: Sleazys have this terrible habit of allowing bar staff to change beer kegs during a band's performance (the store room is at the back of the stage) and so Babylon's crew formed a chain in front of the stage until the band had finished.

We also set up our new HQ, an office in Gairbraid Avenue in Maryhill next to Pet Sounds studio.

Despite the fact that the one-off live gigs and the rock nights at the Bruce were doing well, I still hankered after a bona fide Glasgow rock club and so I approached Stuart and Tam at Henry Afrikas. Their place had just been refurbished and looked ideal as a wee club in direct competition with the Cathouse, playing all the stuff it didn't.

Because Grunge music, emanating from Seattle, was all the rage back then, we called our new venture Not Seattle. It worked well until the place was sold and the building flattened!

Thankfully, we had another iron in the fire, forging the careers of Glasgow's youngest bands by organising showcase gigs for them in the Big Smoke. In fact, through the Nineties hundreds of bands from all over Scotland got the chance to play various venues, such as the Marquee, the

Swan, the Kings Head, the Orange and, the one we used most, the Underworld in Camden, where one of my most loyal friends, Jon Vyner, was doing the business for us.

The formula was simple. We hired a double-decker coach, a suitable venue, made 300 VIP invites, posters and press releases and organised a local band to headline. With everyone sharing the one backline, we shoved all and sundry on the bus. We left Scotland at midnight on a Sunday, picking up stray musicians from all over the place en route and arrive in London at 10.30 the next morning. We set up stage, enjoyed a couple of hours in the Big Smoke before soundchecks at four. All bands were off-stage and the gear packed up again for our departure back up north at midnight.

Les, meantime, was offered the chance of some part-time work with the Music In Scotland Trust and not long after secured a full-time position, with the opportunity to put together a Scottish music directory.

At this point Lee McLean, of IMS and soon to be of Ico Ico and Nemis fame, gave me a wee office in Gordon Street, for which I was extremely grateful and I ran Face Two Face from there. They also had a magazine operation in the building called Monitor and next door was another mag called Bigwig.

One of my first ventures from the new HQ was to put together START (Scotland the A&R Tape). This was a compilation of six new artists, which I regularly sent down to record companies with a reaction sheet for their comments and thoughts. It was a great idea, the kids in the bands loved it, of course, but after just a few months the A&R folks began to rubber it because it did their jobs for them. Soon, it had to be cancelled, due to a lack of response on the reaction sheet.

One band, however, elicited a response from rock music lovers, response sheet or not. Amid the daily entourage of bands and hangers-on coming in and out at Gordon Street were Subway and they really were something special.

Originally, a four-piece – Ewan Galbraith (vocals), David Sherridan (guitar), Steff Mellan (drums and who went on to play briefly with Twin Atlantic) and James Riddell (bass) – managed by local video producer Robbie Moffat, they released their first single 'Something, Nothing, Everything' in 1993. It received a great review in the Evening Times and soon they were being lauded as Glasgow's answer to The Damned.

Subway became a five-piece with the introduction of William Codona on rhythm guitar and played as The Permissive Society at a charity gig at the old Cathouse in Brown Street for 'Cash for Kids' in December 1993.

My old mucker Tom the DJ Russell appeared on the night to lend his support to the event that raised hundreds pounds for charity. The band also played at a special gig on Calton Hill in Edinburgh that ended unceremoniously in drunkenness with the band playing catch with the buses on Princes Street. Due to the band's antics, James Riddell decided, for his own safety, to leave.

Subway played the Glasgow and Edinburgh circuit many times with no discernible success – this was the catalyst for a radical change that drummer Steff spearheaded. He saw the future for a three-piece punk band in 1994, drawing influences from Hüsker Dü but adding a songwriting style that owed more to the Buzzcocks.

Ewan was asked to leave the band in favour of David on vocals and guitar and William on bass. David Sheridon, William and Stef Mellon went on to record an album of material at Busby's Riverside studios with brilliant engineer Johnny Cameron (formerly of Sneeky Pete and The Force), but the magical songs that were recorded sadly never ever saw the light of day.

It was at this time that David began displaying a talent as a songwriter, a skill that was enhanced by William's input. They became the core duo, with a great understanding of what was required musically for the band.

Subway began to play more high-profile gigs, with support slots to The Macc Lads, Kinky Machine and The Supernaturals. After many line-up changes, the band settled with the following members in 1996: David Sheridon on vocals and guitar, William Codona (guitar/backing vocals), Steve Doyle (keyboards), Joe Connor (drums) and Lewis Rankine(formerly of the Silencers on bass).

David and William also joined a music business course in Glasgow City Centre that was fronted by the now defunct Monitor music magazine. It was there that surrealist author Jack Blade and ex-Primal Scream guitarist James Beattie began managing the band. James instilled a real sense of dynamics into the band's music and John found the core duo the perfect foil in the shape of keyboardist Steve Doyle, who had been in The Right Stuff (signed to BMG in 1990).

Subway recorded and released a two-track tape with the stunning opening track, 'From the Heart' and B-side 'Dolly', though a mere 200 copies were produced and sold. The band played storming gigs on a mini-tour of the UK that included Glasgow, Edinburgh, Newcastle and the Isle of Arran. It was at a packed Trillions bar in Newcastle that Guy Holmes of Gut Records saw the band and took an interest in signing them. However, band tensions were rising. Joe left Subway after the Newcastle gig but William stayed on for the love of the music and because of his friendship with David.

After a visit to Glasgow to see the band rehearse with a new drummer at Steve Doyle's Stuffhouse Studios, Guy asked the band to set up a gig so he could come back and watch them play live – each time the band booked a gig, Guy couldn't make it (Gut Records' attention was on the well-known Liverpool band Space) and, after several attempts to play for the record company, the band unilaterally ended the interest from Gut Records.

Subway lasted more than eight years, until 1999. David and William went on to recruit new members but their last gigs were a T in the Park T-Break competition at my own club, Strawberry Fields, followed by a London showcase in the Underworld in Camden attended by Geoff Gillespie from Atlantic Records, who was even then interested in signing the band, but who a few weeks later lost his job in an A&R cull.

David and William reformed as The Dream Society in 2007, with William's wife, Rachel Codona, on bass and Steve Doyle back on keyboards. Steve lasted one rehearsal. Kyle Calderwood was recruited instead on keyboards (he now plays with former Soup Dragons and Teenage Fanclub drummer Paul Quinn's band, The Primary 5).

The band re-recorded 'From the Heart' at Riverside Studios and the track won XFM radio's uploaded track of the week, winning almost 10,000 votes.

Sadly, the band broke up again in 2008, due to David's ill health.

Steff went on to play drums for Glasgow outfit Twin Atlantic. David, Euan and James are now back together for a Surfing Gnomes reunion.

William and Rachel, meanwhile, are now enjoying new careers in band management and promotion.

Who Let The Cat Out The Bag?

After just a few months running Not Seattle, I was in the Cathouse one night and, much to my surprise, found myself asked to come back into the fold as a DJ. I guess it made good business sense to both parties: I still had a loyal following of guests who wanted to hear rock music. I accepted.

At the same time I was approached by Stuart Adams, who was opening a rock club along the Clydeside next to the old Daily Record building. I went along, but didn't fancy the location – back then this was smack bang in the red light district. So I gave Stuart the phone number of Peter McLean, so it was he who opened the quite excellent Power Station.

Back at the Cathouse, old Harry Margolis had now left the building and the bottom floor was vacant. This meant we had a three-floor club, which was unique in Glasgow and so Lee and I took our Not Seattle show into the Catty basement and made it the busiest and best floor of the three.

With increasingly high rents, however, a new venue had to be found and it was decided that the Cathouse should be re-housed in the old Disco Viva, in Union Street. Now, this venue only had two floors and it was Lee and myself who got the short straw and there was no place for us behind the decks. To make up for this slap in the coupon and to aid with the relocation process itself, I was offered a management position.

And so the Catty moved to Union Street, but I realised very quickly that my contribution would be, let's just say, minimal. So minimal, it wasn't long before my time was up.

And as the cat flap shut, another door slammed too. After ten years the Bruce Hotel was bought over and I was usurped by a young pretender DJ. He pleaded his own case to the new owners and I was out on my bahookie.

Undeterred, I approached my old friend Paul Watterson, who owned the rival Stuart Hotel and my live band nights were moved there on a Sunday, with Fridays and Saturdays spent DJ-ing.

It was at this time that I met a Jack Daniels rep by the name of Stevie Davidson, who let slip that the owner of Ivory Black's, in Oswald Street, Glasgow was looking for someone to re-launch it. A meeting was set up and, though I'll not bore you with the details, it saw me re-mortgage the family house and go into partnership with Jack Flanagan who owned the building.

Thus was the Strawberry Fields nightclub born.

First the ageing PA was ripped out and replaced by a new one. Fitted by my old pal Wilson Reid, it doubled up as the sound system for the club.

My son Lee's colour schemes for the new interior were spot on and we opened with an amazing In the City show, which featured Alex Dickson's Fling.

From the very beginning we had a great local music scene going. Initially, I let the bands keep their ticket money, but these nights were soon losing a fortune because the bands weren't pulling in the punters.

I changed the deal to a £50 deposit, returnable if there were 30 tickets with the band's name on them. It still didn't work; the bands would rather lose the deposit and get the chance to play than make any effort to pull in the bodies I needed to cover costs, in the region of £400 just to open the place.

When finally the bands cottoned on to the fact it was a good idea to have an audience, the live gig night was complemented by a '60s/'70s/'80s nightclub. Things were soon going so well that I brought in my sister Joyce and her lovely big man Chris to partner me in the club and we said goodbye to the owner.

In fact, we were doing so well that we were having to turn punters away and needed to increase the size of the place to a capacity in excess of 500.

The year was 1999 and it was the best of times. I called Alex Dickson, who by this time was touring with Robbie Williams and I offered him and his entourage a private party after his SECC gig. It was Robbie's 25th birthday party and so the invite to celebrate at my place was gladly accepted. Alex, Robbie and the gang came down and played an hour of covers for an invited audience.

Robbie sang cover versions of songs by The Who and Elton John. He even did a punk version of the Take That hit, Back for Good along with half-a-dozen of his own songs, including the massive hit, Angels.

It was the first time I had met Robbie and when he arrived at the club, he came up to me straight away and said: 'You're Robbie - I've heard so much about you.'

I replied: 'No, you're Robbie and I've heard even more about you! But I'm the good looking one.'

He just winked and said: 'But I'm the rich one with all the money.'

At that, we had a right good laugh together.

I knew Robbie was a huge Star Wars fan, so we decked out his dressing room in the club with Star Wars posters and memorabilia. He loved that and took all the posters with him at the end of the night with a big thank-you.

At one point in the night Robbie started a food fight in the dressing room when he lobbed a trifle all over a girl in a white dress. She retaliated by picking up a pizza and throwing it in his face. That's when he shouted: 'Food fight' as half his entourage made a hasty exit out the door while the other half joined in the buffet battle. I suppose it's one way to get through a £500 spread in double-quick time.

There was also a poster on his dressing room wall of the Rat Pack and when Robbie saw Peter Lawford on the poster he smashed a champagne glass off the picture. I asked him why he did that and he said that Peter Lawford had helped cover up Marilyn Monroe's murder.

I asked him if he was a fan and he said he worshipped Marilyn Monroe. So I took him into my private office and showed him my little shrine to Marilyn. There was a life-size cardboard cut-out of her, posters and books on her life and we spent about 20 minutes talking about Marilyn.

I gave him a book called The Assassination of Marilyn Monroe, by Donald H Wolfe that had been signed by the author 'To Robert'. Robbie said he couldn't take it as it was signed to me, but I told him you're a Robert as well, so he thanked me and took it.

Robbie was so down to earth and a lovely guy. It was amazing. I never in my wildest dreams thought Robbie would come to my club.

Celebrations there may have been that night, but a dark cloud was looming on the horizon. We had applied for a £60,000 loan from a drinks company against sales so we could enlarge the place – there was an empty garage next door and by moving through we could increase the capacity. But someone from the drinks company overheard my conversation with Alex about Robbie Williams coming over and told me that if I got a photograph of Robbie holding one of their bottles in his hand, we would not only get the entire loan in double-quick time, but I would get a grand for my back pocket and two season tickets to Ibrox.

Robbie, the star that he is, was more than happy to pose for a few pictures, despite the fact that he was earning millions in sponsorship deals for doing just this very thing.

Unfortunately for me, the £60,000 loan didn't come through all at once and instead, was paid in three £20,000 instalments. By the time I realised this was the case we had stripped the place down for the big refurb and very soon I was £40,000 short. If I had known the entire £60,000 wasn't going to be forthcoming all at once, I wouldn't have closed the club and ripped the place apart.

In the end, we got the Strawberry Fields refit finished, as I made up the shortfall by using money we had in the bank that had been set aside for other bills we had to pay. That meant we were heading for financial trouble. Heading into the 2000s, life in the Glasgow rock scene was, on a personal level, fraught with worry.

Thankfully, there were enough minstrels, poets and vagabonds in the new millennium to fill my heart with hope and excitement and some measure of optimism. Let's find out who they were . . .

THE NOUGHTIES

At The Other Extreme

I HAVE to admit that the punk and hard core-death-extreme metal scenes in Glasgow were not really my bag. I did work with some of the top international punk bands – Eddie and the Hot Rods, the Buzzcocks, Rancid, Dog Eat Dog, Sick of It All – and thrash bands of the era – Nuclear Assault, Death, Carcass, Cancer, Mordred, Dark Angel, Death Angel – but, in truth, the local outfits never really came on to my radar.

It seems only fair, therefore, to enlist the able help of two men in the know, a duo who can shine a strobe light on their respective scenes.

Gerry 'Atrick' Rodden is a veteran of the Glasgow punk scene and has been with the same band, Fire Exit, for 30-odd years – they have a new 15-track CD out, which features Knox from The Vibrators, who played with Chris Spedding in the early Seventies.

Currently writing a book about growing up a punk rocker in Renfrew, Paisley, Glasgow, then London, he remembers his first ever gig at the Apollo in Glasgow was a bill featuring Nazareth and Heavy Metal Kids. Here are his memories of the pick of the punk . . .

'Well, we can't start the punk scene in Glasgow without a mention of some of the Seventies outfits. After all, they set the foundations for a new wave of local bands to 'spread the word' in the Glasgow area.

'It was hard starting out as punk rockers. The earlier punk rock movement was made up of kids from Glasgow, Paisley, Renfrew,

Johnstone, East Kilbride, Motherwell and other surrounding areas and coming from the schemes was hard. It still is for anyone 'different', even today.

'They would meet at Bruce's Record Shop or Listen in Glasgow to find out the latest gossip: what bands were playing and where. It was all very underground, unlike today.

'You see, Glasgow City Council had banned punk rock bands from playing in the city until they gave the thumbs up after an arranged gig in the late Seventies in Candleriggs.

'If you wanted to see bands, you had to travel to the Silver Thread Hotel in Paisley on a Wednesday night; Disco Harry had all the punk bands on so it was the only place to see the bands legally. Unknown to Glasgow City Council, however, some Glasgow venues were putting bands on: The Grafton, Mars Bar and Chivagos among them. Good on 'em!

'These places were full of various individuals with slashed tops, bin bags, safety pins, all-colour hair and shirts they made themselves. Punks would be drinking in the audience one week and form a band and play the following week: Dennis Boy (The Provoked Stank Lifters), Gerry Attrick (The Pencils), Rev Olting (The Backstabbers), Big Frank (The Shock) and Jock Strap (The Straps).

'Through the years new venues opened their doors to the punk scene and among them were Hurricanes, the Amphora Tiffany's, Burns Howff, the Mars Bar, Rock Gardens, Glasgow Tech, Art School, QMU, 13th Note, Cathouse (Rat Trap) Rooftops-Nite Moves, Barfly, Arena, Strawberry Fields (now Ivory Black's), Rockers, Nice 'n' Sleazy, the Garage, ABC, Classic Grand, King Tut's.

'The Paisley area, too, was booming – as well as the Silver Thread, there was the Bungalow Bar (this hosted most bands up to the late Eighties), the Arkleston Inn, Jorries, Paris, TUC Club and Paisley Tech, to name but a few.

As rock in the Glasgow area developed, it was clear punk rock influences were an integral part of the music scene throughout the Eighties and Nineties and even to the present day and the venues have catered for every taste.

You know punk rock bands don't all bawl and shout. Real music and styles came shining through over the past 33 years in bands like Ex-

Cathedra, 3D Scream, Fire Exit, Pink Kross, Burning Boy, Machine Gun Etiquette, 4 Past Midnight, the Red Eyes, the Zips, Defiant Pose, Gun Rubber, the Snipes, the Destructos, Roxette, the Haemorrhoids and, of course, the Amphetamines, Defiant Pose, XS Discharge.

All these bands slotted into the punk scene, but each had a very different style and all were original.'

Our second aficionado is Kelvin Cooke, who is recognised as the main man in his field of extreme rock. He plies his trade in Ivory Black's and is Glasgow's top hardcore, death and black metal promoter. This, then, is his case for the defence:

'Scott Kennedy stands precariously balanced on one foot on the edge of the security barrier and gazes at the carnage in front of him with a big grin on his face, which I can just see peeping through his black mop of sweat-drenched hair. The date is 1 August 2009 and Ivory Black's is crammed full of young metal fans destroying each other.

'Scott is in complete control, with Ali Richardson blasting away on the drums behind him, Craig 'Goonsy' Gowans and Dave Lennon on either side, shredding on guitar and David Provan on bass. He is on top of the world. With more than a million hits on their MySpace site and an acclaimed performance at this year's Download festival behind them, Bleed From Within are back home to launch their new album Humanity to a hungry Glasgow audience baying for more of their frenzied, technically brutal metal.

'I look at them and at the sea of bodies in front of me and part a wee grin myself, because this is why I love what I do.

'In 1994 I came to Glasgow to do a 'normal job', but coming from the tiny town of Duns in the Scottish Borders, where nothing much happens, I soon immersed myself in the Glasgow nightlife and, as I was playing bass in a death metal band, Engulfed, at the time I sought out local gigs to see what bands were around that we could play with.

'One such band was Confusion Corporation. Hailing from Dumbarton, they were an amazing blend of aggression and melody, with highly talented musicians. With Malcome Douse on vocals, Alan McFarland on lead guitar and backing vocals, Charlie Perrat on guitar, Dougie on bass (replaced by Danny McNab after the 'Confusion Begins' demo 1994) and Derek Quizzy Hughes on drums, I saw them for the first time in Nice 'n' Sleazy's some time early in 1994 and was blown away.

'They had everything that I wanted to hear in a metal band at that time: they mixed death metal and thrash with beautifully crafted melodic passages; they had clean vocals mixed with manic squeals, grunts and chants, usually delivered insanely by Quzzy while torturing his snare drum with incessant blast beats.

'This band had to be signed but, alas, in the greater wisdom of the time, they were overlooked for countless run-of-the mill bands from south of the border. It's a real shame that this band were never given the recognition worldwide that they deserved, but their influence is still to be felt in the Glasgow scene today. Alan McFarland and Danny McNab are now playing in Man Must Die, while Charlie Perrat and Quzzy are the mainstay of the insanity that is Co-Exist.

'Throughout 1994 and into 1995 I went to hundreds of concerts, from small underground gigs to major events at the Barrowlands and I put my first gig on in Glasgow in 1995 in Nice 'n' Sleazy's (thanks, Mig!).

'In early 1996 my constant gig-going and subsequent hangovers played a part in the demise of my proper job and I plunged myself headlong into concerts. In the early days I was organising gigs in Sleazy's, Ragnarok (which became the 13th Note Club, then the Barfly), the Rat Trap (Brown Street) and then later on in the Arena (Oswald street), the Cathouse, the Garage, the QMU, Strawberry Fields (which is now Ivory Black's) and, in that time, I have met literally hundreds of local bands all of whom I won't be able to remember or mention here, but there follow some of the ones that have caught my eye and ears over the years.

'**ACHREN** play 'blood metal', a crushingly heavy blend of black metal, death metal and thrash. They formed in 2003 with the aim of forging raw, filthy, 'heavy as f*ck' metal. They released Fury of the Northmen and Wings of War. After reviews such as 'brutally technical black/death/thrash with the shredding and violence turned up to 10 . . . a fearsome live act' (Metal Hammer) it was obvious they had something good going on, but I always thought they wouldn't be complete without a bassist to help provide a solid foundation to Gordon's pounding drums. We had a chance meeting with them in 2005 in the 13th Note – they were upstairs drinking while I had a gig downstairs with a folk band called the Sulphur Children, featuring bassist Miranda Bradshaw. I persuaded them to go down and see her play; they did and quickly added her to the line-up.

'In 2006 they were voted by Terrorizer readers into the Top Ten in their unsigned metal bands category and supported bands such as Onslaught, Dismember, Devil Driver and Destruction, which enhanced their reputation further.

'They toured Finland in 2007 with Perfect Chaos and in 2008 recorded Blood Soaked Banner with Dave Chang as producer. Miranda left in early 2009 to be replaced by John Clark Patterson.

'Achren will continue to pulverise throughout Europe and spread the word of Blood metal for a while to come yet I hope.

'**BLOB** – They were nuts, death metal, grind and stupidity all rolled into one. The first time I saw them I loved them – I was chuckling all the way home, but you had to see it live to get it. Mad vocals and humorous song titles ('I Jizzed on the Duracell Bunny') were mixed with squeals, mad expressions, furious grinding and lots of catchy riffs. The line-up was Cha on vocals, JJ (of Co-exist) on guitar and Johno on drums. Blob invented Slut Metal/Porn Grind . . . 'nuff said.

'**BROKEN OATH** – I first met vocalist Lee Marshal way back in 1998 when she was about 16 and in a school band called 187. I remember I booked them for a gig at the Arena alongside much older extreme bands and the band started getting funny looks when this wee tiny 'fragile' girl gets up on stage. Two seconds later all their jaws were on the floor when she delivered a brutally aggressive and controlled vocal performance worthy of the most extreme male singer.

'She also scared them half to death with her diving antics. It was obvious she was a natural, but 187 didn't really do her justice as she was always more extreme than the music. So she moved on and in 2001 she helped set up Broken Oath – this band suited her style way more with their mix of Hardcore and Metal. They balanced her powerful delivery with music to match and they released their first demo, which sold out almost instantly.

'After some line-up changes they toured throughout the UK, meeting up on their travels with Eviscerate AD from Peterborough, which spawned a split CD release with them on Unity Worldwide Recordings.

'A tour of Europe followed and then Blood Cleanse the Streets was released in 2006 through Runktion Records. This gave Broken Oath a much higher profile throughout Europe and they rapidly built up a big fanbase. They toured with Burning Skies and appeared at the Filled with

Hate Fest and BFLBU festival in Belgium.

'In 2007 they released Given Half A Chance, also on Runktion Records and continued playing destructive live shows to enthusiastic crowds. On 12 August 2008, Broken Oath split up. It's a shame; they were a great Glasgow band.

'**CEREBRAL BORE** – They play death metal/grind, have self-funded tours all over the world and last year I was glued to their blogs on MySpace as they got themselves to the States and toured for a month or more across thousands of miles in a van entirely powered by cooking oil topped up from various diners and fast food joints. Over the years Bore's Paul and I have had a few run-ins but it's all cool now and I wish Paul, Mcdibet, Kyle and Davie all the best.

'**CHURN** – Formed around the mid to late Nineties, the line-up stabilised around 1999 with Rab Kennedy on vocals, Scott Walker (guitar), Gerry McGrath (drums) and Graham Lapper (bass). They were an angry bulldog of a band: furious guitars and drums, all marshalled by Rab's unique vocal delivery. I saw them play many times and watched them get better and better with various tours down south, always winning new fans on every trip.

'Their most famous moment was announced to me in a phone call from Scott, when he told me that McVities wanted to use one of their songs in an advert. You may have seen it. It was the one with the girl playing the record backwards to reveal the message 'Don't Eat the Biscuits', then when she releases the record you can hear Churn playing loud and clear: I would recognise Rab's vocals anywhere. All was good but it came to a sad end when Rab had to quit singing due to throat problems after advice from doctors. Their final gig was on Saturday, 20 September 2003, at the 13th Note Cafe.

'**CLAN D** – My memory is a bit vague here but I remember them having about seven members with the bassist, guitarist and drummer looking like Slayer and the front three singers looking like East 17 . . . and then their was a guy on decks. Metal meets Rap and Dance in the Nineties. They were different from anything else in Glasgow.

'**CO-EXIST** – Founded by Charlie Perrat after the demise of Confusion Corporation, the first incarnation was more of a hardcore band fronted by John Heeney (of Clan D). So on what Charlie regards as the first actual Co-exist demo, he thanks 'John Heeney's Co-exist R.I.P. Because the new animal was a much more vicious beast, with the omni-present Quzzy on drums and Danny McNab on bass, they proceeded to perform some of the most violent, insanely crazy gigs I've ever been to.

' I remember during one of my Six Hours of Hate gigs at Sleazy's, Quzzy taped a microphone to his mouth and dived into the crowd with arms flailing and squealing pig noises, scaring the hell out of a bunch of unsuspecting kids at the front. Over the years they have delivered brutal demos of grindcore/metal and released their first album, Surgical Removal of the Teeth, Nails and the Drilling of the Kneecaps, featuring Paul Catten (Medula Nocte, Murder One) on vocals to much acclaim.

'Following ups and downs, the line-up is now back to three and the lads have just recorded their new album and are hoping to get a new deal. I hope they do, because they are one of Scotland's and the UK's nastiest bands.

'**DAEMONOLITH** – They play old school black metal without compromise and have supported Mayhem, Gorgoroth, Taake, Averse Sefira, Throneum, Infernal War and Negura Bunget, to name but a few.

'**DIONYSUS** – They played heavy metal/power metal/black metal heavily inspired by dragons and fantasy stories, with keyboards to add to the atmosphere, but have now split up. The line-up was Big Gee (vocals and bass), Graeme (keyboards), Danny (guitar), Starezy (guitar) and Mike (drums).

'**GODPLAYER** – After Confusion Corporation split up, Alan McFarland formed Godplayer in 2001 along with Joe McGlynn, Darryl (bass) and Stevie (drums), later replaced by Danny McnNab (Confusion Corp) and Gerry Mcgrath (Churn). They also added a second guitarist in Rob Coverdale. They played very technical metalcore/death/thrash with angry-as-hell vocals. Recently Joe, Alan and Danny have been concentrating on their other band, Man Must Die, but I'm sure Godplayer will rear its head again for another storming gig or two.

'**MADMAN IS ABSOLUTE** – I've known Jimmy Madman for a long time, though I can't quite remember when I met him. If anyone deserves to get his band signed its Jimmy. The band is made up of cool and technically brilliant musicians delivering complex and brutal metal and they work as hard as anyone touring up and down the country, blowing away crowds wherever they go. The line-up has changed over the years, with many drummers coming and going, most recently Kevin (Mendeed) replacing Matt (now with Man Must Die). Original vocalist Tony left in 2008 for personal reasons but Jim has a new solid line-up with vocalist Adam Holt and I'm hopeful they can get a good deal. They have played hundreds of gigs and have supported many bands, most notably Napalm Death, The Haunted, The Berzerker, The Black Dahlia Murder, Stamping Ground and Raging Speed Horn.

'**MAN MUST DIE** – Formed in 2002 with Alan from Confusion Corporation/Godplayer on guitar, Danny from Confusion Corp on bass, John from Regorge on drums and Joe on vocals, they play brutal technical death metal akin to Suffocation and Kataklysm and right from the start things looked good for them. Their first demo was recorded in early 2003 and a song was placed on MP3.com – within a few weeks it was number 1 in the worldwide death metal charts.

'From this they were invited to play at the Maryland Deathfest of 2004 but before that were signed by Retribute records in August 2003 and released their debut album Let's Start Killing in 2004. This and their numerous live shows up and down the country, brought them to the attention of US label Relapse, one of the most respected extreme metal labels in the world – it would be the dream of many an extreme band worldwide to be signed to them. In fact, up to 2005 no UK band had been signed to Relapse and so when Man Must Die put pen to paper that year they became the first UK band on the auspicious label.

'In 2006 they headed to Canada to record their next full-length album, The Human Condition, their first on Relapse. They were happy with the result and felt it captured both their melodic and brutal sides perfectly. The Human Condition was released in 2007 and they promoted it heavily by touring Europe.

'After this prolonged bout of touring they parted company with John Lee and brought in Matt Holland (Madman Is Absolute/Sons Of Slaughter) on drums and started work on their third album, No Tolerance for Imperfection, recorded in 2008.

'They went back to play at the Maryland Death Festival in May 2009 and toured in Europe with Macabre and Japanische Kampfhörspiele. This is when they met guitarist Rene Hauffe of Japanische Kampfhörspiele and a friendship developed on tour. He learned the new material and joined Man Must Die as a second guitarist.

'No Tolerance for Imperfection was released on Relapse in the US on 4

August 2009 and in the UK and Europe on the 10th.

'Having known Alan and Danny since the days of Confusion Corporation and Joe and Matt for a good ten years, I'm immensely proud of the lads and what they have achieved. I knew how much Alan wanted this but I thought it wasn't going to happen after Confusion Corporation didn't get the recognition they deserved.

'Hopefully, there is more success to come for them and they continue to proudly represent the Glasgow/Scottish extreme metal scene worldwide.

'**MENDEED** – This band were from Dumbarton and I ended up knowing them pretty well. They formed around 2000 and started as more of a nu-metal band with their first demo and then in 2002 released their first EP, Killing Something Beautiful. They got a good bit of stick locally for being a nu-metal band but they progressed, getting heavier and heavier, scrapping old stuff faster than I could keep up with so, unless you had seen them that first day, then you didn't know them at all.

'They worked harder than any other band I know and it paid off in 2003 when they released the As We Rise EP through Casket Records – this attracted the attention of Rising Records, who signed them in late 2003 and they released the From Shadows Came Darkness EP.

'Their style was much more melodic death metal/power metal by now and they supported Dragonforce on two full tours. Their music was getting played on rock radio stations and their popularity was growing by the day. They made a video for the single 'Ignite the Flames' and it made it on to the playlists of MTV2 and SCUZZ. I got a call one night from an excited Chris, who told me: 'I've just seen myself on Headbangers Ball', which obviously doesn't happen to many bands from the Glasgow scene.

'They continued to tour, supporting more well-known bands: Cradle of Filth, Slipknot, Anthrax, Napalm Death, Trivium, Fear Factory, Avenge Sevenfold and Bleeding Through.

'In 2005 they released their first full-length album, The War Will Last Forever, on Rising records: it was well received and attracted the attention of Germany's Nuclear Blast Records. The album was released worldwide through Nuclear Blast in 2006. This was amazing – a wee band from Dumbarton sitting in the same label roster as Manowar, Messuggah, Testement, Nile, Exodus and Enslaved, to name but a few.

'They were nominated for best newcomer at the Kerrang! and Metal

Hammer awards in 2006. Alas, it was all to turn sour. Not long after they had released their second album, The Dead Live By Love, in 2007, the band issued a statement saying:

'Mendeed have regrettably broken up due to irreconcilable differences with our manager. We would like to thank all of our fans for believing in us and helping us get as far as we did. I really wish things would have turned out differently for us. Thanks to everyone who had faith in us. We'll miss you all.'

'**PIGSCUM** – Formed in 2002, they mixed elements of grindcore, hardcore and metal. The line-up was Scott (Churn) on guitar, Quzzy (Co-Exist) on drums, Alan 'gtr' Darryl on bass and Deek (from Goatfucker.com) on vocals.

'**SYTH** – They are unashamedly a heavy metal band in the classic style of Iron Maiden, Judas Priest and Helloween, with gallopy riffs, widdly widdly guitar solos, tales of battles and warriors delivered with high-pitched, ball-bursting vocals. Fantastic . . . I love my cheese! The current line-up is Niall Russell (vocals and guitar), Barry Fitzsimmons (guitar), Allen Bell (bass) and Mark Connelly (drums).

'As I write this, I realise how much fun I have had over the 15 years I've been in Glasgow. I've booked and seen so many great gigs and Glasgow has had and still has an amazing amount of extremely talented and extremely brutal and heavy bands.

'I just wish that some of them had had a few more breaks. I was fed up of seeing crap English bands getting signed much more than the bands up in Scotland, but hey, maybe, I'm biased.

'I'm sorry if I haven't mentioned your band, I only had a short space to write about the extreme metal scene in Glasgow but here are some more of the notable bands that I've had the pleasure to meet along the way: Amok, Paradox, Pig God, Ripcage, Divide, Regorge, Serenade, Concept of Time, Pathogen, Evidence Of Trauma, Argonath, Covenant, Azriel, Chaosphere, Embolysm 2005–2008, Dirt, Sinthetic, Sanguinus, Scordatura, Spacejunk, Black Sun, El-Chupacabras, The Threat Remains, Delay Is Fatal, Burning earth, Maelstrom, Grant me Revenge, Switchblade, Scream, Anihilation, Stillborne, Splitbac, Alba Gu Brath, Left Hand Element, Farseer, Attica Eage, Circle Of Tyrants, Chasm, 15 Times Dead, Novella.'

ROCK AROUND THE CLOCK

E'VE come a long way from the days when rock and roll was just a wean, bravely singing and strumming into the wind. In the 2000s not only has the genre grown up, it has spawned an entire new family. And so now we have underground, progressive, metal, nu-metal, emo . . . basically, this brave new decade has music to satisfy every taste.

Bands leading the pack at the outset of the decade were Linkin Park, Papa Roach, the Foo Fighters, In Me and Puddle of Mud. A bolshie wee boy called Eminem was also bringing his commercial hip hop rantings into the equation, while Zak Wylde's Black Label Society have kept the heavies in dreamland. Supergroups, such as Audioslave and Velvet Revolver, jumped on the band wagon, being horsewhipped by Wolfmother and The Answer in keeping alive the memory of Zeppelin, Free and Cream, with a retro sound steeped in the early Seventies.

Glasgow's up-and-coming bands, naturally, have been influenced by all of these sounds and the early days of the 2000s saw the emergence of Logan, Yashin, Hiding Place, DB Sixtyeight, The Ivans, The Cosmic Rough Riders, Dead City Riots, Flood of Red, Red Snowman, Ampersand and the Hedrons. Sticking to their trad rock guns and God bless 'em for it, were God's Twin, Attica Rage, Ernest and Nightrider.

The Solid Rock is 22 years old this year, while the Cathouse is 19 years young and the city has never had so many rock clubs and pubs going at the same time, which is great news for all of us, punters and promoters. Joining the Rock and the Catty were Rufus T. Firefly, Rockers, The Crow,

Maggie Mays, Firewater, Ivory Black's and Sin at the Soundhouse.

It's not all shiny and new, however. Many of the acts we met at the start of this book have taken to the stage once more. Cream re-formed, as did Led Zeppelin and Northwind. SAHB are still selling out shows and Maggie Bell is still touring, as are Black Sabbath, Deep Purple, Judas Priest and Aerosmith.

This year alone I've seen live gigs by loyal members of the old guard: Uriah Heep, Iron Maiden, Whitesnake, UFO, Mötley Crüe, Journey, AC/DC and most recently Robin Trower, with our very own prodigal son returned, Jack Bruce.

Glasgow now also has its own dedicated Rock Radio station, playing classic rock 24 hours a day and still featuring our very own rock warrior, Tom Russell.

With the excitement of the new decade came, too, the sadness of saying goodbye to old friends. We said our farewells to Jimmy Dewar, James Brown, Dimebag Darrell, Joey Ramone, Dee-Dee Ramone, Paul Samson, Lee Jon, Stuart Adamson, Robin Crosby, Tim Rose, Ian Dury, John Entwhistle, Mickey Finn, Mick Tucker, Noel Redding, Kelly Johnson, Pepsi Tait, Brad Delp, Michael Lee and Tommy Tee, Joe Kilna, Geraldine Kane and George Harrison.

But the rock has never stopped rolling and there are still minstrels, poets and vagabonds of the so-called Noughties.

Strawberry Fields Ain't Forever

John Lennon famously once warbled 'no one loves you when you're down and out'. Well when I lost everything in the year 2000, many of the people I'd considered friends, whom I'd known for decades, seemed to lose a lot of their love. While not quite hitting down and out rock bottom, it came pretty close and I nearly lost my house.

As the Easter weekend approached, we were doing great in Strawberry Fields. The club had just been refurbished – it was looking great and now had a capacity of 500. But we were also up to our eyes in hock, however, because of the grief we suffered over the loan fiasco. The £60k did eventually come through, but it was just too late.

I decided to bring in a great friend, Graham Boyle, who is a financial consultant. After reading the figures Graham came to the conclusion we could trade out of the hole. What's this: could it be the light at the end of a long, dark tunnel? No, it was a bloody great big locomotive hurtling towards us.

On the Monday morning of the Easter weekend I discovered the safe had been emptied.

I was told the next day by the detectives precisely who their prime suspect was, but I just couldn't bring myself to believe them. Which just goes to show the truth in the old adage that in business trust no one, not even people you have known for years.

Strawberry Fields was already haemorrhaging money and when £18,000 does a runner from the safe, it's a death blow.

The bank were characteristically sympathetic – aye right! Having read in the Press of the robbery, they phoned up to commiserate and ask how much was going to be paid into the club account this week.

'How much do you think?' I asked. 'We've just been f'n robbed!'

They took our circumstances into full consideration before billing us £6,000 in bank charges over the next 14 days.

Well, that was the end of a three-year dream and drowning in debt, I had to sign the club over to the brewery to pay off the £60,000 I owed them.

There were one or two who tried to brighten the day with offers of help.

At the SECC, there to see Robbie Williams perform his first show in Glasgow since his private gig at Strawberry, I was greeted by his manager, Andy Franks who had put me on the guest list. He said how sorry he was to hear that I had lost everything and that Robbie, too, sent his best wishes. He told me if there was anything either of them could do, just to let them know.

At the same gig my old friend Stuart Clumpas also took me aside and told me to get in touch later that week. He wanted to put on a show at the Barrowlands so that he could donate all the takings into paying off my debts.

To say I was emotional would be putting it mildly and I gave him a big cuddle and told him I'd never forget his offer, but I was going to try to get out of the mess by myself. Fine man that he is, he understood and said he respected my decision.

We shook hands, went in to see Robbie and that was the last time I ever saw Stuart before he emigrated to New Zealand.

So it was back to the drawing board for Robert Fields. They say we should learn from our mistakes, so the first thing I did was get myself back into learning. Confronting my worst nightmare of finding myself back at school, I enrolled in a one-year course at Stow College, in Glasgow where, after two years I finally gained an advanced diploma in music industry management. Okay, I confess I chucked it in halfway through the first year to see a band called Quarantine through their development deal, then went back the following year.

The next nine years would see me living a nomadic working existence trying to pay off my debts. I worked in various factories by day and putting on club and band nights in places such as Hielan'man's Bar in Glasgow, Hudson's and Thrum's in East Kilbride and even the Bruce Hotel. I also fulfilled a lifetime's ambition when I got to DJ the Solid Rock Café for seven months.

Of course, I was also still plugging away at promoting this new decade's crop of young and talented bands. I became a musical vagabond myself, spreading the word on the new minstrels and poets to anyone who would listen.

Nowhere To Hide

One of the young bands, the outfit for whom I absconded from my Stow College studies for a while, were Quarantine, later to be called Hiding Place, who originally hailed from East Kilbride. In actual fact, with this band I was coming full circle, for I'd gone to school with the mums and dads of some of the members and had even lived next door to their guitar-playing twins, David and Derek Somerville, since the day they were born.

D&D were joined by Paul McCallion on vocals, Gary Kelly (bass and vocals) and Iain Wilcox (drums). The lads were very young at the time and, like most rock bands of their age, they were into the nu-metal scene and so everything was down-tuned, a trick learned from the master himself, Tony Iommi of Black Sabbath.

I kept bumping into the D&D twins and finally gave in to their incessant requests to go see them in Universal Connections, which in my young days in East Kilbride had been called the Key Youth Club. I must admit that they were okay, but something was niggling me in the back of the head about them, so I got them on at the Cathouse with a few other bands from East Kilbride and took along a couple of industry bigwigs for a second opinion.

I got a positive reaction from my people and the band, on the third time of asking, persuaded me to manage them.

I put into place an 18-month plan with a view to hitting my contacts in major labels with a demo of quality songs. The first thing that needed attention was to lay down a quick two-track demo, as there was a T Break competition being held in Hudsons Bar. Being based in an East Kilbride venue, we had been told that this was to scout East Kilbride, Hamilton and Motherwell bands for a potential slot in the T in the Park that summer.

I took Quarantine to Terminal One Studios in Blantyre, which was run by Andy McAfferty, one-time bass player for Zero Zero and lead guitarist with The Almighty. Now with a cracking demo in hand, I offered it in to be judged.

It got knocked back. In fact, to add insult to injury, I was told by the T boy minion that my band simply were not good enough for the competition in their home town.

When I subsequently discovered that two of the bands who were chosen for the six-strong talent night were not even from the area, it's fair to say I went ballistic.

I bypassed the foot soldiers and made an official complaint straight to the top -- I phoned T in the Park supremo, Geoff Ellis, who said he would look into my complaint. When one of the local band members told the local newspaper that a group from Dundee had won the East Kilbride contest, I was approached by a reporter for a comment.

I told them straight that I was unhappy and I thought they should contact Geoff Ellis for a comment. Shortly afterwards, I received the following letter from him.

16 May 2002

Dear Robert,

We were interested to read your criticism of T Break in the local press. Perhaps you might want to enlighten us on your comments. I thought you were well aware of how the activity is organised / co-ordinated and that it is very fair and certainly, in my opinion a great initiative to support young talent in Scotland.

It is obviously disappointing when we end up getting a boot in the swingers as a result

Regards,

Geoff Ellis

Weirdly, the missive made me feel like a naughty wee schoolboy. I immediately got in touch with Geoff again and recounted what had gone down in the heat held in Hudsons. But it was me who got the boot in the swingers. When I applied for my passes for that year's festival I was told that all of my privileges for events organised by DF Promotions (including T in the Park) had been withdrawn.

Well, there might not be a summer festival slot but there were plenty more opportunities for Quarantine and I was determined to make sure the lads grabbed every chance going.

The next step was to expose the band to the wizard that is Sandy Jones who, along with Graeme Duffin at their Music Foundry Lab studio in Motherwell, saw the huge potential in Quarantine and ripped apart their five and six-minute epics into three-minute commercial rock songs.

Now armed with four killer songs and a new name – we'd discovered that three bands used Quarantine, one with albums out who wanted paid for changing their moniker, so we decided on rechristening the band Hiding Place – I sent two tracks to my good mate Dave Shack, who liked what he heard and passed them on to BMG's head of A&R David Field.

David, in turn, asked me to set up a showcase for four songs in the Core studios in Glasgow and that started a three-month courtship reaching a climax when the band who weren't good enough to play their own local T Break contest, won a major five-album deal with BMG International.

The lads enjoyed a short, but amazing, two years, culminating in a slot at the Download festival, with Metallica headlining. It was shortly before this gig that Gary decided to leave and was replaced by Dougie Thompson.

At this point the band still hadn't signed our management contract, a move agreed on the proviso I get them signed. In a classic divide-and-conquer movement by the record label, who had discovered our situation, a female friend of the A&R people was foisted on the lads in my place.

Heartbroken that I was being so unashamedly pushed aside after all our work together, I handed in my notice. When young Iain discovered what was going on, he announced he'd had enough. He told me the only reason he was in the band was because of me. He made up a story about having a sore arm, insisting he had to rest it on doctor's orders and he, too, quietly left the band.

Iain was replaced by Jason Bowld, formerly of Pitchshifter and Hiding Place lasted a few more tours, with the odd single and video. The end came when Sony merged with BMG and a huge cull was put into effect. Like a lot of the rest of the bands in the BMG stable, as well as the A&R, office and canteen staff, their tea was oot.

The parting gift was a £100k album – produced by Al Clay, of bands Feeder, 'A' and Stereophonics fame – that was never released commercially (worry not, dear rocker, for the best track is yours to hear free on the listening post).

At least the lads got to live the dream for those two years. David, Derek and Paul, along with Alex Dickson, were probably the most gifted people I have ever worked with. I fear they were really too young to appreciate what they had in front of them – I'll never forget drummer Iain's mum Glynis having to sign his long form contract for him, as he was only 17.

Hopefully, they will find inspiration in all the highs and learn from some of the lows and come back with the nuclear-sized bang I know they're well capable of.

Ready, Steady Eddie

If it wasn't for the tenacity and talent of people like Eddie Trainer, a man who just doesn't know when to stop the rock, there wouldn't be a book like this. Having starred in Weeper, Lyin Rampant and Danger through the Nineties, his next career move would be God's Twin.

What began as a bevy-inspired notion in a flat in the east end of Glasgow, soon transmogrified into a bona fide band. Seeking a pastime to alleviate their boredom, Thomas T-Bone Moonan, former bassist with Dr Pop and The Day I Snapped and Martin 'The Pony' Hutchison, former drummer with Chain, began seeking like-minded rockers to join them in a new venture.

Tommy McNally sent them a demo of him performing an acoustic version of 'Down in a Hole' by Alice in Chains and they had their third man. The trio began writing songs and recording them on to an old Tascam four-track, while the search continued for a guitarist: no one, it seemed, could step up to the plate with enough aptitude, never mind attitude.

Enter stage right Eddie Trainer, who had bumped into T-Bone at the Solid Rock Café's annual barbecue. One audition later the band was whole.

A four-track demo with the somewhat bizarre title Scoof was recorded at Park Lane Studio in Glasgow, mixed and engineered by the talented Kenny McDonald. Influenced by artists such as Alice in Chains, Soundgarden, Audioslave, Mötley Crüe and Stone Temple Pilots, the recordings were well received. Passing the demo around the gig promoters of Glasgow brought them much acclaim and phone calls and they went on to play gigs in the Cathouse, the Garage, the Renfrew Ferry, Barfly and the Solid Rock Café, as well as a support slot with Wednesday 13 at King Tut's.

Five months after Scoof was recorded, the lads recorded another four-tracker, this time with an even stranger title: Funtering Fum Feesh. Quite! A shared sense of humour seemed to be the gel that held God's twin-talented musicians together, but even the best jokes can grow stale and, when things turned a little sour, T-Bone jumped ship.

His slot was filled by the talented Billy McFarlane and the band continued to play shows at places like the Garage and anywhere else they could.

About a year later, when they had all cooled down, T-Bone was reunited with the Twin and they went on to play shows at the Cathouse, Camden Underworld, where they did an amazing show for me, completing the circle for drummer Hutch, who as a wee boy had played the same venue with me many years before, in his first band.

Their final gig was in the Arches as part of Witchfest, but by then all four of the divine Twins felt thoroughly fatigued and admitted the band had become more of a chore than fun. They all trundled off on their separate ways.

There have been a few, half-hearted attempts to get the boys back into a rehearsal room together, just for the craic, as it were and to see what happens, but as yet nothing has come of them. Who knows what the future holds but while they were together God's Twin made some amazing rock music and gave Glasgow some killer shows.

Check out their downloads. Phwoarghhh! Now, that's what I call heavy metal!

The Importance Of Being Ernest

Now Ernest might sound like a long lost great uncle renowned for dressing in Harris tweed and sucking on an unlit pipe between tales of how he fought off the Boers, but in actual fact, it was also the name of one of the heaviest metal bands I've ever heard in Glasgow, a power trio who could blast a sonic hole in a Bar L wall.

William Hitchell was singer and guitarist, Alan Moffat was on bass and Douglas MacFarlane was on drums. Tireless showmen, they formed in 2003, refugees from the broken pieces of Planet Fuse, Flu Jag and Engine and their mainstay gigs were in Arta, the Scotia Bar and the Solid Rock Café.

A limited edition debut single, 'Swords', was released in July 2005 on the lads' own Masquerade label. With only 500 copies, 'Swords' would end up selling for £40 a pop on eBay. A follow-up double A-side 'Lonely Town/Draggin' Me Down' was released six months later, heralded by a riotous launch party in the Arches.

One guest who managed to blag one of the 800 tickets that sold out within two-weeks, was Ian McCulloch. His verdict after the gig? 'Ernest are the best band I've heard in Scotland in 20 f*cking years!' Their sound obviously cut some ice with the Echo and the Bunny Men frontman.

As well as being a constant highlight in Glasgow's live rock scene, the lads allowed me to fulfil a life-long ambition. At one of their legendary Sunday jaunts in the Solid Rock, in front of a packed house, they asked me on stage and I experienced the thrill of a wild reception to our unrehearsed rendition of Blue Suede Shoes.

What might be a short party piece to many was a moment of magnificence to me. I was so overcome with emotion, I presented William with a wee novelty Elvis watch I was wearing.

Ernest remain a tour de force in the Glasgow scene and I hope the King is still helping William to get to the gigs on time.

A Spoonful Of Sugar

When I started out on this rock 'n' roll journey, there were few signposts to help the music fan discover new bands or gauge the mood of the day. As we've seen, however, through the years, a great swathe of magazines and papers became our bibles, leading us into the spotlight and dispensing words of wisdom.

For the young music fans of the Sixties, the most important legislator of the musical world was the NME. In the Seventies it was Sounds, followed by Kerrang! in the Eighties, aided by Metal Hammer. In the Nineties we saw the short-lived RAW but at the tail-end of the decade and into the 2000s we were blessed with a new magazine.

Classic Rock is a magazine dedicated to the radio format of classic rock, published by Future Publishing, who are also responsible for its sister publication Metal Hammer. Although firmly focusing on key bands from the 1960s through the early 1990s, it also includes articles and reviews of contemporary and up-and-coming artists it deems worthy of note. It recently published its 100th issue and now has a higher circulation than the NME.

Classic Rock was an idea formulated in 1998 by ex-Metal Hammer deputy editor Jerry Ewing along with colleague Dave Ling (a good friend of mine) and art editor Andy Ryan at Dennis Publishing –their one-off title dedicated to classic rock. When it sold better than expected, it was continued.

Along with the tangible organs of the press – if that sounds bad, let's just say that alongside all the good guys, there are also a lot of w*nkers working in that industry – the Internet has found its own place as an incredible tool for both rock punters and promoters. In fact, one of the most important things in my career development around this time was learning to use the MySpace website as I got right into it. No longer did I have to hound bands for demos, photos and potted biographies; just log on to their website and there it all was.

It also helped enormously when trying to track down lost bands and friends from long ago. This was certainly the case of early to mid-Seventies cult rockers the Heavy Metal Kids, whom I'd met many times when they were supporting Uriah Heep. They were fronted then by the wayward, original Cockney wideboy Gary Holton, who would go on to worldwide fame as Wayne in the TV series Auf Wiedersehen Pet before, aged 33, falling foul of a lethal cocktail of drink and morphine in 1985.

I logged on to the Kids' MySpace in the hope of finding out if their label, Atlantic, had ever released their first two albums on CD and got cyber-conversing with keyboard player and original member Danny Peyronnel.

Danny remembered meeting Carole, baby Lee and me at the gigs and he was chuffed I was in touch again. Although the first two albums were not available, a potential new album, Push the Right Button, was on the go. They were without a label, however and so I told him to send on a couple of copies and I'd tout them around for a licensing deal. I gave one copy to an old friend, Paul Birch, of Heavy Metal Records America, who signed Drunken State and one to Dave Ling, of Classic Rock.

They both loved it so I brokered a 50/50 deal with Paul and reported back to Danny. He told me the Kids' manager would be in touch to run through everything and he would require help in setting up a showcase in London and in Glasgow with the necessary press support.

And so I awaited a call from one of the biggest music legends of my generation, Dave Dee. It was a Thursday night when it came through and I recognised the voice right away: this was the guy who signed AC/DC to his label! He had also been the lead vocalist in Sixties pop band Dave Dee, Dozy, Beaky, Mick and Titch.

Actually his adventures in music followed a career in the police force, which ended one dreadful night when he was first on the scene of a car crash in Chippenham in Wiltshire on Saturday, 16 April 1960. Eddie Cochrane had been killed outright, while his girlfriend Sharon Sheely, along with Gene Vincent, survived.

Constable Dee (the name the Heavy Metal Kids would always use when name-checking him) carried Eddie's guitar to the police station, thus ensuring that the rock legend's family would receive one of his most treasured belongings intact.

As luck would have it DD, D, B, M and Titch were touring in Glasgow a couple of weeks later; I'll always remember that huge grin and the wee gap between his front two teeth. When we met he still looked and sounded as fit as ever. In actual fact, he was battling cancer (the fight was lost early this year and another great rock icon lost).

Anyway, on Dave Dee's behalf, I set up two major gigs, one in the

Underworld in Camden and the other in the Cathouse in Glasgow. I also asked my old mucker Dave Ling if he'd do an interview and feature on the new Kids CD – it was great to see him in the Underworld, where he always looked immaculate in his beloved Crystal Palace scarf and flowing ginger locks.

I also approached Martin Jarvis, a dear old friend I'd known from the Eighties, when our paths frequently crossed at Trident gigs and offered his band Blue Sugar the opportunity to support both of the Kids' shows.

Now, Martin had spent nearly 15 years playing his way around the local scene, in one format or another. He recalls: 'For too many years I've been working with people who just want to play whatever is current at the time. After a while you realise that you're not going to get anywhere because by the time you're ready, there's a new fad on the scene.'

So forming Blue Sugar came with a clear plan; simple songs played well and don't follow any trends. That's timeless.'

Formed from the ashes of many local bands, the line-up was Pete Sneddon (formerly of Sonic Temple on drums), TJ Stirling (of Sweet Mercy on bass), Mark Borland (of Everlone on guitar) and music scene newcomer Lynsey Dolan (vocals).

Early on, it was obvious that Lynsey didn't quite do justice to anyone else's songs but the style she brought to her own was outstanding. It was decided she should bring her own songs to the band, with Martin working with her to keep a rock edge to them. Very quickly, they began to build a reputation as one of the best and hardest working live bands in the country.

Indeed, such was their impact that, after only their first live gig, Blue Sugar were booked to support the Heavy Metal Kids on their UK tour. The highlight of that was playing to a sold-out Glasgow Cathouse, where the audience was made up almost entirely of their own fans. All this, after only three months in existence.

However, as is the way of the rock world, things didn't quite go to plan. Just six months later, while busy working on the debut album, Lynsey upped and left to pursue a solo career, eventually taking with her the band's original second guitarist.

Undeterred, Martin and TJ recruited singer Kirsty Pirie and former guitar tech Matt Grady just in time to headline a sold-out gig at Glasgow's

Renfrew Ferry. Kirsty lasted just one gig. However that parting was amicable and the band effectively kept a low profile.

TJ by that time was working on some theatre shows, Martin was getting more and more involved in artist promotion and Matt was writing and recording music for fashion shows, amongst other things. Drummer Mark Devine returned to his own band, the Twilight Sad. To everyone, including their legion of disappointed fans, Blue Sugar had become a footnote before they even got off the ground.

In a new capacity as an agent, Martin had booked Eighties outfit Doctor and the Medics to play a show just outside Glasgow. This was due to take place the day before Martin and TJ departed on tour with former Georgia Satellites frontman, Dan Baird. The week before the gig, TJ mused out loud: 'Hey, it would be fun to do the Medics gig.' A couple of quick phone calls found that Matt was available and long-time friend Davy Gray, currently on sabbatical from the Pete Loaf Band, agreed to do the gig, 'for a laugh and to play real rock 'n' roll again'.

After just one rehearsal, with TJ on lead vocals and a new song, Blue Sugar took the stage. Their show went down a storm.

Despite this success, however, with TJ and Martin now working with Dan Baird and Homemade Sin and Martin also working with former Mott the Hoople legend, Ian Hunter, there wasn't much time to seriously consider a Blue Sugar renaissance. However, a song written about their exploits in Europe convinced Martin and TJ at the very least to do some recording, even if the results were to be for their own pleasure.

Decanting to Frielance Studios, run by writer and producer, Greg Friel, the band laid down three tracks. 'To be fair,' recalls Martin, 'whenever I've been in the studio before, it's been with engineers who just do as they are told. As such, you don't really get an outside ear giving you constructive advice. Working with Greg meant that he was challenging me all the way, including the use of keyboards, which I had never really thought about before. As such, I think we have better songs as a result.'

Finishing the tracks coincided with a call to join rock legends Nazareth as special guests on their 2006 tour in Glasgow. This time Matt was unavailable so, with Davy Gray back on drums, the band was completed by former Easy Tiger keyboard player, Steve Lightbody and the baby of the band, Craig Griffin, on bass.

This was arguably the strongest line-up of the band yet and this was ably demonstrated by the gigs played. More new songs and gigs with other great touring acts, Blue Sugar had soon developed a reputation for stealing everyone else's audience wherever they played.

However, things derailed in spectacular style when Martin and TJ agreed to a parting of the ways, a move that coincided with Davy Gray emigrating to Australia.

Martin tried to keep things going, bringing in a new singer, Emily Campbell and a drummer in Kev Woods, who was also Steve's nephew, but the sound was not gelling in the right way.

'I think the magic was gone when Davy moved away,' says Martin. 'He was virtually irreplaceable and one of my best friends.'

After just a couple of low-key acoustic gigs, Martin's suspicions were confirmed and he effectively fired himself from Blue Sugar, bringing to an end yet another great band that never quite fulfilled their potential. Not all good things in life can stay sweet forever.

All The Rage

Enjoying a career that has been the polar opposite to that of Blue Sugar, one of our longest lasting bands are Attica Rage. I go way back with the earliest line-ups in the late Eighties with young Ritchie Rage and his chums supporting Drunken State in the Village Theatre in East Kilbride. I have to admit, they are the perfect examples of rockers sticking to their guns throughout a 20-year career.

Before their 2000s incarnation, the original Attica Rage of 1989 formed around the core trio, a mainstay throughout the band's lifetime of Richie Rage (drums), Bob Kidd (guitar) and Nathan Elliot-Ling (bass).

During the late Eighties and influenced by the heavy metal scene of the time, the band covered songs by Accept, Wasp, Metallica, AC/DC and Ozzy, gigging around Ayrshire and Glasgow. At this point Attica included guitarist Dougie and singers Jim Anderson and Paul McGale.

By 1989, they'd recruited Jon Henderson as lead vocalist and guitarist and established themselves on the gig circuit. Leaning more towards their thrash metal influences – Metallica, Anthrax, Megadeth – the band recorded the Activated four-song demo at Ca Va Sound Workshops, Glasgow, becoming one of the very few heavy bands to record in a studio best known for Scottish popsters such as Wet Wet Wet.

Activated gained regular airplay, with band interviews on West Sound FM with Tom Jones and our old mucker Tom Russell on his Clyde 1 Rock Show. It was also voted into the final of the UK-wide Radio 1 Rock Wars demo competition, presented by the late, legendary Tommy Vance.

The band hired the Magnum Theatre in Irvine for a week to film a promo music video for the track Killing For Company, inspired by the story of yon nasty serial killer Dennis Neilson. The video was picked up by an American metal mag, Metal Forces, for their first music video magazine Metal XS, which was distributed worldwide and saw the Attica lads featured alongside interviews and videos from Motörhead, Helloween, the Cult, Gamma Ray, Iced Earth and fellow Scots rockers, The Almighty.

Shortly afterwards, Lanarkshire guitarist Dave Pollock joined the band, allowing Jon to concentrate on the vocals. Attica Rage started gigging further afield across Scotland and North England. However, Jon was forced to leave the band due to university commitments (he would later become a senior university lecturer, so I guess he made the right decision, bless his brainy wee heid!).

The search for a replacement singer began in earnest and the lads tried out a couple of local chanters, first Scott Reardon, then the promisingly named Gary Couper, but after a few gigs and recording efforts, it wasn't working out.

To find a permanent solution to the role of frontman and vocalist, Richie realised the answer had been in front of him all this time. It was someone he'd known all his life, who had been to loads of the gigs from an early age and had all this time been waiting patiently for a chance - his younger brother Jonny.

In July 1993, Jonny joined Attica Rage just in time to record vocals for the new five-song demo Dreams of the Guilty. Despite being only 15 years old (his age was put down officially as 19 on the band's press pack to save any problems from venues and promoters!), Jonny had already been a regular at nights out with the drinking crowd and was accepted into the band with no hesitation, bringing a new lease of energy and life into the band.

His first gig at Jonesy's in Ayr (now called Harleys) introduced him to their fans. With a big hoodie of charity thrown over his blushing napper for forgetting the lyrics to their cover of Testament's Trial By Fire, he was an immediate success.

Over the next year and a half, the band gigged in Ayrshire and Glasgow, also taking part in a bands battle at the Sax venue in Cumbernauld. Major headline slots followed, both in King Tut's and the Catty.

In December 1994, Attica Rage played, unknown to them at the time, what would be their last ever gig at the Crown in Irvine. Personal circumstances and changes with the band members brought a close to the chapter of this version of Attica Rage.

They regrouped in Glasgow in 2003, with a line-up of Jonny Parr, Richie Rage, Big C and Stephen Bell. Their debut album, Ruin Nation, brews a potent blend of hard rock riffs, melodic anthems and infectious metal power-grooves with an occasional dose of darker, epic soundtracks. Produced by Big C, mastered by Ace (of Skunk Anansie fame), the album also features artwork designed exclusively by legendary Motörhead artist Joe Petagno.

Attica Rage's growing reputation has been built with their consistently solid, tight and energetic live performances at shows across the UK and Europe. They have also shared festival bills with Thin Lizzy, Black Label Society, In Flames, Opeth, Arch Enemy, Clutch, Carcass, Orange Goblin, Firewind, the Wildhearts, Apocalyptica and Ministry.

The band have continued to promote Ruin Nation throughout 2009 but have already started writing new material, with plans to record and release a follow-up album early next year – and I can't wait to hear the tracks.

The New Kids

If Blue Sugar and Attica Rage represent the old school, then this little lot are the new kids on the rock block. DB Sixtyeight were formed in Glasgow in 2000 and comprise Andy Cannon (vocals and guitar), 'Marshall' (guitar), David Gillespie (keyboards), Dave McTaggart (bass and vocals) and Pete Cannon (drums and percussion). I'd known their bassist Dave from a local band in East Kilbride called Downiner and had even approached him at one point to ask him to join Hiding Place – I'd needed to replace Gary Kelly, who had left just as we were starting to record the debut album with BMG.

Dave, however, had college and Specsavers work commitments, so he knocked us back. Anyway, months later he got back in touch and asked me to check out his new band DB Sixtyeight at Core studios.

I was impressed. Maybe Specsaver Dave hadn't been shortsighted after all? DB Sixtyeight had everything going for them; a great image, original songs and superb musical ability. We clicked right away, the only problem being their annoying habit of calling band members, mates and even curmudgeonly old rock promoters by their surnames and so it was Fields this and Fields that.

I put together a six-month plan, leaving those who knew best to concentrate on the songwriting and stage show. I raised their profile through the press and radio and the publicity machine was cranked up several notches in a bid to secure a T Break showcase later on in the year.

All of this and more was achieved, yet after a climactic London showcase, still no one had shown any real interest. Oh and, surprise of all surprises, they didn't get to play T in the Park that year!

Near the end I wanted them to try to kick things up a level by getting the lads to record with Sandy and Graeme, but they insisted they had a mate who had done all their recent demos and they were sticking with him and so we drifted apart.

Later they would secure an album deal in Japan (Banzai! That's always the kiss of death for unsigned bands, just ask Kobai!) and have recently split up. I wish them all the best, whatever they get up to.

Another young band appearing on the gig circuit in Glasgow in the latter half of this decade were SpearBrave, who originated in my home town and whom I took down to the Underworld in Camden a couple of years ago.

It's refreshing to see how they have come on leaps and bounds since they formed in 2006. They're fronted by the amazing singing twins, Sean and Declan Cleary. Sean is also the songwriter and rhythm guitarist, while Michael Timmons is lead axeman Andrew Robertson the bass player and Scott Duff the drummer.

The band have played venues all over the Glasgow area and were a highlight of the Emergenza music competition, playing alongside 14 other bands in the Scottish final, held at the Glasgow Carling Academy in 2007.

The band also appeared in the National Live and Unsigned Final held in Newcastle and were nominated for best live and unsigned band at the Vodafone Music awards in 2008. The latest demo was recorded in Chem19 studios, by Andy Miller, who has recorded and produced for bands such as Mogwai and Camera Obscura.

With such a meteoric rise in such a short time, there can only be better, bigger, bolder things to come from SpearBrave. Watch this space . . .

Joining the ranks of 2000s' new kids are Flood of Red, a six-piece consisting of Jordan Spiers, Graham Griffith, Calum Doris, Jamie McGowan, Dale Gallacher and Sean McGroarty.

Formed from the remnants of the Psychotic Pandas (what a brilliant name, shame they were always an endangered species!), they have displayed a real hunger for success rarely seen in Scotland's underground rock scene.

Quickly building up a fan base through MySpace, Flood of Red have grown from playing local shows in Glasgow to touring the UK, booking their own shows through the internet and their own tours with bands like Enter Shikari and The Blackout – by simply swapping show spots all around the country. In their first two years of existence, Flood of Red have played around 400 shows throughout the UK. God bless 'em, but they'll be the death of old school promoters like me!

In 2007 the lads released their debut EP, Lost in the Light, through independent label Smalltown Records and were quickly tipped in Rock Sound, Kerrang! and Metal Hammer as a band to watch.

This year they spent the whole of January in Baltimore, USA, recording with legendary hardcore producer, Brian McTernan, in his Salad Days studio. The result of this has been Leaving Everything Behind.

A single, 'A Place Before the End', was released on 20 July 2009. I was at the single's launch in Tut's, where I was told that simply being a 56-year-old codger doesn't qualify me to buy more than one pint at a time: house rules said my similarly-aged compadres had to buy their own individually. Honest to goodness!

Anyway, a braw time was had by all, the band played an electrifying set, fully loaded with lots of new material. Even though, I must admit, I liked best their earlier, heavier material, this is another band to keep an eye and two ears on.

Logan's Fun Run

In every decade a band rises from out of nowhere, sets off on a quiet journey, unnoticed, through the foot hills and, after lots of hard graft, arrives suddenly and quite without warning to sit proudly on the top of the entire pile.

Logan are one such band. I've been lucky enough to see them live when they supported Thunder at the O2 in Glasgow recently. To say they went down a storm would be a terrible pun, but the truth is these lads are out-and-out rockers and worth their weight in the heaviest metal.

I first encountered their singer Kenny Collins when I did his first ever band's gig in Strawberry Fields in the late Nineties. Back then I certainly wouldn't have put the contents of my soon-to-be-empty safe on Kenny developing into the rock star he is today. But all credit to him and his band, for they are more than worthy of inclusion in this history of rock heroes.

Kenny started off as the singer in Buzzer, while Mick Coll was the chanter in fellow Glasgow band Greebo. Truth be told, both bands had been around for several years and achieved pretty much nothing. Kenny texted Mick one night in 2003 and suggested they form a new band together. Logan was born.

Early rehearsals saw instant chemistry and songs were created in those first few weeks that would stand the test of time and go on to become Logan classics, most notably the anthem When I Get Down.

Here Mick himself picks up the tale for us:

'From day one, we decided not to be the kind of band that did every gig we could, just for the sake of it. Instead we chose to work on songs and record. I had a working relationship with a great sound engineer called Steve Reilly – I had recorded all my previous band's music with him and I wouldn't go anywhere else to record.

'Steve took to the band instantly, proclaiming we were the band 'he'd been waiting ten years to find'. Hearing the songs recorded confirmed what we already knew . . . we had something special. Steve stepped into a full working relationship with the band, becoming our manager and producer, while his brother, Al, would drop by to listen to some of our stuff at the time and he seemed impressed.

'Not being a lead guitarist myself, Steve asked Al if he would consider laying down some solos on the songs to help fill them out. The songs that were already great now sounded even better.

'Around about this time Kenny and I were growing increasingly unhappy with our present drummer. Loveliest guy on earth, but we were having to cancel more and more rehearsals and recording sessions in order to work around his lifestyle and this didn't suit us at the time. Logan needed to be everyone's number one priority.

'Right around this time, we received an invitation to head over to America to showcase for a guy called Pete Ganbarg. He was VP of Sony A&R and made his name by being the brains behind Santana's 13 million-selling Supernatural album. This put us in a position where we had to make the choice between doing Logan as a hobby or going for it as a career.

'We chose the latter and this meant replacing our drummer. It was the hardest thing that we had to do. Kenny did the talking that night and I've never heard from that drummer again. I hope he's doing good.

'Waiting in the wings was young Iain Stratton. I had struck up a friendship with Iain myself but also, on a totally separate note, he was also working with Steve in his studio. On Steve's recommendation we invited Iain to join the band and come to America with us. He did.

'The final piece of the puzzle (almost) came in the form of Al joining the band. He had laid down some solos on our first album and one night he came into rehearsal and jammed with us live. After that, Kenny and I talked about how good it would be if Al would become a band member, but we didn't think it a possibility. A few days later, the night before we flew to America, we met up with Steve and Al and Al expressed an interest in joining the band. We were delighted.

'The trip to America went very well. We impressed the A&R at Sony but not enough. In the VP's words, we weren't ready and, in hindsight, I can see that he was totally right. Upon our return to Scotland, Al came to his first rehearsal with us and brought with him the music for what would become fan favourite, 'Hey Mary'. Again, we were delighted.

'We trundled along doing the rounds in Glasgow to pretty much no avail. At this point in Logan's career we had many more fans in America than we did in the UK. We needed exposure.

'Exposure came along in a way that I would never have dreamed of. My favourite guitarist, Mark Tremonti of Creed, was coming to the UK with his new band, Alter Bridge. I was lucky enough to have a friendship with Mark's brother and when Alter Bridge came to the UK, I was invited along to the show. Myself, Al and his wife attended and at the after-show party I mustered up all the courage I had in me and asked Mark if we could support his band when they came to Glasgow. He said yes! The three of us went out that night and partied with the guys in Alter Bridge. It seemed so surreal at the time.

'The Alter Bridge gig came and we looked upon it as a test, make-or-break kinda thing. Fortunately, the crowd went mad for Logan and we now found ourselves as a known band in Glasgow. Our own shows started selling more and we had developed a following. We got to support Alter Bridge again and then on their third trip to the UK we got the whole tour. If we thought that first Glasgow show was make-or-break then this UK tour really was! Again, we triumphed every night and, lo and behold, three years after we started, we were a known band throughout the UK.

'We were now at a level where momentum was everything. To keep up that profile we needed to be out there, in people's faces, all the time. Unfortunately, that couldn't happen due to the fact that we all needed to work day jobs. So slowly we slipped back down off the radar for a while. This was hard for everyone. We'd been out there, touring and selling albums. We even had a video on the TV and a single in the rock charts. It was so frustrating because, despite all of this, we still couldn't get any kind of industry backing.

'Once again, fate dropped in and delivered us a gift, just at the right time. A new radio station was being advertised all over the place here in Glasgow - Rock Radio. What a wondrous thing! It seemed, to me at least, that this was a way for us to get back into the mindset of the rock community that didn't require us to be out touring. As soon as it launched I bombarded every DJ at the station with emails and one of them got back to me - it was the one-and-only Tom Russell.

'Tom has been a legendary figure in rock music for decades, so I was pretty excited. The outcome of our email conversations was to be an interview, live on the radio. Myself and Al attended this interview and on that day we crossed paths with someone who was to change all of our lives.

'We were sitting in the studio across from Tom; I was focusing on not speaking too quickly when a long-haired, larger-than-life guy in a suit bounded into the room. This fellow turned out to be Billy Anderson, managing director of Rock Radio. He wanted to say hi to Al and me and added that if we ever needed anything, to email him. Later that same day I was doing just that and pretty quickly I had struck up a friendship with him.

'Around about this time Logan had another line-up change. Things in the camp were tense and, without going into any detail, things needed to change. At this point our one-time manager, Steve Reilly, stepped in to become the full-time bass player.

'A few months down the line, our relationship with Rock Radio was strong and we were getting a decent bit of airplay. It was announced that Bon Jovi were doing a show and there was a contest to win a support slot. The timing for us couldn't have been better. We were getting airplay on Rock Radio quite a lot just before the contest, so I knew we had a decent chance of winning. After several tense weeks, it was finally revealed that we had won the contest. We were going to play at Hampden, opening for Bon Jovi!

'Now, the first show with Alter Bridge was a test and we passed it. The first tour with Alter Bridge was a test and we passed that too. Now this was Hampden stadium, 40,000 people: this was the test of all tests!

'Once we stepped out on to that stage we did our thing, just like we do at every gig and at the end of it, everyone in the stadium, pretty much all 40,000 people were singing along to 'When I Get Down', that same song that was written on one of the band's first ever rehearsals, five years previously. Success!

'After that show we were signed up to Guardian Angel Rock Management, a company started for us by Billy Anderson and his long-term friend and business partner, Cameron Pirie. Three months later we were in LA filming a music video and the week after that we were out on a three-month tour around Europe.'

It's certainly been a fun run so far for Logan but I'm not the only one in the industry who is certain the lads are going on to even bigger and better things. In an age-old Glasgow phrase, right now Logan are the berries.

Hazy Daze

Donald MacLeod and myself have a lot in common: we both love our rock music and love working with rock bands. His latest charges are The Haze. A Glasgow five-piece, they've spent the past few years learning their craft on the road, touring anywhere and everywhere they can across Britain.

'I'd say that we've played almost every major city and most of the bigger venues,' says singer James Cairns. Through supporting the likes of Idlewild, Eagles of Death Metal, the Cult, the Hold Steady, The Haze have become a focused and articulate rocking crew. Led by James's distinctive lead vocals, their sound is one of menace and soaring guitars, with a backline of heavy rhythms.

'When we started out, our main influence was Oasis,' reveals James. 'But now we're much more into the classic giants: Zeppelin, the Doors, the Stones, The Who, Dylan. It means that we've managed to get interest from older fans, as well as pick up a large young following. It's a great mixture.'

In actual fact, James almost joined the band as a guitarist.

He recalls: 'I was invited down by John Paul Hunter (guitarist and Haze co-founder). I knew his cousin and so got asked to come along for a bevvy and a sing-song, because they were looking for more band members. I went along and actually just started to sing along to some of the tunes. That was it. I got the job . . . as the vocalist!'

Having never sung before in public, James needed some severe anaesthetic intake to calm his nerves before doing his first ever Haze show. Consequently, his recollections are, well, hazy.

'Don't ask me to tell you anything about that,' he says. 'I was so out of it. I can't recall that gig at all! But I've learnt my lesson. These days, we all party hard, but only after doing the show.'

The current line-up – James, John Paul, Mark Miller (guitar), Ross Duffy (bass) and Robert Mitchell (drums) – have been together since 2004 and the aim is to spread the word far and wide.

'We want to go to America, Japan, Europe . . . in fact, anywhere they love their rock music,' says James.

Things are certainly heading in the right direction for world domination. They've just recorded their debut album, Spirits Will Rise, with producer Chris Tsangarides.

'Man, that was amazing. He's worked with Sabbath, Thin Lizzy, Judas Priest as well as tons of new acst', says James. 'He has so many stories that it could keep us in lyrics for the next six records!'

Let's hope The Haze will have their very own tales to tell. Billed as the natural successors to so many great names who've graced the British scene over the past 40 years – from Thin Lizzy to Led Zeppelin, Nazareth to the Pink Fairies – they also form an integral part of Glasgow's new rock scene. And as long as we have bands like this plugging away, the future of rock 'n' roll is in safe hands.

Hot And Cold

There are a lot of great young bands happening just now and none more so than Ampersand, with Paul Shields (vocals), Chris Diamond (guitar), Richard Fowler (bass and vocals) and Darren Gowrie (drums and vocals). Together they make a splendid noise. I did two great shows with them in the Cathouse and the Underworld in Camden where they impressed everyone from the sound engineer to a scribe from Night Magazine 200 who wrote the following:

'Ampersand started way before but the current Ampersand have been together since October 2007. Since shedding some heavy weight, Ampersand have concentrated on becoming what they set out to be - a great rock band. The aim is simple: to write good music with a good tune to go with it. Ampersand enjoy playing live. Bringing life and energy to their music is essential to what they are about. Fusing their love for the Big Rock Sound with great melodies, Ampersand create a sound of power and grace with ease.

'Roaring into life the band opened with 'Taking Over', creating a wall of sound that filled the room to bursting point. A good rock song with strong vocals and great three-part harmonies from the lead vocalist, drummer and bassist, it was a sign of things to come.

'Ampersand are, literally, a big band built for a bigger stage. A potent mix of Pearl Jam, Soundgarden, Led Zeppelin, Deep Purple and Black Sabbath, they blend seismic riffs to perfect melodic choruses and screaming guitar solos. Their gigs are a master-class in how to do stadium-sized rock in a club-sized venue.

'Singer Paul Shields cannonballs around the stage, often straight through the permanently head-banging and brilliantly named guitarist Topher Diamond. Songs like 'Believe', 'Damn Time' and definite future anthem 'Devil and I' were made to be played on a massive stage with so much pyro that there's barely a second passes when something isn't on fire. Definitely one to watch in 2008, this five-piece exudes confidence, talent and, most importantly, the songs to go very far indeed.

'Reviews such as this are not alien to the band and in the past year they've grown even bigger and stronger. The only thing that is in any doubt is whether Glasgow has rock venues that are big enough to hold on to these lads much longer. Of all the bands to have emerged on to the scene in the 2000s, it's fair to say that Ampersand may well be the outfit most likely to be mentioned in dispatches in the next decade as homecoming headliners at Hampden.'

Sadly, the same cannot be said for their contemporaries, a band I worked with for two years. The only rule I have when I'm working with a band is that they make the hair on the back of my neck stand and Red Snowman had the nape fairly tingling. The only problem we had is that before I started working with them they had been together for more than five years and, even after my two years of varied success, the Snowman had perhaps been left out in the sun too long.

A rather convoluted line-up saw singer David Pollock also playing guitar and keyboards, Fraser Gamble on guitars, drums and vocals and his brother Ross Gamble also on guitars, drums and vocals, while Ronnie Phipps stuck to the bass and Craig McLachlan focused on guitar.

They really were quite different: think Lizzy meets Yes meets Radiohead and you get some idea of the sound. With the Ross bros playing drums and guitars in equal measure, they also had superb vocals and harmonies.

The lads had known each other from school and college days and, when I first saw them in Tut's. As with any band I've worked with, I listened to all the songs then fitted the best into a well balanced set. Job done, it was up to Snowman to begin writing new material, all the while weeding out the weaker songs and replacing them with better ones.

With the shows doing well, Ampersand soon reached such a level it was almost scary and they were soon facing the two most important gigs of their life. The first was a T Break competition where my heart went out to them. They blew everyone away but deep down in my heart I knew they had as much chance of winning as there I had. And they didn't. Next, at the Underworld in Camden, on a bill alongside Ampersand, they produced a killer set. Of all my London shows, this was the greatest night, with the best sets from two unsigned bands I've ever witnessed.

So it was rather unsettling when, shortly afterwards, Red Snowman decided to call it a day. That's showbusiness, I guess. Every Snowman melts away one day.

Rock On The Radio

Radio, of course, has always played a big part in the formative lives of rock fans. In the Sixties I relied on Caroline, Luxembourg and then Radio One. In the Seventies it was Kid Jensen, Alan Fluff Freeman, then the great Tommy Vance. The Eighties saw Tom Russell take to the airwaves on Clyde, though this was knocked on the head in the Nineties. Then, just a couple of years ago, someone had the balls and vision to give Glasgow a radio station we all could 'rawk to'. The all-new 96.32 Rock Radio was born. Here Martin Kielty describes how it all came to pass:

'Maybe it's the spirit. Maybe it's the drink. Maybe it's the weather or the legacy of working in loud shipyards to power the empire (as was). But the west of Scotland has always been up to its ears in rock music – and in 2007 someone finally had the guts to repay that belief with a dedicated radio station.

'It's a matter of fact the city fathers tried to stamp out Glasgow's love for hard and heavy noise. They stomped on punk, they strangled the Stranglers, they closed the Kelvingrove Bandstand and they let the Apollo die. But when Radio Clyde also abandoned ship by ending Tom Russell's Friday Night Rock Show, it really did feel as if the old noise was dying down at last.

'No f*ckin' chance!

'As ever, the people of Glasgow turned it round and rock music lives again. The saviours this time were Jay Crawford and Billy Anderson of GMG Radio, owners of Real Radio. As a former pirate DJ, Jay understood the passion for rock in the area; and as a fan of the music, Big Boss Billy was happy to support. Together, they made Rock Radio a reality.

'And this wasn't to be a case of lip service to sell adverts. To prove they meant business, the station brought Tom back from the edge of the wilderness – and not just for his legendary Friday Night Rock Show . . . for every day of the week.

'They backed him up with Nazareth star Billy Rankin – who's been there, done that and won't shut up about it – David the Captain Grant, Father Ted, the Crack and a host of rock-endowed worthies who live, breathe and eat rock music. They even brought me in on the writing side, to look after the website, so that every base possible was covered by someone who rocks as a way of life.'

Now known as The Beard of Doom, Tom could be forgiven for relaxing a little in the throne he's earned. Not so. In 2009 Rock Radio was invited to provide the on-site radio station for the Download Festival at Donington Park. As well as cementing the station's position in the rock world – as a small unsigned act with a ferocious audience and a sound worth hearing – Download FM showcased Tom's knowledge and inspiration with a playlist which he spent weeks over perfectly accompanying the vibe of the event.

And he doesn't intend slowing down yet. The veteran festival MC and Apollo house DJ says: 'One of the great things about Rock Radio is we've been able to make contact with some of our lost followers. Over the last two years I've been approached by people who've told me: 'I last came to a gig 20 years ago, then I got married, or moved for a job, or whatever. I heard about this gig on Rock Radio and I bought a ticket – and I haven't had such a great time in years.' And that's not just happened to me once or twice, it happens a lot and it happens at every gig. That's something to be proud of.'

Of course, it's not all plain-sailing. With the UK's legendary stiff rules on what can and can't be played on air, when and how much, with only one frequency to play with it's tough to please everyone.

'Rock is such a broad church,' Tom says. 'Every time you please a Beatles fan you'll annoy an Anthrax fan. If you play an AC/DC track someone will have wanted a Megadeth track. Or if you make a Shinedown fan happy you'll make an Answer fan mad. Like everything else, Rock Radio is a work in progress. But the nice thing is we all care enough to argue over how we should stretch the rules as far as we can. In fact, we fall out over it – but then we remember it's only because we all live for rock music, just like everyone who's listening.'

Girls Cool

Not since Pink Kross has Glasgow had an all-girl rock band to boast about, so it's with great pleasure and some pride I introduce to you The Hedrons. The girls are managed by one of my all-time loyal and most trusted friends, Dougie Souness from 'No Half Measures'. Dougie and I go way back to the Howff and Venue days, though I'm sure he will claim that he's a lot younger, if not better looking, than me.

Dougie came to me in the late Nineties, when he was managing a local singer-songwriter called Yvonne Tipping. We put on a major showcase for interested record and publishing companies in Strawberry Fields but nothing of import came of it. This was quite a shame, as Yvonne is very talented.

Thankfully, she is also very determined and wasn't about to give up. Her next move was to set about recording a solo album in 2005. This started off very promisingly, until one day in the rehearsal studio she met three other girls in a band in the next room and fate took a new twist. Discovering they were all equally disenchanted with the way their respective careers were heading, they decided to throw their lot in together.

Yvonne changed her name to Tippi and, from a very insecure, shy but vastly talented musician, she adopted a wild stage persona second to none. Joining this wild child Tippi were bassist Gill, lead guitarist Rosie and drummer Soup.

The NME has described them as 'an all-girl four-piece who sound like Patti Smith meets Penetration with a dash of early Blondie and a smidgeon of the Runaways'. The girls themselves describe their sound as the 'modern love child of the Foo Fighters and Joan Jett'. What they produce live is certainly a headstrong, heart-driven roar of a sonic attack. Rosie sums it up best when she says: 'If you listen to us, you wouldn't realise it was girls until Tippi starts singing – you'd think it was a bunch of big hairy guys playing.'

If they sound like big hairy guys, they certainly don't look like them and, with a relentless gigging schedule, back-to-back Top 5 UK Indie singles chart success and an entry in the Top 40 of the official UK indie album chart with debut album One More Won't Kill Us, the four-piece have established themselves as one of the country's foremost emerging rock bands.

And, Finally, The Ones To Watch

Yashin leads our list of 'ones to watch' in the 2000s. Another quaintly named young Glasgow band making a name for themselves nationally and in Europe. They've just returned from Italy and have a full British tour lined up for the end of this year. I first saw them in the old Saints and Sinners in St Vincent Street, when they played an excellent set for a T Break competition.

They followed this with a priceless slot on The Orange Unsigned competition. Although, in the manner of such shows, they were voted off, Radio One's Jo Whiley pleaded with the rest of the cardboard judges to give them a second chance – sadly to no avail. Jo has since described Yashin as 'a band to watch, up there with Enter Shikari and the Gallows'.

The band are Harry Radford (vocals), Kevin Miles (vocals), Paul (guitar) andy (bass and vocals), Lewis (guitar) and Dave (drums).

Another young band making waves are Twin Atlantic. Formed in March 2007, their line-up is Sam McTrusty on guitar and lead vocals, Barry McKenna (guitar, cello and backing vocals), Ross McNae (bass, piano and backing vocals) and Craig Kneale (drums). All the lads have history in other bands: Sam was in Arca Felix, Ross in LongStoryShort, Barry in Think:Fire and Craig appeared in Ernest.

During 2007 they built up a strong reputation both locally and nationally, with tour support slots with Circa Survive and mewithoutYou before recording their debut EP, A Guidance From Colour at Long Wave Studio in Cardiff with producer Romesh Dodangoda. Their first single, 'Audience & Audio', was released on Christmas Eve the same year.

Building on support from Kerrang!, the band's profile was boosted enough for them to land support slots with Biffy Clyro and they were personally chosen by Jimmy Chamberlin to support the Smashing Pumpkins at Glasgow's SECC.

Early this year they were signed to Red Bull Records and began pre-recording for their debut mini-album in Los Angeles, working alongside producer John Travis. It's not surprising that they're looked upon by many critics as Glasgow's 'most likely'.

Not quite yet in the same league, but promising greatness are Jocasta Sleeps, who met in a practice studio in the west end of Glasgow. Featuring Callum Wiseman on vocals and guitar and the excellent rhythm section of John McGinley and Niall McGarvie, the lads have spend the majority of their short time together locked up in bedrooms and rehearsal studios, honing their craft, while dedicating their precious few remaining hours to raising their profile on the gig circuit. Following a fantastic reception at T in the Park and the critical acclaim that greeted their debut single, 'Crayfish Cocktail', the world's their smorgasbord.

Like their more infamous next-door neighbours, the ill-fated Red Snowman, We Throw Stones hail from Renfrewshire. While still very much a work in progress, they have spent the past year away from the gigging scene, tinkering with their songs in garages and studios, but now look ready to emerge from hibernation.

With Patrick Rodger on vocals, ably backed up by Mark Sinclair (guitar), Russell Phipps (bass and vocals) and Scott McClements (drums and vocals) they wowed at a sold-out King Tut's gig, supporting Nine Black Alps. With an EP in the offing and showcases lined up, they've earned their place among our ones to watch.

Back at the heavier end of the rock scale are young Glaswegians Black Cherry Group, a new band on the scene who cite AC/DC, Metallica, Deep Purple and Pearl Jam as their primary influences – and that, dear reader, is more than good enough for me. Founded by songwriter DR Webster in 2005, who sings and plays guitar, the band have Bradley Smith on bass and Tony Cocozza on drums.

They are currently working on their debut album, entitled Cinemas Everywhere Now. They are also busy gigging around Glasgow in venues such as Barfly, King Tut's, Cosmopol, Pivo Pivo, Box, Rockers, Ivory Black's, ABC2 and the O2 Academy.

Most recently, they supported The Sword on the Metallica World Magnetic Tour at Tut's and they're also in talks to join festivals abroad, including Midpoint Music Festival in Cincinnati, Ohio.

I really like this wee band – with a sound that evokes Rush or Deep Purple at their best, they embody all that's good about modern rock bands, while never forgetting their musical forefathers from the late Sixties and early Seventies.

Another of the Glasgow bands who fall into the should-have-been-huge category are The Grim Northern Social. With two albums earning critical acclaim, they also proved themselves in the live arena, appearing as special guests of big-name artists such as Elvis Costello and Simple Minds. Other live highlights included T in the Park appearances and sets at the South-By-Southwest Festival in Austin, Texas.

With a phenomenal line-up that incorporated Ross Baxter (guitarist), Ewan MacFarlane (vocals), Paul Crawford (drums) and Pete Cowan (bass), it was entirely justified when Music Week proclaimed the band 'a fine live act and decidedly the best the country has to offer'.

Unfortunately, the band split up in 2007 and, just like one-time label mates the Cosmic Rough Riders, they failed to make the premier league. Ewan is currently pursuing a solo career and has just secured a major publishing deal, while Pete, Andy and Paul are now playing with Joe Gallacher in a band called Mr Kil.

I first saw Joe Gallacher when he was supporting The Grim Northern Social in the Arts Centre in East Kilbride. I was standing next to his justifiably proud mum and I was blown away by his vocal prowess. After the gig I discovered he was moving down to Brighton where my old mates from Little Angels days, guitarist Bruce Dickinson and his mentor Kevin Dixon had opened the Brighton Music Academy and so I passed on their numbers.

Based in Brighton for a couple of years, Joe forged a reputation supporting the likes of The Turin Brakes and Martha Wainwright. A few years later I bumped into him in Glasgow's HMV store, where he told me he had hooked up with the former Grims. Joe's news really excited me, as both Paul and Joe are stunning musicians.

Mr Kil's sound came together very quickly, after just three months of intense rehearsals in the spring of 2008. Songs such as 'Who'll Start All the Fires', the twisted lullaby 'Turn the Screw' and the grinding, howling 'She Cries Wolf' are awesome tunes, but the stand-out song for me is the simply stunning 'Boat Song'.

Being widely tipped nationally is usually the kiss of death for any local band but Mr Kil, who by the time you read this will have launched their debut EP, The Homespun Tales, have my hollering and hooting support.

Another of our ones to watch is 16-year-old Zoë Bridget McFadyen, who is already proving a force to contend with. Having hijacked her English teacher at St Paul's High School in Glasgow to play guitar for a battle of the bands contest they won - which isn't surprising since her teacher was none other than Robert John Getty, aka Punky Mendoza, formerly of Heavy Pettin' – her new focus is a magnus opus, due to be unveiled next year.

She has reinvented herself as Revelare, which is, I'm told, Latin for 'to reveal' and helping her is her new manager, the very same Punky.

Shortly after winning the YROCK Battle of the Bands, Revelare wanted to make a demo of cover songs to see how she felt working with Punky. The demo was recorded at A-Side studios in Maryhill. Imagem Music granted the synchronisation rights for the Kaiser Chiefs' song 'Love's Not A Competition (But I'm Winning)' to Zoë and her manager in order for them to film a showcase video to be viewed by music business personnel. The video received very positive feedback from various people in the music business, who have asked to be kept informed of Zoë's, sorry Revelare's, progress.

The track I've chosen to go along with this book is 'Firebird'. It was co-written by Revelare and Punky and is a belter of a tune. If this lass from St Paul's continues to grow and be nurtured by the great team around her, I've no doubt at all that in the fullness of time, all really will be revealed when she joins the ranks of all the minstrels, poets and vagabonds who have blessed our dear, green place all through the past five decades.

Raw Glory are as visceral as their name suggests, with a great rock pedigree flowing through their veins. Three Glaswegians have, at one time or another, passed through their ranks since they formed in 2006.

The band's Mick Underwood, who began his career with The Outlaws in 1961, has been one of the most influential figures in the British rock genre ever since.

Guitarist Cosmo also started working professionally in the 1960s when he was 13 years old and, as so many guitar prodigies of his generation, such as Jimmy McCulloch and the Young Brothers, left Glasgow early in life to pursue the rock 'n' roll dream playing some of the legendary circuit venues such as the Marquee and the Star Club in Hamburg, Germany. He further established his reputation during the Seventies, touring with the Heavy Metal Kids, former Jimi Hendrix band member Curtis Knight, Frankie Miller, Free's Andy Fraser, Phil Lynott of Thin Lizzy, Sweet's Brian Connolly and the Jordanaires (Elvis Presley's backing group). Although he retired from the music business, he was persuaded to return to performing by manager Peter Grant, who had been listening to old demos he had recorded.

The third original Glory member, Glaswegian Johnnie Heywood, first worked with Underwood in Quatermass II, along with former Deep Purple bassist Nick Simper, originally as singer only, though he took on bass duties when Simper left to concentrate on his band The Good Old Boys.

When Heywood left, the Glory line-up was completed by singer Paul Manzi, who didn't start singing until he was 23, when he joined a local prog rock band called Barchetta. Paul then made a living doing session work before getting the call to join Raw Glory.

Now filling the vacant bass spot is a loyal and trusted mucker o' mine, Ronnie Garrity, who, after dabbling in management and playing with original Thin Lizzy guitarist Eric Bell, has decided to pack in the mastering and recording side of the rock business altogether to get back to doing what he does best - playing bass guitar.

As I write, a British tour is on the cards for Raw Glory, which will include a Glasgow homecoming, sure to be an emotional night . . . be there or be square.

A mention must be made in this chapter of Bleed From Within. Formed in Glasgow in 2005, this young death metal band consist of Scott Kennedy on vocals, Dave Lennon (guitar), Craig Gowans (guitar), Ali Richardson (drums) and Davie Provan (bass).

They've toured all over the UK and, even sojourned in Europe, while their debut album Humanity has had the critics waxing lyrically in the music press.

Our penultimate band, Kobai, were formed in 2004 from various local outfits, including Kiness and Road Kill Pandas and consist of Ross Hinton (vocals), Stephen Morrow (guitar/synth), Chris Jarvie (synth/guitar), Robert Taylor (guitar and, rather oddly, cowbell), Ricky McBride (bass) and Jamie Finn (drums).

Kobai set out to make original, hard-hitting music and within a matter of months they'd won the UK-wide Emergenza unsigned competition, playing in front of thousands at the Glasgow Carling Academy and then the London Astoria.

The year 2006 saw the band touring throughout Germany, Austria, Italy and finally the UK, promoting their enthusiastically received debut single 'Serotonin', which is included on the book's listening post.

After spending the first half of 2007 writing new material, the band recorded a 12-track debut album with producer Kevin Burleigh, who in the past has worked with Dirty Pretty Things, Simple Minds, Mogwai and the Supernaturals as well as currently working with the likes of Glasvegas and the Hussy's. Misadventures was released as a Japan-only release in January 2008, selling more than 10,000 copies within the first few months. This led to Kobai signing a licence deal with Tokyo's Fabtone records.

Our last band formed in Glasgow in 2006 and, in just a short space of time, Wired Desire have become one of the fastest rising and most talked about young rock bands in the UK, touring with Nazareth, Wishbone Ash and Bad Company.

The line-up includes Kieran Daly (vocals), Jam (lead guitar), Eddy (bass) and Jeeves (drums). Their debut EP, Barely Illegal, was released on 6 October 2008 and, as of May 2009 the lads have been in the studio writing and recording their debut album. It promises to be huge – Tom Russell summed it up best when he said: 'Rock 'n' roll is back!'

Fresh Fields

And so we near the end of the Noughties and, even as I write, there are new acts popping up everywhere. But the lights are on and the roadies are dismantling the backline so I'm going to have to end it here.

I should say that, despite the trials and tribulations of my life in the world of rock, on a personal level I've never been happier. Carole and I have been blessed with becoming grandparents for a third time by Lee and his lovely wife Angelique, in the shape of a gorgeous wee girl Madeline, who's now six months old. She joins Cheryl's two girls, Charmaine and Siobhan, both now in their teens, in being as mad about music as their granddaddy.

Indeed, in the last couple of years I've taken them to see such diverse acts as Fall Out Boy, Darren Styles, Ultrabeat, 50 Cents, Westlife and Boyzone (ha, ha . . . what a cool papa!), thus ensuring the Fields rock gene will live on and on.

Perhaps in another few years, they'll produce a book themselves with pictures of an old geezer in the corner of Solid Rock Café, suppin' his pint through a straw, while nodding away to Heep. They'll certainly be hard-pressed to hear their papa singing Elvis songs in the Horseshoe Bar, unless it installs an escalator.

It's not all about Robert Fields rolling gently into dotage, mind you. Rock is in my blood and it would be a shame not to share an invincible enthusiasm. To this end, I've recently set up SMASH, the Scottish Musicians Advisory Service & Helpline, which is aimed at any college or university brave or mad enough to take me on so that I can offer hard-earned advice to students thinking of pursuing a career in the industry.

'Please sir, but how do you lose a nightclub that was taking in a million pounds a year?'

'Well, gather round you young rock kiddies you. Are you sitting comfortably? Then I'll begin. You see it was way, way back in the Sixties and there was this plastic Beatles wig . . .'

So, what's all this about a free internet listening post with loads of tracks from bands featured in this book? I've kept you waiting too long, so here's what you do – log on to www.minstrelspoetsvagabonds.co.uk and the login password for music access is mpv1967. Enjoy.

ACKNOWLEDGEMENTS

A thank you list for a book this size could become of War and Peace proportions, but there are some special people who merit a wee mention and so in no particular order let me introduce you to the 'A' team.

Dave Shack, Mark Plunkett, Ronnie Garrity, Robert Alexander, Billy and Margaret Forsyth, Dave Ling, Steven Flanagan, George McStravock, Dougie Souness , Donald MacLeod, Michael Pagliocca, Kirsty (Kat) Smith, Mhairi Cowley, Rab Andrew, Tom Russell, Duncan McCrone at M.C.P.S, Derek and Wendy Chalmers at Chow Productions, Sam Burrows, Linda Anne McConnell, Graham Boyle, Richard McKail, Mick Box, Ally McCoist, Cliff Smith, Kimberly Turri, Lesley MacKenzie, Allison Morgan, Big Iain and Kenny at the O2 Acadamy, Lee Maclean, Ailsa McInroy, Lesley and Alan McAteer, John Shearer, Stuart Eadie, Jim Downie, Barbara Mathieson, Paul Black, Richard Whiteside, Mairi Hitomi, Davey Arthur, Fiona Shepherd, Craig McLachlan, Willie and Rachel Codona, Russell Leadbetter, Martin Kielty, Sandy Jones and Graeme Duffin at MFL, Irene and Gunter, Norman Paton, Dutch Michaels, Andy Willisher, Danny Chestnut, Duncan Chambers, Andy Buchanan, Mr Flynn, John Barr, Paul Webster, Tommy Devlin, Douglas McMahon, Melanie Hunter and all the bands who gave me tracks and pictures in good faith. Oh and aye Raymond and Charlie in the Horseshoe Bar for letting me sing Elvis (brilliantly).

Norman Macdonald, my publisher, who had the balls and the vision to see the merit of this wee book and Dominic Ryan, who flicked his magic wand (and sweat) over all the words and made it interesting and credible.

And finally to the most important person in my life - my wife, soulmate and best friend for nearly 40 years, Carole Doris Fields, without whom I'd be a very lonely and sad person.

I dedicate this book to the memory of my parents, Robert and Isobel Fields – never a day goes by that I don't shed a wee tear for both; my big brother-in-law, Chris Watson; and special friends John Toal and big Davie McGhee, who sadly all passed away in the last few years without seeing the fruits of my labour (say hi to Elvis and John Lennon for me guys, and keep a wee pint of lager on tap and a bar stool warm for me).

Robert Fields,
October, 2009

DON'T STOP THE ROCK

We'd like to add a couple of legends of our own to Glasgow's rock story.

Tom Russell... who's introduced you to hundreds of your favourite songs.

Billy Rankin... who's played in all the city's great venues, and the shit ones too.

We never stop rockin'. Join us on air or online, day or night and help us add some new chapters to the legend.

www.rockradio.co.uk

96.3 ROCK RADIO

If the stories in Robert's book mean anything to you then you'll already know who we are, where we are, what we do and how long we've been doing it.

And it's probably your round.